Barcod **W9-ANT-765**

1

Alcohol Advertising and Young People's Drinking

Also by Barrie Gunter

LOOKS COULD KILL: Media, Body Image and Disordered Eating (*with M. Wykes*)

ADVERTISING TO CHILDREN ON TV: Content, Impact and Regulation (*with C. Oates & M. Blades*)

DIGITAL HEALTH: Meeting Patient and Professional Needs Online

MEDIA AUDIENCES: Volume 1–4 (*co-edited with D. Machin*)

GOOGLE GENERATION: Are ICT Innovations Cultivating New Information Search Perspectives? (*with I. Rowland & D. Nicholas*)

TELEVISION VERSUS THE INTERNET: Will TV Prosper or Perish as the World Moves Online?

ADVERTISING TO CHILDREN: New Issues and New Media (*co-edited with M. Blades, C. Oates & F. Blumberg*)

Also by Anders Hansen

NEWS COVERAGE OF THE ENVIRONMENT: A Comparative Study of Journalistic Practices and Television Presentation in Danmarks Radio and the BBC (*with O. Linné*)

THE MASS MEDIA AND ENVIRONMENTAL ISSUES (*edited*)

MASS COMMUNICATION RESEARCH METHODS: Volume 1–4 (*edited*)

ENVIRONMENT, MEDIA AND COMMUNICATION

MASS COMMUNICATION RESEARCH METHODS (*with S. Cottle, R. Negrine & C. Newbold*)

Alcohol Advertising and Young People's Drinking

Representation, Reception and Regulation

Barrie Gunter
Anders Hansen
Maria Touri

First published 2010 by
PALGRAVE MACMILLAN

Palgrave Macmillan in the UK is an imprint of Macmillan Publishers Limited, registered in England, company number 785998, of Houndmills, Basingstoke, Hampshire RG21 6XS.

Palgrave Macmillan in the US is a division of St Martin's Press LLC, 175 Fifth Avenue, New York, NY 10010.

Palgrave Macmillan is the global academic imprint of the above companies and has companies and representatives throughout the world.

Palgrave® and Macmillan® are registered trademarks in the United States, the United Kingdom, Europe and other countries.

ISBN 978–0–230–23753–7   hardback

This book is printed on paper suitable for recycling and made from fully managed and sustained forest sources. Logging, pulping and manufacturing processes are expected to conform to the environmental regulations of the country of origin.

A catalogue record for this book is available from the British Library.

Library of Congress Cataloging-in-Publication Data

Gunter, Barrie.
    Alcohol advertising and young people's drinking: representation, reception and regulation/Barrie Gunter, Anders Hansen, and Maria Touri.
        p. cm.
        ISBN 978–0–230–23753–7 (hardback)
    1. Advertising—Alcoholic beverages.   2. Youth—Alcohol use.
3. Advertising and youth.   I. Hansen, Anders, 1957–   II. Touri, Maria,
1977–   III. Title.
        HF6161.L46G86 2010
        363.2920835—dc22
                                                                    2010027516

10   9   8   7   6   5   4   3   2   1
19   18   17   16   15   14   13   12   11   10

Printed and bound in Great Britain by
CPI Antony Rowe, Chippenham and Eastbourne

Contents

Acknowledgements

The authors and publishers would like to thank Oxford Journals/Oxford University Press for granting permission to reproduce as Chapter 8 a revised version of an article originally published by Hansen, A. & Gunter, B. (2007), 'Constructing public and political discourse on alcohol issues: Towards a framework for analysis'. *Alcohol and Alcoholism*, 42(2), 150–7.

We acknowledge the ELSA Project (2005–7) of STAP (National Foundation for Alcohol Prevention in the Netherlands) as the source of the alcohol marketing regulation monitoring framework outlined in Chapter 9.

We are grateful to the Alcohol Education and Research Council (AERC) for funding the research project which provided the starting point and much of the research for this book, and to the AERC's external advisor, Professor Gerard Hastings, for input in relation to the project.

Many thanks to our editor Christabel Scaife and her colleagues at Palgrave Macmillan for continuous guidance and support, and to our anonymous reviewers for their insightful comments on an earlier draft of the book.

Notes on Contributors

Barrie Gunter is Professor of Mass Communications and Head of the Department of Media and Communication, University of Leicester. He has written or edited 50 books and more than 250 refereed journal papers, book chapters, non-refereed articles and technical reports on media, marketing, management and psychology. His research interests include advertising and young people, social marketing effects, the impact of television on public opinion and social behaviour and the use of the Internet across generations. He has recently published books on *The Google Generation* and on *Television versus the Internet*. He is currently co-editing a new volume about children and advertising.

Anders Hansen is Senior Lecturer in the Department of Media and Communication, University of Leicester. Much of his research has focused on media roles in relation to health, science and risk communication. He has published widely on media representations of alcohol and alcohol consumption. His recent books include *Environment, Media and Communication* (Routledge, 2010) and *Mass Communication Research Methods* (edited four-volume set, Sage, 2009). He is currently completing a jointly authored book on media and communication research for Palgrave Macmillan.

Maria Touri is a Lecturer in Media and Communications at the University of leicester. Her research interests are focused on the effects of media representations and framing on social and foreign policymaking. She has done research and published in the area of advertising effects, media-government interactions and new media technologies. She has also worked as a consultant in the area of development communication for the Panos Institute.

1

Alcohol Consumption and Youth: Key Issues

There is growing concern about problems of alcohol misuse and abuse among young people. In the new millennium, government and medical authorities have highlighted the health and social problems associated with excessive alcohol consumption, and the issue has received increasingly widespread media attention (see Prime Minister's Strategy Unit, 2003; BMA, 2008). While some evidence points to a reduction in prevalence of alcohol consumption across young people in general, occurrences of excessive consumption or 'binge' drinking are on the increase. Reports for the UK in 2008, for example, catalogued significant increases in hospital admissions due to drinking (BMA, 2008; Ford, Hawkes & Elliott, 2008). In tackling the causes of problematic alcohol consumption, critics have often turned their attention to the role played by alcohol advertising and other forms of promotion (Hastings & Angus, 2009). Such advertising is often blamed for driving irresponsible use of alcohol by encouraging people to start drinking when still very young and by making alcohol consumption seem an attractive and fashionable pursuit. Despite these calls for greater control over alcohol advertising, in many parts of the world, the alcohol that is consumed most often is locally made and not advertised at all.

Furthermore, in spite of the impression often given by contemporary debates about alcohol that excessive consumption is a recent phenomenon, alcohol abuse and dependence have been recognised as significant health issues for many years. Alcohol consumption represents normal behaviour in many countries. Historically, it has been embedded in the social and cultural fabric of many communities for centuries (Heath, 2000). Although many cultures encourage and condition the sensible and responsible consumption of alcoholic drinks, when appropriate role models and social parameters are missing, alcohol consumption may get out of control.

The BMA (2008) reported that alcohol consumption was high in the early years of the twentieth century, fell away during the period including and between the two world wars and then increased steadily from the 1950s into the twenty-first century. In 1950 average consumption per capita in the UK was 3.9 litres a year. This rose to 9.4 litres in 2004 and dropped slightly to 8.9 litres by 2006. These figures however were based on sales of taxable alcoholic products. They did not include home brews, black market purchases and illegal imports. From 1970, beer consumption declined and wine consumption increased markedly. Cider and spirits consumption also showed modest increases.

While the health benefits of moderate drinking are well known, irresponsible, excessive consumption can produce damaging health consequences at great cost to the individual, their family and society (see Educalcool, 2005, 2006). Medical authorities such as the Royal College of Physicians and the BMA in the UK have long been vocal in their calls for government action to combat the health and social problems caused by excessive alcohol consumption (Waterson, 1989; BMA, 2008).

In addition to the health-related side effects of alcohol abuse, there are in many ways equally serious social behaviour consequences as well. Drunkenness is associated with antisocial conduct. Research among children and adolescents in the UK has indicated that youngsters who drink alcohol commit a disproportionate number of criminal offences (Sivarajasingam, Matthews & Shepherd, 2006). Drunkenness in particular is strongly associated with not just general offending but also violent crime (Richardson & Budd, 2003).

At the root of these calls for more control over alcohol is the perception that its consumption has increased relentlessly and that the prevalence of harmful levels of consumption has reached a dangerous level. Whether or not this is true and, if it is true in some degree, how significant a social problem it represents tends to be judged via selected consumption statistics. As with any statistics, however, it is probably unwise to accept any such data at face value. We should question the popular measures of alcohol consumption to ascertain that they really do reveal the actual nature of public involvement with alcohol.

Some measures attempt to ascertain how many people drink alcohol. Others examine how much drinkers reportedly consume. Yet other measures focus on the frequency of consumption or on consumption to what are defined as excessive levels. The latter thresholds identify consumption levels above which alcohol can pose serious health risks. These levels, however, have varied over time and vary also with the nature of the individual. We need to understand more about the types of alcohol people consume and how strong different beverages are in terms of their alcohol content. Hence, when reported alcohol consumption data are obtained from people who are questioned about such things, we can be sure that different alcohol consumption reports are translated into probable volumes of alcohol exposure in each case. It is also important to ensure that when people are questioned about their drinking habits they are given an opportunity to stipulate a time period over which such habits have prevailed. An individual's level of alcohol consumption might vary from one time to the next.

One particular issue of concern is the prevalence of underage drinking. Young people have always consumed alcoholic beverages. Challenging the age-related restrictions on drinking is often seen as a rite of passage for many adolescents. However, risk-taking is also prevalent at this stage of life (Martinic & Measham, 2008a). Uncontrolled periodic bouts of excessive drinking – or binge drinking – can have particularly serious consequences. Adolescent drunkenness is associated with reckless and antisocial behaviour that can cause harm to those who get drunk and to others around them. Early onset of patterns of excessive alcohol consumption can also store up problems for health in later life, particularly if a dependence on alcohol persists. Concern about youth drinking is also fuelled by evidence that they experience disproportionate harmful side effects associated with alcohol consumption compared to older age groups (Wyllie, Millard & Zhang, 1996).

In considering steps to be taken to tackle problems of alcohol abuse and underage alcohol consumption, many lobbyists and governments have turned their attention to the role played by alcohol advertising and marketing. The role of advertising is a central focus of this book. As well as reviewing existing published evidence on the nature and effects of alcohol advertising, new research is presented that examines the nature of alcohol advertising in the UK and its significance for young people.

A considerable research literature has built up over the past four decades that has produced empirical evidence that alcohol advertising can influence young people (Hastings & Angus, 2009). Some of this research has also indicated that children and teenagers under the legal alcohol purchase age pay attention to, remember and often enjoy alcohol advertising. Advertising, however, is one of many factors that might influence young people's interest in alcohol (Houghton & Roche, 2001). Alcohol consumption can be shaped by a range of social-psychological factors in the individual's environment. Parental and peer influences are especially powerful (Adlaf & Kohn, 1989; Smart, 1988). It is also controlled by the different stages of life. While consumption of alcohol may be a part of their social culture for many adolescents and young adults, as they grow older and take on more responsibilities in their private lives and at work, people's alcohol consumption patterns change and often decline (Casswell, 2004). Furthermore, excessive or risky alcohol consumption may disappear naturally as young people grow older and take on greater personal responsibilities (Fillmore, 1988; Fillmore et al., 1991; McMahon, Jones & O'Donnell, 1984).

It is not simply the advertising of standard alcoholic drinks that is a source of concern, however, but also the marketing of alcoholic products directed at young drinkers. The primary example of this phenomenon has been the popularity with teenagers of a new range of 'alcopops' and other 'designer drinks' in the 1990s and the emergence of marketing strategies used to promote these drinks to young people (BMA, 1999). UK teenagers have one of the highest levels of alcohol consumption for their age group in Europe (Alcohol Concern, 2002; Plant & Miller, 2001). There is further evidence that the new designer drinks, that overcome the traditional taste barrier to early alcohol consumption, may encourage underage drinkers to start drinking earlier (McKeganey et al., 1996).

In the UK, the government recommends that an adult man should not regularly drink more than three to four units of alcohol per day, and the recommended daily intake for an adult woman is two to three units. Harmful drinking for men is regular consumption of eight or more units a day (or 50+ units a week) and for women six or more units a day (or 35+ units a week). Binge drinking involves drinking large quantities of alcohol in a short space of time (i.e., in a single evening) that leads to drunkenness (Department of Health/Home Office, 2007).

Alcohol consumption issues

Alcohol consumption is an established behaviour that permeates most sectors of the population. In the UK, although most people consume alcohol, rates of consumption have been found to vary with age, gender, socio-economic class and ethnicity (Office for National Statistics, 2006). Hence, studies have shown that men were more likely than women to report having had an alcoholic drink during the previous week and to have drunk alcohol on more days of the week (Office for National Statistics, 2008; NHS National Services Scotland, 2007). Perhaps the biggest variances in consumption of alcohol are associated with ethnicity. While fewer than one in ten of white British people (9%) were found to be teetotal in the General Household Survey of 2005, this proportion was far higher among many ethnic minority groups rising to nine out of ten (90%) among people who originated from Bangladesh and Pakistan (Office for National Statistics, 2006).

Most people in the UK consume alcohol in moderation. There are, however, people who drink to excess and who do so on a regular basis (BMA, 2008). Estimates of the prevalence of this problem have varied. The Prime Minister's Strategy Unit (2003) estimated that around one in seven people (14%) in Britain exceeded recommended daily guidelines and a similar proportion was estimated to engage in so-called binge drinking, that is consumption of eight or more units of alcohol per day for men and six or more per day for women. Seven per cent of people were classified as 'alcohol dependent'. The 2004 Alcohol Needs Assessment Research Project estimated that nearly four in ten (38%) of males aged 16–64 and around one in six (16%) of females in this age range in England exhibited an alcohol use disorder. This amounted to one in four (26%) of adults overall (Department of Health, 2005). At around the same time, the Parliamentary Office of Science and Technology (2005) estimated that nearly one in four (23%) men and nearly one in ten (9%) women in the UK engaged in 'binge' drinking.

In its report of 2008, the BMA presented further statistics to confirm that drinking in excess of recommended health guidelines was prevalent in the UK to a worrying extent (BMA, 2008). The problems of unhealthy levels of consumption were age-related. The BMA (2008) noted particularly high levels of alcohol consumption in the UK among men and women aged 16–24 years and 25–44 years. In 2006, for instance, four in ten of men (42%) and of women (39%) who exceeded recommended daily guidelines on at least one day in the previous week were aged 16–24 years. Even high percentages of people consuming at this level were contributed for men (48%) and women (40%) by the 25–44 age group. Quoting data from the ESPAD surveys conducted between 1995 and 2003, the BMA (2008) concluded that the UK was one of the worst offenders in Europe for alcohol consumption in excess of recommended health guidelines. Smith and Foxcroft (2009) reported a steady increase in prevalence of a drinking problem in the UK population that began in the 1990s and was especially pronounced among young people aged 16–24 years. Here, the gap between men and women was closing.

Further data on alcohol consumption among school children in England showed that both the prevalence of drinking and the average amount of consumption among 11- to 15-year olds increased significantly between 1990 and 2006 (ICHSC/NCSR/NFER, 2007). By 2007, more than one in three people aged 16 and over in Great Britain (37%) reported exceeding the recommended maximum for a single drinking session as part of their weekly alcohol-consuming routine (BMA, 2009). It is not simply the fact that most adolescents have sampled alcohol by their mid-teens that is worrying, but the fact that most report having got drunk even at 14 (McKeganey et al., 1996), and many claim to down at least 10 units of alcohol in a typical weekend session at 15 (Boys et al., 2003). There are potentially both immediate and longer-term repercussions of such behaviour for personal health and well-being (BMA, 1999; Jefferis, Power & Manor, 2005). Moreover, the prevalence of this regularity of heavy drinking is a cause of much concern. It is not restricted to a single age group, although it displays a particularly problematic rate of occurrence among teenagers and young adults.

One reason for the particularly acute concern about misuse of alcohol among children and teenagers is that they are more vulnerable to the adverse effects of alcohol consumption because they may be insufficiently experienced as drinkers to regulate their consumption effectively. Further, drinking to excess early in life can also set down a pattern of behaviour that if repeated later can materialize into health problems later in life (Bonomo et al., 2004; Wells, Horwood & Fergusson, 2004). Clear associations have been established between the heavy alcohol consumption in adolescence that leads to early dependency and continued drink-related problems in later life, including poor physical and mental health and involvement in antisocial and criminal behaviour (Jefferis et al., 2005).

There are concerns about alcohol misuse that extend beyond the immediate health-related effects that it can bring to problem drinkers. Excessive alcohol consumption has also been linked to violent and antisocial behaviour, dangerous driving and sexual promiscuity (BMA, 2008; Hastings & Angus, 2009). Between 1991 and 2005 the number of alcohol-related deaths more than doubled from 4144 in 1991 to 8386 in 2005 (National Statistics Online, 2006, November). Numerous factors have been identified as contributing towards the onset of underage drinking, with advertising and marketing factors being among them. Youngsters may be more susceptible to the effects of advertising than adults (Atkin, 1993). Advertising can cultivate favourable social climate towards alcohol and its consumption (Dring & Hope, 2001; Hill & Casswell, 2000; Jackman & Hill, 2003).

What effects do advertising and marketing have on the onset, regularity, quantity and type of alcohol consumption among young people? This question has been addressed in whole or in part by numerous published investigations. Most of the research derives from the US, with a few additional studies mostly from Australia, Canada, New Zealand and the UK. Before we consider the parts played by alcohol advertising and other forms of marketing, there are significant issues relating to the definition and measurement of alcohol consumption that need to be addressed. We must have confidence in the quality and veracity of consumption data before we can draw conclusions about if and to what extent such alcohol-related consumption behaviours might be influenced by the way alcohol is promoted.

Alcohol consumption: Measurement issues

Assessment of alcohol consumption in any population can be assessed in terms of production and distribution statistics for alcoholic beverages and through self-report data from survey samples questioned about their drinking behaviour (Midanik & Room, 1992; BMA, 2008; Hastings & Angus, 2009; Smith & Foxcroft, 2009). Although survey data among national or subnational samples are not perfect, they do allow some investigation of statistical links between drinking behaviour and other personal, social and environmental factors at the individual consumer level. Macro level societal data can demonstrate trends over time in consumption and measure degrees of association between consumption levels and societal and economic interventions such as price increases, changes in the performance of the economy and legislative and regulatory controls over the sale of alcohol and marketing practices. Such data do not reveal anything about the nature of alcohol consumption at the individual level and cannot therefore reveal anything about specific factors that may drive drinking behaviour.

Drinking behaviour can be highly diverse in the form it takes. Some individuals may be non-drinkers, others may be light or occasional drinkers and others might be regular or heavy drinkers. Heavy drinking is usually defined in terms of consumption of alcohol at a specified multiple of the medically recommended maximum average daily or weekly intake, expressed in units of alcohol. One unit of alcohol is equivalent to a half pint of beer, lager or cider, a glass of wine, a single glass of spirits or one can or bottle of alcopops or pre-mixed alcoholic drinks (see Office for National Statistics/Department of Health, 2004). The maximum recommended daily dose is four units for men and three units for women.

In practice, a person who drinks the maximum weekly amount for a man (28 units) could do so at a steady rate of four units a day or might consume this quantity of alcohol in two or three sessions of heavy drinking. The latter pattern of consumption, manifest in terms of bouts of 'binge' drinking, would be regarded as much less healthy compared to a steady rate of consumption throughout the week. In research into drinking habits and their health implications, it is important to establish not only overall amounts of consumption but also the patterns of consumption in which individuals engage and, in particular, the extent to which they consume large quantities of alcohol within a single day.

In a survey of drinking patterns around the world, the UK finished 22nd out of 189 nations in terms of total recorded alcohol per capita consumption among individuals aged 15 years and over, in terms of litres of pure alcohol consumed per annum (World Health Organisation, 2004). Turning to very heavy drinking episodes, the WHO collated national statistics for 46 countries. Among males aged 15+, the UK finished 13th in terms of the proportion of individuals within this social group who were classified as heavy episodic drinkers (at 24% of males, aged 15+). Among females aged 15+, classified as heavy drinkers, the UK finished in 12th place (9%).

According to more recent government statistics, the majority of men (73%) and women (60%) in England had consumed an alcohol drink 'on at least one day during the previous week' (National Statistics/ Department of Health, 2004, p. 2). Thus, a majority of adults aged 16+ in England were found to be drinkers. Furthermore, nearly one in four men (23%) and one in seven women (14%) had reportedly drunk alcohol on five or more days during the previous week. In England in 2002, the average weekly consumption of alcohol was 17.0 units for men and 7.6 units for women.

It is not simply the regularity of drinking that is critical, however, but the volume of alcohol consumed. Even more specifically, it is important to know how often alcohol consumers drink to excess. In this context, government statistics indicated that nearly two out of five men (37%) in England had drunk more than four units of alcohol at least one day during the previous week. This proportion increased by a significant margin among young men, aged 16–24 (48%).

Women were much less likely than men to drink above recommended levels. The same survey found that just over one in five women (22%) said they had drunk more than three units of alcohol during the previous week. Again, though, this proportion increased dramatically among young women in the 16–24 age group (40%).

One of the critical areas of concern is the occurrence of binge drinking. This phenomenon relates to the consumption of a large quantity of alcohol in fairly limited period of time. In the process, binge drinkers tend to get drunk. There is particular concern about binge drinking because of the health implications of the large intakes of alcohol involved.

Monitoring of youth drinking

The monitoring of alcohol consumption among young people has received special attention in a number of countries. What has sometimes made comparisons between surveys difficult is their failure to define 'youth' in the same way. The Health Behaviour in School Children (HBSC) study began in 1982 and has been conducted by international teams with the World Health Organisation in Europe. These surveys have been carried out every four years among samples of children aged 11–15 years. Questions probe a number of issues including health, well-being and the social situation of youngsters, with some questions about drinking included (see WHO, 2004).

The European School Survey Project on Alcohol and other Drugs (ESPAD) was launched in 1995 and repeated in 1999 and 2003. It examined alcohol consumption (and other drug use) among 15- to 16-year olds in Europe. By 1999, 30 countries took part and the survey questioned over 90,000 young people (Plant & Miller, 2001). It focused on 15- and 16-year olds. All respondents completed a core questionnaire under supervised classroom conditions. UK teenagers were among the heaviest consumers of alcohol alongside teenagers from Denmark, the Faroe Islands, Finland, Greenland, Iceland and Ireland. Alcohol consumption remained stable within the UK, however, over the period of the surveys (Miller & Plant, 1996, 2001; Plant, 1997; Plant & Miller, 2000).

In the US, key surveys that have examined youth drinking include the Monitoring the Future Survey (13- to 17-year olds), the Youth Risk Behaviour Survey (14- to 17-year olds) and the Harvard Public Health College Alcohol Study.

On a wider scale, the World Health Organisation launched the Global school-based health survey (GSHS) in which 16 countries have participated (Bahamas, Botswana. Chile, China, Guatemala, Guyana, Jordan, Kenya, Mozambique, the Philippines, Swaziland, Trinidad and Tobago, Uganda, Venezuela, Zambia and Zimbabwe). The survey examines health behaviour and behaviour risk factors among young people aged 13–15 years.

There is growing concern that the health and well-being of young people are being threatened by excessive consumption of alcohol and that this is a worldwide problem. Historically, while some countries have experienced a drinking culture, especially the wine-producing regions, cultural changes have produced a shift in drinking patterns. In Mediterranean countries such as France and Spain, the adoption of beer over wine among young people has created a drinking environment in which intoxication has become more prevalent.

Alcohol Concern (2003) reported a relatively small-scale survey of 540 youngsters aged 15–17 years. These teenagers were recruited from five secondary schools in the south of England and their drinking behaviour was tracked over 18 months. An initial face-to-face interview was followed by two self-completion surveys conducted after nine months and 18 months. At recruitment, an overwhelming majority (94%) said they had drunk a whole alcoholic drink at some point in their lives. At the start of the research, 59 per cent reported drinking once a week; it had increased to 80 per cent by the end.

In a survey of 27 countries by the World Health Organisation (2004), the UK (30%) was placed fourth in terms of the proportion of young males who engaged in heavy drinking episodes at least weekly or in the past month, behind Denmark (62%), Poland (41%) and Hungary (39%). The UK (27%) was placed third in terms of the proportion of young females who said they had engaged in bouts of heavy drinking recently, behind Denmark (54%) and Ireland (32%). In the case of the UK, the age group covered was 15–16-year olds, as it was in 13 other countries. In the remaining countries, the most frequent age range was 14/15/16–19s with two countries surveying drinkers as young as 11 years. The heavy drinking threshold in the UK was the consumption of five or more drinks in a row three times or more in the last 30 days, a threshold also used by 10 other countries. The consumption of at least five drinks in a single sitting was the most frequently used qualifying threshold for heavy drinking (either within the last week or last month).

Evidence from the ESPAD surveys of 15 to 16-year olds in 30 European countries conducted in 1995, 1999 and 2003 (Hibbell et al., 2000, 2004) found that over one in four school children (28–9%) below the legal drinking age claimed across this period to have got drunk at least 20 times in their lifetime. This placed the UK in second place in Europe in 1995 and 1999 and in fourth in 2003. Over one in five of these respondents across 1995–2003 (22–4%) claimed to have got drunk at least three times in the past 30 days.

Statistics on early teenage drinking from the UK produced by the NHS Information Centre (2007) indicated that while the prevalence of alcohol consumption was decreasing, the amount being drunk by those who did consume was increasing. More seriously, binge drinking during early youth was on the increase. The data reported in this case were for 2006 and were taken mainly from a survey of Smoking, Drinking and Drug Use among Young People in England (SDD). This survey questioned over 8000 children aged 11–15 years.

Just one in five school children aged 11–15 years in England (21%) said they had drunk any alcohol in the week before the survey, with virtually no difference between girls (21%) and boys (20%). There was, however, a dramatic rise in this type of report with age, increasing from 3 per cent among 11-year olds to 41 per cent for 15-year olds. The overall prevalence of alcohol consumption figure for 11- to 15-year olds, though, represented a fall from 2001 (26%).

Although the prevalence of reported alcohol consumption among 11- to 15-year olds in England fell, among those teens who do drink, the average amount of consumption displayed a further increase in 2006 to 11.4 units in the week prior to the survey, up from 5.3 units in 1990 and 10.4 units in 2000. A particularly notable increase in reported amount of consumption occurred between 2000 and 2006 among 11- to 13-year olds (from 5.6 units to 10.1 units). The most popular drinking days for English teens were Friday (51%) and Saturday (62%). Drinking was much less likely to occur on other days of the week.

The most widely endorsed types of alcohol drunk were beer, cider and lager (72%), followed by spirits (63%) and alcopops (60%). Boys reportedly were more likely to drink beer, cider and lager (87%) and girls preferred alcopops (69%) and spirits (67%). It was the popularity of spirits that displayed the most significant increase over time, growing from 35 per cent in 1990 and 59 per cent in 2000 to the 2006 level of 63 per cent (NHS Information Centre, 2008).

The increased prevalence of what has been termed 'problem' drinking among young people aged 16–24 years has been observed by other writers, with the next age group (25–44) also displaying heavy drinking patterns (Robinson & Lader, 2009; Smith & Foxcroft, 2009). Further, even among those aged 11–15 years, more than one in two (54%) have been found to acknowledge that they had started to consume alcohol (Fuller, 2008). This statistic disguises the dramatic increase in prevalence of alcohol consumption that has been observed to occur across this age range. One study of Scottish teenagers found that well over half of 13-year olds (57%) said they drank alcohol, while by age 15 an overwhelming majority (84%) admitted doing so (Maxwell, Kinver & Phelps, 2007). Among acknowledged drinkers aged 11–15 years, the average amount of consumption in England was 9.2 units and in Scotland 14.5 units. At the younger end of this age spectrum (11–13 years), it was observed that by 2006 in England this age group was drinking twice as much as in 1990 (Smith & Foxcroft, 2009).

The concept of 'binge' drinking

There has been growing concern about excessive alcohol consumption among young people. This concern goes beyond any examination of drinking per se to consider how extensively young drinkers consume large quantities of alcohol in single drinking sessions or over concentrated periods of time. This concern has been expressed in many different parts of the world. In the US, for example, children have been observed to begin trying alcohol at progressively earlier ages. The average age of the first-time drinker in 1967 was 18. By 1999, this had dropped to below 16 years of age. The rate per 1000 12- to 17-year-old first-time drinkers increased from 75 in 1965 to over 200 in 1999 (Health Care Technology, 2002). Across Europe as well, most countries have witnessed increases in binge drinking and drunkenness among adolescents from the mid-1990s into the new millennium (Anderson, 2007).

Whereas alcohol consumption was once a pastime enjoyed as part of a social culture that also featured food and family, drinking has become an activity in which young people engage with the primary purpose of getting drunk. One European study has found that young people today show a higher propensity to get drunk than did their elders when young (Leifman, Osterberg & Ramstedt, 2002).

One of the problems with any analysis of 'binge drinking' is the lack of consensus with regard to its operational definition. According to the BMA, binge drinking 'was often used to refer to an extended period of time, usually two days or more, during which a person repeatedly drank to intoxication, giving up usual activities and obligations' (BMA, 2005, March, online citation). One commonly used definition (though by no means universal) of binge drinking is the consumption of more than five alcoholic drinks on a single drinking occasion (Alcohol Concern, 2004; BMA, 2003; Hibbell et al., 2004).

Episodes of binge drinking, defined as consuming five or more drinks in a single session, were reported to have increased 17 per cent among all America adults between 1993 and 2001, but rose by 56 per cent among 18- to 20-year olds. Binge drinking among all American adults in 2001 aggregated to 1.5 billion episodes (from 1.2 billion in 1993), averaging more than seven times per person. Around one in six American 13-year olds (16%) reported binge drinking in 1996, with this figure doubling among 17-year olds. Male 17-year olds (37%) were more likely to engage in binge drinking than female 17-year olds (23%) in 1996 (Health Care Technology, 2002).

Peer pressure to drink alcohol has been found to start even earlier. In the US, one-third of children aged nine years and over half of those aged 11 years claimed to have been pressured by friends to drink alcohol (Center for Substance Abuse Prevention, 1993). Despite fairly widespread awareness that over-indulgence in alcohol consumption carries a health risk, significant minorities of American children and teenagers nevertheless admitted to experiencing drink-related problems. Two-thirds of 12-to 17-year olds thought that drinking four or five alcoholic drinks nearly every day posed a risk (National Institute on Drug Abuse, 1998). Despite this, 13 per cent of 12-to 17-year olds admitted to having at least one serious problem related to drinking over the past year and an even larger percentage (39%) of established drinkers admitted to such a problem (Substance Abuse and Mental Health Services Administration, 1999). In addition, one in three 12- to 17-year-old Americans (34%) said they had got drunk in the past month and a similar proportion (30%) said they had engaged in binge drinking in the two weeks prior to the survey (National Institute on Drug Abuse, 1998).

In an attempt to deal with the issue of binge drinking, the UK Government changed its advice about levels of recommended drinking from weekly to daily rates of consumption, in its report on *Sensible Drinking* (Department of Health, 1995). In doing so, the emphasis was shifted from calculations of weekly alcohol intake to daily ones. This measure took into account that a weekly average rate of alcohol consumption may not necessarily represent a healthy drinking pattern if that weekly intake is consumed in just one or two heavy drinking sessions. Whether or not young people take any notice of such guidelines, however, is a debatable point. Indeed, survey evidence compiled not long after these new guidelines were published indicated that many young British drinkers still drank heavily and consumed in excess of eight units of alcohol (in the case of men) and six (in the case of women) in a single recent drinking session (Office for National Statistics, 1999).

Research conducted by the Department of Health among 11- to 15-year olds from 1988–98 showed a drop between 1996 and 1998 in the percentage of youngsters within this age range who had reportedly drunk alcohol in the past month from 26 per cent to 21 per cent. The 1998 figure also matched that for 1988. Average alcohol consumption was 1.6 units per week which amounts to modest consumption, and the great majority of children said they drank under parental supervision.

Only small percentages of boys (4%) and girls (2%) claimed to have drunk over 15 units in the last week. These figures indicated the presence of an 'at-risk' group that needed to be targeted by health services, but there was no indication of a young person's drinking problem spiralling out of control (Alcohol in Moderation, 2003).

The Office for National Statistics (1999, 2002) used the definition of eight or more units of alcohol in a single drinking session for men and six for women. On this basis, it was found in 2002 that significant minorities of 16- to 24-year-old men (36%) and women (27%) in the UK engaged in binge drinking (Office for National Statistics, 2002).

The ESPAD surveys (1997, 2000, 2004) asked youngsters about binge drinking which in this research was defined as the consumption of five or more drinks in a row. The proportions of 15- to 16-year olds claiming to engage in this pattern of alcohol consumption at least three times in the previous 30 days increased from 1995 (22%) to 1999 (30%) and then dropped away again in 2003 (27%). This same pattern was observed for boys, but not for girls. Girls showed no signs of any decline in reported binge drinking from 1995 (20%) to 2003 (29%). By 2003, they had overtaken boys (26%).

In the UK, research by Alcohol Concern (2003) among a sample of over 500 teenagers aged 15–17 years, over an 18-month period, found that a significant majority (84%) at the end of the study admitted to being drunk recently. Drinking mostly took place at the respondent's home (50%, 75% and 80% across the three survey waves) or a friend's home (69%, 83% and 87% respectively).

Those who claimed to drink six or seven days a week increased from 0.4 per cent at wave one to two per cent by wave three. The most commonly consumed drinks were lager, beer and spirits, with just six to nine per cent across waves claiming to drink alcopops. Interestingly, the proportion claiming to drink 10 or more units of alcohol over a weekend fell from one in three at the start of the research to 18 per cent by the end, but the consumption of five to six units in a single session became more widespread.

In 2004, the UK government defined binge drinking as the consumption of twice the recommended maximum amount of alcoholic units within a single relatively short drinking session – or eight units. National Statistics/Department of Health (2004) reported for England that over one in five men (21%) reported having drunk this amount of alcohol in a single day during the previous week, with just under one in ten women (9%) reporting a drinking session during the past week in which they had consumed more than six units.

Based on this definition, binge drinking was found to be more prevalent among young people than anyone else. One in three men aged 16–24 years (34%) said they had consumed eight units in a day and over one in four (26%) women in this age group reported consumption of more than six units in a day over the previous week. Binge drinking is associated with being economically active or gainfully employed. Among those aged 16–64 years, more economically active men (26%) and women (15%) had engaged in binge drinking in the previous week than had economically inactive men (16%) and women (7%) (National Statistics/Department of Health, 2004).

From 2006, the UK government updated its methodology for calculating units of alcohol consumed to bring its measurement techniques in line with changes in the strengths of some alcoholic drinks, the emergence of new types of alcoholic beverage and changes in the quantities that are sold to consumers (NHS Information Centre, 2008). Statistics from the 2006 General Household Survey showed that in England at that time, 72 per cent of men and 57 per cent of women aged 16 and over reported that they had drunk alcohol on at least one day during the week prior to the survey interview. People aged 16–24 years were less likely to say they had had a drink in the previous week than were those aged 25–64 years. Those aged 65+ were also less likely to have had a drink at all during the previous week. However, among those who did drink, those aged 65+ (21% of men and 11% of women) were more likely to report having drunk every day in the previous week compared with those aged 16–24 (4% of men and 1% of women).

In 2007, the UK government highlighted the alarming extent to which young adults aged 16–24 years were more likely than any other age group to consume twice the recommended sensible drinking limit. Among young men, three in ten (30%) and among young women, over one in five (22%) had drunk at a harmful level on at least one day in the previous week (Department of Health/Home Office, 2007).

The data reported above derive from research that has presumed a clear and common understanding of a key concept – 'binge drinking'. Some writers have challenged this notion and dispute whether a common understanding has been reached and indeed whether the operational definition of 'binge' drinking used by government is grounded in a robust measurement of consumption habits (see Martinic & Measham, 2008a).

The notion of 'binge drinking' has been defined in different ways by different studies and different jurisdictions. Terms such as 'binge' or 'bender' have entered common parlance, but are often used to represent what are in behavioural terms different amounts or styles of drinking. Martinic and Measham (2008a) noted, for instance, different definitions emerging for this concept in the US and the UK. In the US, the threshold for a drinking 'binge' has been set at five or more drinks for men and four or more for women within a single drinking session in the past two weeks. Anyone acknowledging such behaviour within the past two weeks would be classified as a current 'binge' drinker (see Wechsler et al., 1994; Wechsler & Nelson, 2006). In the UK, said Martinic and Measham, 'a binge has been defined as either drinking more than half the recommended weekly maximum intake or (more usually) more than double the recommended daily maximum in a single session' (2008a, p. 5).

A further complicating factor is that even when two sets of definitions make references to different numbers of units of alcohol consumption within their respective definitions of 'binge' drinking, the actual difference could be more or less than that stated if the definition of 'unit' varies in each case. There are cross-cultural differences in what a single drink of alcohol means in terms of the actual volume of alcohol consumed. As Martinic and Measham (2008a) pointed out, one drink in the US is equivalent to 1.6 units in the UK. In addition, if recommended intakes of alcohol are to provide useful guidance to consumers, it is important that they can be readily translated from actual consumption patterns. This translation can prove to be problematic when the alcoholic strengths of different types and brands of alcoholic beverage can vary widely. In terms of the clinical effects of alcohol consumption that exceed recommended thresholds, the body size, alcohol tolerance and experience of the individual must also be taken into account.

Many surveys of alcohol consumption behaviour attempt to ascertain the prevalence of drunkenness. Such measures may be used in addition to or instead of reports of drinking given in terms of numbers of alcoholic drinks consumed within specified time periods. This subjective concept however can be interpreted by respondents in different ways. Hence asking people how often they have been drunk will depend upon the subjective yardstick that is used in this context to reach such a judgement. There is mixed evidence on whether subjective reports of drunkenness provide better or worse indicators of potential harm (Midanik, 1999; Hammersley & Ditton, 2005; Wright, 2006).

Martinic and Measham (2008a) offered the term 'extreme drinking' that goes beyond the idea of standardised measures of drunkenness or binge drinking and acknowledges the significance of cultural distinctions between acceptable and unacceptable levels of alcohol consumption as well as recognising that clinical harms can be predicted to some degree, though not exclusively or always comprehensibly, by the amount of alcohol consumed. Part of the definition of 'extreme drinking' is that alcohol consumption to a point of intoxication takes place. In addition, however, there are motivational factors that underpin the behaviour that also need to be taken into account. Drinking to a point of intoxication can occur as a result of socially positive activities or for more negative reasons. People can get drunk by accident if they do not realise how much they have consumed and if they are inexperienced drinkers. Much excessive drinking, however, takes place among individuals in pursuit of pleasurable experiences. It may be part of a regular scene in which others also drink heavily and where such behaviour carries a degree of social cache.

Concern about young women

Alcohol consumption, and especially heavy drinking, is mostly associated with men. As the statistics reviewed above clearly show, women and girls tend to consume less alcohol than men and boys. This pattern has occurred consistently within the UK and other countries around the world. Even so, there has been growing public concern about the increased prevalence of heavy drinking among young women. Dramatic news headlines have highlighted increased female fatalities from excessive alcohol consumption in the UK. Drink-related deaths have been reported to have soared from the mid-1990s to middle of the first decade of the new millennium, particularly among women aged 35–54 years. Drinking alcohol to excess has been linked to teenage pregnancies and lost days of schooling (MacRae, 2007). These problems do not stem simply from alcohol misuse among young men. The gap between men and women in terms of volume of alcohol consumed and propensity to consume above recommended health guidelines is closing (Robinson & Lader, 2009; Smith & Foxcroft, 2009).

This trend was highlighted by GINA (2005) in its review of young women's alcohol consumption in Britain. Data from the General Household Survey examined by GINA not only indicated a steady increase in alcohol consumption among young women aged 16–24 years between 1998 and 2002, but also that young women had almost caught up with young men in the same age group by 2002 in terms of the proportion of those who were drinking above weekly recommended benchmarks.

Key statistics quoted by GINA (2005) were that young women increased their alcohol intake from an average of 7.3 units per week in

1992 to 14.1 units per week in 2002. In 1992, just 17 per cent of 16- to 24-year-old women drank more than 14 units per week, whereas by 2002, this proportion had grown to 33 per cent. Even more seriously, few young women (4%) in 1992 drank more than 35 units per week, but by 2002, one in ten (10%) regularly consumed this amount of alcohol.

The problem of heavy episodic drinking was even more serious in Scotland than across the rest of the UK. Here, the overwhelming majority of young women (91%) said they drank alcohol (GINA, 2005). Around two-thirds of these women (63%) reported being drunk in the previous three months. Significant numbers of teenage girls drink alcohol in Scotland. In 2004, one in five (20%) 13-year olds reported drinking alcohol in the previous week. By the age of 15, the latter percentage rises to 46 per cent (an increase from 25% in 1990). Moreover, more 15-year-old girls than boys reported drinking in the previous week in Scotland (46% versus 40%). A subsequent Scottish study conducted among a small sample of female undergraduates found that the majority of those who provided self-reported data about their drinking (70%) said their drinking could be classified as binge consumption at least once a week (Gill et al., 2007).

Statistics for Irish university students, in contrast, indicated marginal decreases in the percentages of females who drank alcohol and who drank alcohol above the recommended weekly intake for their gender (O'Brien et al., 2001).

By 2005, however, government statistics for alcohol consumption in the UK indicated that drinking trends among young women had stabilised and even showed signs of being in decline. Figures produced by the Office for National Statistics revealed that one in five young women aged 16–24 years (20%) said they drank more than the recommended daily limit of three units of alcohol during the week before they were polled, compared with higher proportions who answered in this way in 2004 (22%) and 2002 (28%) (Steele, 2006).

By 2006, reports emerged that among 10–15-year olds in the UK the prevalence of alcohol consumption per se continued to fall, but that heavy drinking among alcohol drinkers in this age group had increased. More significantly, for the first time, the proportion of girls who drank exceeded the proportion of boys. Research was carried out by the Schools Health Education Unit in Exeter conducted among 68,000 children across the country. This survey found that the proportion of girls who drank at least once a week continued to fall in 2006 (37%, down from 52% in 1991), as with boys following the same trend (35%, down from 55% in 1991). While boys preferred to drink beer, girls had developed a taste for distilled spirits. Among 14- to 15-year-old girls, 28 per cent reported in 2006 that they consumed at least five measures of spirits per week. In comparison, 35 per cent of 14- to 15 year-old boys claimed to drink at least five pints of beer a week (Iredale, 2007).

A survey reported by Ofcom (2007) found that 'regular' drinking of alcohol was reported by a steadily growing percentage of young people across the age bands of 11–13 (4%), 14–17 (24%) and 18–21 (62%). Self-reported drinking patterns of a national sample of over 1,500 young people in the UK did not differ greatly between males and females. Compared with an earlier survey in 2005, however, an important finding emerged that the proportion of 11- to 13-year olds who said they had never drunk alcohol increased from 31 per cent to 46 per cent in 2007. This result indicated that more young people may be starting to drink at a later age. By the time the young people reached 14–17 years, around half had become either Occasional (25%) or regular (24%) drinkers. In this age group, the proportion of 'never' drinkers was much smaller at 17 per cent (a slight increase from 2005 – 14%).

Minorities and alcohol consumption

Alcohol consumption on the part of young people varies between different countries and these cross-national differences are often associated with dominant cultural values associated with alcohol, the way it is used and how much it is appropriate to consume in general or on specific occasions (Martinic & Measham, 2008a). Some of the cultural factors associated with the use (or non-use) of alcohol are also linked to ethnicity and can give rise to marked differences in the use of alcohol between different social groups within the same country.

One relevant set of insights into ethnic differences in alcohol use derives from surveys of 15- and 16-year olds in the East Midlands of England in 1990 and 1997 (Denscombe & Drucquer, 2000). The samples of both occasions were drawn from the same 12 schools that represented different locations and ethnic mixes. Data were based on a usable sample of 1009 in 1990 and 1648 in 1997. All participating teenagers were classified as non-drinkers, occasional drinkers (once a week or less frequent consumption) and regular drinkers (drank more than once a week). Around one in four members of each sample were from ethnic minorities in 1990 and 1997 compared with around seven per cent of the national age-group population in these categories (based on 1991 census data). Around nine in ten ethnic minority respondents were of south Asian origin, divided between Hindus, Muslims and Sikhs.

All ethnic groups (whites and minorities) exhibited clear signs of drinking more in 1997 than in 1990. Occasional or regular alcohol consumption was reportedly undertaken by 66 per cent of males and 57 per cent of females in 1990 with drinking prevalence growing to 73 per cent and 63 per cent respectively by 1997. Among 'south Asian' groups, just six per cent of males and four per cent of females were occasional or regular drinkers in 1990, and these figures grew to 11 per cent and eight per cent respectively in 1997.

Among the south Asian communities, Sikh respondents were the most likely to report alcohol consumption in 1997 (males = 13%; females = 21%). In 1990, Sikh males were more likely to report drinking than males in any other south Asian groups (17%), but no Sikh females indicated occasional or regular drinking. Hindus were the most likely overall to drink in 1990 (males = 8%, females = 10%) but fell behind the Sikhs in 1997 (males = 13%; females = 15%). Muslim respondents indicated very low levels of drinking, with just one per cent of males in 1990 and three per cent in 1997 saying they were occasional or regular drinkers, and no females saying this in 1990 and just one admitting to it in 1997.

Research with larger and more representative samples of people across the UK has confirmed that many ethnic minority groups consume smaller quantities of alcohol than does the white majority and drink less frequently (Office for National Statistics, 2006).

Designer drinks and 'alcopops'

Many factors can contribute to alcohol consumption among young people, but some degree of responsibility has been attached to the manufacturers. The development of new alcohol drinks targeted at young people has been identified as having an important influence. So-called designer drinks based on ciders and fortified wines used new attractive packaging styles to appeal to young drinkers over the legal drinking age, but also attracted underage drinkers (Mosher & Johnsson, 2005).

Newly branded beverages that combine alcohol with sweet and carbonated drinks – collectively known as 'alcopops' – have become fashionable. They have become the drinks of choice for many young drinkers. Their sweet flavours often disguise their alcohol content and render them attractive even to relatively inexperienced young drinkers and they may then serve as a bridge to eventual consumption of harder alcoholic products. They are particularly popular among teenagers aged 13–15 years (Hughes et al., 1997). There is concern in particular that these beverages are targeted at young people by marketers (McKeganey et al., 1996).

During the 1990s, a range of new alcoholic drinks products were released in the market that combined sweet, fruity flavours with fortified wines or that were based on strong white ciders. These products were branded with names such as 'MD20/20', 'Mad Dog', 'Ice Dragon' and 'White Lightning'. Collectively they became known as 'designer drinks' and they were targeted in terms of their packaging and flavouring at young consumers. The fortified wine-based drinks tended to have a 13- to 21-per cent concentration of alcohol by volume but their potency was frequently disguised by their sweet, fruity taste. Not surprisingly, these drinks were found to have appeal for underage drinkers whose immature taste buds took more readily to sweet-tasting drinks than the more bitter-tasting traditional alcoholic beverages that are an acquired taste.

Drinking alcohol in adolescence is a not a new phenomenon associated with these marketing developments, but concern was generated by their appearance because they seemed to be directed at young drinkers (Barnard & Forsyth, 1998). At the time designer drinks appeared, the extent to which adolescents drank alcohol had not exhibited significant shifts, but there was emergent evidence that the prevalence of excessive drinking among teenagers was on the rise (Lister Sharp, 1994; Newcombe, Measham & Parker, 1995).

In the US, surveys have confirmed the popularity of designer drinks or alcopops among young drinkers. While most surveys of drinking behaviour reveal greater consumption among males, there is mounting evidence that alcopops have established a particularly strong appeal among young female drinkers to the extent that they have also been referred to as 'girlie drinks'. Two nationwide polls issued by the American Medical Association revealed that around one in three teenage girls reported having tried alcopops at some time and one in six had done so within the six months prior to being polled. Teenage girls (31%) were more likely than teenage boys (19%) to have tried alcopops in the past six months.

Interestingly, while alcopop was the most popular alcoholic drink among teenage female drinkers, it was the least preferred among those aged 21 or over. This finding suggested that designer drinks may play a part in the initial establishment of alcohol consumption among girls, but it represents a short-term fad from which they emerge as drinkers of other, more traditional alcoholic beverages. Although not providing evidence for the effects of advertising, this research indicated that girls aged 16–18 years (49%) were more likely than women aged 21 and over (34%) to claim to have seen advertisements for alcopops on television (News-Medical.Net, 2004).

In Scotland, a profound impact of so-called designer drinks has been observed among teenage drinkers. There is evidence that young people aged 12–15 years who consume these products are more likely than others to engage in more frequent and heavy drinking (McKeganey et al., 1996).

A further survey among teenagers (12–17 years) in Scotland reported that more than half had tried the brand 'Mad Dog' (a fortified wine) and over four in ten (42%) had tried at least one of four brands of strong cider. Once again, consumers of such brands reported drinking more overall, were more likely to engage in heavy drinking sessions and to report loss of behavioural control while drunk. When asked to choose between a number of soft drinks, high-energy drinks and alcoholic drinks, one designer alcoholic brand 'MD20/20' emerged as being especially popular among 13–15-year olds, although declined in popularity among 16- to 17-year olds who increasingly moved towards drinking standard forms of alcoholic drinks (e.g., beers) (Hughes et al., 1997). The evidence from this survey indicated that designer drinks or 'alcopops' had a strong appeal for individuals at the youngest end of the teenage spectrum before being superseded by other forms of alcoholic drink.

In a further report from the same survey, the researchers indicated that drinking was widespread among the 14- and 15-year olds they surveyed, with almost three in four (74%) having tried alcohol and one in six (17%) drinking at least once a week. There were peer group influences and drinking alcohol was driven by a need to be part of the drinking subculture in their age group. There were signs of distinctive subcultures defined by the type of alcoholic drink usually consumed. Teenagers aged 16–17 years regarded themselves as more mature drinkers than 14- to 15-year olds and defined themselves therefore in terms of what they drank. Thus, the older teenagers were less likely to display an open preference for designer drinks if they were perceived to be an immature drinkers' drink. Instead, they wished to associate themselves with experienced drinkers and the drinks and brands they were perceived to prefer. Designer drinks were likened by 16- to 17-year olds more to soft drinks than hard drinks and hence were less likely to be named among their favourites (MacKintosh et al., 1997).

Whether consumption of alcopops leads to heavier alcohol consumption in general has been questioned by research conducted in Switzerland. Comparisons of consumers of alcopops and consumers of other alcoholic drinks (but not alcopops) found no significant differences between them in propensity to engage in risky drinking patterns or to suffer alcohol-related consequences such as involvement in anti-social behaviours. Overall amount of alcohol consumed, regardless of type, was the key predictor of negative alcohol-related consequences (Wicki et al., 2006).

In the UK, research has shown a declining interest in alcopops among young people. One survey reported that among those who said they had had a drink in the last six months, the percentages who said they had consumed alcohol declined from 2005 to 2007 among 11- to 13-year olds (from 53% to 37%), 14- to 17-year olds (76% to 62%) and among 18- to 21-year olds (69% to 61%). In the meantime, consumption of cider increased dramatically especially among 14- to 17-year olds (14% to 30%) and 18- to 21-year olds (11% to 31%) (Ofcom, 2007).

Summary

There has been growing concern about alcohol consumption among young people in the UK and other countries. This concern has been reinforced by large-scale surveys of national youth samples that have indicated that many teenagers experiment with alcohol and significant minorities drink on a regular basis. While some signs have emerged that more young people are starting to drink later, by the time they reach their mid-teens around one in two consume alcohol at least occasionally. Furthermore, growing numbers of teenage drinkers periodically drink to excess to the point of drunkenness. A number of factors have been identified as underpinning the onset of alcohol consumption among children and adolescents. The advertising of alcoholic products and the marketing of products deliberately targeted at young adult legal drinkers are among the factors believed to play a part in creating a climate in which alcohol consumption is regarded as normal, and that serves to trigger an interest in alcohol among those legally too young to purchase alcoholic products.

The availability of so-called designer drinks has been pinpointed as a particularly significant development that has encouraged young people to drink. These drinks not only have appeal because they are promoted with marketing messages that play on themes known to capture the attention of young consumers, but also provide alcohol-based products with varied flavours that attract inexperienced drinkers.

The provision of drinks that do not taste like normal alcoholic drinks – that for most people are an acquired taste – introduce under-age drinkers to alcohol consumption that is driven by the intrinsic taste appeal of the product as well as responding to social and cultural pressures. Despite the traditional association of heavy drinking with males, recent trends have indicated that female drinkers are consuming as much as their male counterparts.

This chapter has indicated that debates about alcohol-related consumption levels often make narrow assumptions about the nature of consumption and the robust nature of key definitions of consumption patterns, not least about the notion of 'binge' drinking. It is important to be clear about what a 'unit' of alcohol really means. It is also important to understand the social and cultural contexts in which alcohol consumption takes place. Much of the data produced by survey research, which forms the foundation of most of the research literature on this topic, are derived from respondents' self-reports about their behaviour. These reports can be challenged in terms of whether they provide accurate representations of over behaviour. Even leaving aside that evidence, however, financial data have indicated that more money is being spent on the purchase of alcohol. This trend is not accounted for simply by cost inflation. It has been observed that there has been an increase over time in the proportion of household expenditure (by 81% between 1992 and 2006) on alcohol products (Hastings & Angus, 2009).

This financial trend masks other behaviour shifts. The volume of alcohol bought and consumed outside the home has decreased over time while the volume consumed inside the home has increased. Similar proportions of people (25%) had purchased alcohol from supermarkets and from bars in 2007 (Lader, 2009). The heaviest drinkers bought more alcohol than did light drinkers from both locations.

In the context of the present book, the key question being investigated centres on the role played by advertising in priming young people to drink. Much of this book will focus on that question. Before doing this, however, it is important to consider what is known about the nature of young people's alcohol consumption habits. A number of large-scale national and international surveys have been carried out in the past 25 years that have attempted to map the prevalence of alcohol consumption and the frequency and nature of that consumption among young drinkers. It is important to understand the scale of this behaviour and it's problematic manifestations if any. It is also relevant to examine that quality of the research data on these behaviours. In the next chapter, attention is turned to marketing issues and alcohol. We begin by examining the nature of alcohol marketing and how it has evolved. Concerns about the possible role played by alcohol advertising have often centred on the types of appeals used by advertisers. One criticism is that alcohol advertising adopts actors, settings and themes that have strong appeal to young people, including those not yet legally old enough to purchase alcoholic beverages for themselves. In this way it draws in young people and encourages them to consume alcohol prematurely and creates a climate in which excessive alcohol consumption occurs. The following chapter will examine evidence concerning the nature of alcohol advertising to see whether it reinforces these critical observations. It also makes the important point that alcohol advertising cannot be considered in isolation. Alcohol consumption is embedded in and shaped by a range of social and cultural factors defined by the way alcohol is used and valued by social communities.

2
Alcohol Marketing over the Years

The principal focus of this book is the role played by the marketing of alcoholic drinks in shaping the way they are consumed. Marketing activities, however, represent one set of factors involved in the genesis and cultivation of patterns of alcohol consumption. There are other mediated representations of alcohol consumption, that are not components of marketing campaigns, that can nevertheless offer examples for others to follow or associate drinking alcohol with specific social narratives that might lend justification to real-world patterns of consumption. The influence of mediated representations of alcohol use does not occur in a vacuum and must be considered within a wider social and cultural context. This perspective may be especially relevant in the context of excessive alcohol consumption among young people.

For many young people, alcohol consumption is regarded as a leisure activity that is classified as a regular pastime associated with socialising with friends in bars, clubs and when out on dates or at parties. Drinking alcohol is also linked to identification and conformity with a reference group. Getting drunk is regarded as an important feature of making new friends and for strengthening bonds with existing friends. Drinking alcohol in adolescence is also associated with young people having more freedom to choose what to do with their lives as they gain more autonomy from their parents. Drinking can be a hedonistic pleasure in its own right. It can also be used as a form of escape and as a coping mechanism when confronted with problems.

Generally, drinkers tend to report more positive than negative consequences of alcohol consumption. While younger drinkers tend to have a rosier picture of alcohol consumption than do older drinkers, older drinkers seem to be more willing to recognise the negative consequences that can accompany excessive drinking.

Leigh and Lee (2008) also reviewed evidence that indicated that some cultures accept drunkenness more readily than do others. This acceptance of individuals who frequently get intoxicated can create a sense of normality about heavy drinking (Coleman & Cater, 2005). Even when society is perceived to be critical of drunkenness, however, young people tend to reject any suggestion that their consumption of alcohol should be externally controlled. If young people have been raised in an environment where adult drunkenness is commonplace, this too can increase the perception that excessive drinking is both normal and acceptable (MacAskill et al., 2001).

Social opinions about getting drunk have changed over time. Representations of drunkenness in the media are also signalled as playing a part in shaping public attitudes in this context. Social developments throughout the ages have created conditions under which alcohol consumption has been branded as acceptable or unacceptable. In pre-industrial Britain, it became fashionable to drink outside the home among the lower social classes and this was predominantly a male behaviour. Women who drank, particularly to excess, procured a negative social reputation for themselves. With industrialisation, working classes divided into two: those with skilled trades who sought to better themselves and those who remained unskilled for whom life was a struggle. The skilled working classes acquired affluence and also aspired to emulate the higher social classes not only through their growing wealth but also in terms of their behaviour. Drinking alcohol for this social group moved indoors into the private domain, while the unskilled working class continued to meet in public places to drink. For the latter, the alehouses often provided a more comfortable and hospitable space in which to spend one's time compared with the basic premises in which they tended to live. With class divides becoming more apparent, there was also a decrease in the extent to which the different classes shared the same recreational spaces.

Historically, alcohol consumption trends have evolved in line with wider social changes. Over time mediated representations and promotional campaigning have become more prevalent – taking advantage of changes in an evolving media landscape – and form part of the wider social fabric in which alcohol consumption occurs.

The emergence of the industrial era with growing numbers of people working in factories brought with it a need for more regularised control over behaviour both in the workplace and outside it. To operate effectively, routine and discipline had to be instilled in workforces employed in factories, although this was not always achieved. Even so, it invoked the idea of a work ethic that ran contrary to the values associated with hedonistic pursuits. Put simply, drunkenness reduced productivity. There are different schools of thought on this matter, however. For some, excessive drinking could be seen as a relief from the pressures of work and therefore has had an important social function that helped to keep order as much as it might have disrupted it (Campbell, 1987). In the modern era, in which consumer culture has taken hold, the pursuit of instant gratification and hedonism is a normative value system that permeates large sectors of society (Hayward & Hobbs, 2007), and alcohol consumption can be seen as an integral part of this ethos.

Measham (2008) outlines a number of mediated representations of intoxication. These have occurred in news coverage and in dramatic portrayals. Early twentieth-century movies portrayed intoxication positively in comedic, 'good time' scenarios. With the onset of the Second World War, a more sombre tone was adopted in which excessive consumption of alcohol was associated with physical and psychological problems (Rorabaugh, 2003). This trend continued into the 1960s with social commentary films graphically portraying the destructive professional and personal consequences of alcohol abuse (Room, 1989). A decade or so later, there was a shift back to the depiction of alcohol consumption as central to having fun in films such as *Animal House* and *Cocktail*.

Measham (2008) cites a number of examples of movies with alcohol consumption themes to illustrate changes that occurred over time in representations, some of which depicted themes of alcohol addiction and intoxication. How representative these movies might be of cinematic depictions of alcohol use is debatable. They do nevertheless provide some useful illustrations of prominent and in some instances iconic portrayals of alcohol misuse. We return to the topic of representations of alcohol consumption in movies and other entertainment formats in Chapter 7.

Another phenomenon that has driven changes in drinking patterns, not least among women, has been the introduction of a wider array of brands targeted at specific market segments. Alcopops, high-energy fortified drinks and various forms of cocktail have comprised new ways of consuming traditional forms of alcohol – beer, lager, cider, wine and spirits. Such beverages have been closely associated with youth drinking and in particular with increasing rates of heavy drinking sessions among women (Measham, 2006; Measham & Brain, 2005). According to Measham (2008), the media have cast alcopops as a 'temptation for young people' (p. 27). Whether youth drinkers actually behaved as portrayed by the media has been challenged by observation that young, early-stage drinkers continued to opt for cheaper and more traditional alcoholic beverages than the relatively expensive alcopops indicating that price is a primary driver of product choice (Brain & Parker, 1997). Instead of tempting teenagers, alcopops were actually of more interest to slightly older drinkers who could afford these newly fashionable brands.

Interest in the representation of alcohol in the media centres on arguments concerning the way media portrayals individually or collectively can or might affect alcohol consumption and orientations towards alcohol. The representation literature has examined non-advertising as well as advertising content in the media. Detailed examination of media representations has been used to assess the meanings and messages the media might convey about alcohol and its consumption.

This form of analysis is a useful adjunct to the research reported earlier that has focused on understanding the effects of alcohol advertising. For one thing, much of the empirical research literature about alcohol advertising has taken a fairly crude and simplistic view of the advertising itself. Yet, advertising messages can vary dramatically in their content and format. While some distinctions have been made on the basis of the platform for advertising, with comparisons made between the effectiveness of alcohol advertising on television, radio, newspapers, magazines, at the cinema, on billboards and posters and in retail outlets, the nature of the advertising messages themselves tends to be glossed over.

In considering different media or platforms in which advertising can occur, another aspect of 'representation' that we will consider here is the physical placement of advertisements. Advertisers can choose which programmes to set their commercial against on television and radio, which movies to advertise with in cinema theatres, which magazines or newspapers to locate their messages in, taking account of the nature of the readership, and in which communities to place posters or billboard advertising on the basis of the nature of the local consumer population. Although the study of representation of alcohol does not directly investigate the impact of advertising on children and teenagers, it can identify where potential effects might be found. This level of analysis is important in view of evidence that indicates widespread and repeated exposure of young people to alcohol advertising, especially on television (CAMY, 2002; Grube, 1993; Winter, Donovan & Fielder, 2008; Fielder, Donovan & Ouschan, 2009), but also on radio (CAMY, 2007) and in magazines: see Montes-Santiago, Muniz & Bazlomba (2007) on magazine advertising in Spain; Siegel et al. (2008) in the US; and Donovan et al. (2007) on magazine advertising in Australia). It has been reported in the US that viewers aged 12–20 years are likely to see more alcohol advertising than older viewers given the types of programmes in which such advertising most often occurs (CAMY, 2004).

The nature of alcohol advertising

A number of critical questions have been posed about the effects of alcohol advertising. Does it play a part in the onset of consumption among young people? Does it promote enhanced drinking? Does it contribute towards alcohol abuse? Does it create a positive mindset towards alcohol? Wherever such questions are empirically investigated, it is important to know not just whether advertising per se has an effect on alcohol consumption, but whether certain forms of advertising are particularly likely to have such an effect. So far, much of the consumer research evidence on the latter question has derived from studies of audience evaluations of advertising rather than investigations of advertising effects upon consumers.

Having clear and empirically verified insights into how attributes of advertising can mediate the overall impact of advertising on consumers – young or old – will not only enhance our general understanding of the role advertising can and does play in relation to the shaping of alcohol consumption and orientations towards alcohol, it will also provide more valuable intelligence with which to inform codes of advertising practice.

The overall volume of alcohol advertising in the mass media can provide a constant reminder of drinking that, in turn, serves to create the idea that alcohol consumption is a normative behaviour. If alcohol advertisers target media that are widely consumed by young people, including those who have yet to reach the age at which they can legally purchase alcohol, there is an increased likelihood that alcohol will come to be seen as a normal and acceptable aspect of contemporary culture (Montonen, 1996). Research published in the US by the Center on Alcohol Marketing and Youth (CAMY) has been used to reinforce the accusation that alcohol advertisers engage in deliberate targeting of young people. The placement of alcohol advertisements on radio (CAMY, 2007) and in magazines was found to target broadcasts and publications widely consumed by the youth market. This was reported to be true especially in the case of advertisements for beer and distilled spirits (CAMY, 2003, 2005). A recent American study also found evidence that 'the number of alcohol advertisements in magazines increases significantly with the proportion of youth readers, even after controlling for young adult readership. Our results indicate that youths are disproportionately exposed to alcohol advertising and that reducing youth exposure to alcohol advertising remains an important public policy concern.' (Siegel et al., 2008: 482).

It is not just the placement of alcohol advertising that is important in the context of its role in shaping youth drinking. The content of such advertising is also critical, particularly when it is characterised by promotional ingredients and production treatments that may have special appeal to young people. Advertising treatments have often tended to depict alcohol consumption in glamorous or pleasure-filled settings and associate alcohol with social and sexual success (Grube, 1993; Madden & Grube, 1994).

More recently, a study of beverage advertising in popular magazines and television in the US during 1999–2000 (Austin & Hust, 2005) concluded that alcohol is advertised heavily to youth through placement and appeals, and that alcohol advertisements emphasised sexual and social stereotypes and lacked diversity. Alcohol advertising in magazines aimed at women and men respectively have been found to construct women's and men's drinks and drinking behaviours in line with particular gender-stereotypes (Lyons, Dalton & Hoy, 2006). A masculinity and machismo discourse was found to be prominent, as was a discourse of 'drinking as normality'. Lyons, Dalton & Hoy. (2006), in their analysis of popular magazines in the UK, also found that drinking 'was aligned with traditional masculine images, although new kinds of drinks were aligned with traditional feminine images – and derided in men's magazines' (p. 223). Many alcohol advertisements project a particular view of masculinity through associations of consumption with manly pursuits linked to sport or adventure (Hill, 1999). If these treatments associate alcohol with attributes that have special appeal to young people, it is not difficult to conceive the potential roots of impact of advertising on early alcohol consumption.

Analysis of advertising message content is one way of determining whether advertisements contain ingredients that are likely to have special appeal for young consumers. Of course, it is not always easy to distinguish specific content features as young-person oriented where they may also appeal to older consumers. Nevertheless, if advice is to be presented to policymakers and regulators about more effective codes of practice, it is necessary to deconstruct advertising messages in detail.

Magazine advertising

One study of 13 national American magazines identified 454 alcohol advertisements (Breed and DeFoe, 1979). Twelve issues of each magazine were analysed in 1978 yielding a total magazine sample of 156 editions. Each magazine was the most popular publication of its type at that time. Coding focused on the physical size and setting of advertisements in the magazines, whether the advertisements featured people and who these people were and a range of themes indicating that alcohol consumption might be associated with wealth, prestige, economic, social or sexual success and so on.

A later American study of alcohol advertising in magazines covering major publications between 1997 and 2001 found a tendency for beer and spirits advertising to be more frequently occurring in magazines that attracted larger adolescent readerships. Most of the advertising across these publications was for distilled spirits (82%), with much smaller proportions of advertising occupied by messages for beer (13%) and wine (5%). The researchers called for closer examination of advertising policies where magazine advertising of alcohol is concerned to ensure that it avoids those publications where widespread exposure to alcohol promotions among adolescents is likely to result (Garfield, Chung & Rathouz, 2003).

Alcohol advertisements were dominated by lifestyle themes that indicated the possibility of short-term and long-term rewards or gratifications associated with drinking alcohol. The most prevalent theme among lifestyle advertisements was long-term wealth and success, then social approval among friends or acquaintances, relaxation, purely hedonistic pleasure, exotic travel and experiences, individualism and selfish experiences, and finally sexual success. Wealth and success was most often associated with Scotch advertisements; social approval and relaxation were associated mostly with vodka; hedonistic pleasure and sexual success with tequila; and exotic associations with beer and tequila.

The theme of tradition or history also featured in alcohol advertising and was most closely associated with Scotch, gin and American whisky and beer. It contained messages of longevity of establishment through dates when the manufacturing process first started and the use of historical images such as sailing ships, old plantations and literary characters.

Direct appeals to product attributes such as good taste or smoothness of texture dominated rum commercials and also occurred frequently with fortified wine and American whisky advertisements.

Neuendorf (1986) reported research from the US that indicated that some alcohol advertisers were branding their products as 'good food' rather than as a substance that can intoxicate its consumers. The same researcher described the cases she identified in this respect:

> Four sets of specimen magazine advertisements were used; (1) three liqueur advertisements which seemed to evade the issue of alcoholic content (one showed a liqueur being used as a cooking ingredient for *every* course in a large meal, one showed the product next to a large, ripe peach, and one showed the product being poured – a dead ringer for chocolate milk); (2) these same three advertisements with the product name and picture masked out; (3) three typical hard liquor advertisements using the typical appeals to friendship, prestige, and romance; and (4) these same three advertisements with the product name and picture masked out.
>
> (Neuendorf, 1987: 17)

A sample of 11- to 19-year olds were shown these advertisements and asked to comment upon what was being promoted. Those who saw the liqueur advertisements frequently misinterpreted the product as non-alcoholic because of its close association with food in the commercial message. Even when the teenagers knew that the product being advertised was a liqueur, a significant minority (29%) still misperceived it as non-alcoholic.

This kind of analysis reveals the subtle ways in which advertising can disguise the nature of alcoholic beverages and, in turn, distort the impressions formed about them by naïve young consumers. It is important to identify the attributes of alcohol advertising that can trigger these effects and then to catalogue them in terms of their prevalence. Content analysis methodology is the technique usually applied by media researchers to provide a systematic and objective report of the attributes of media content. This technique has been applied to alcohol advertising.

In two early studies, advertisements for alcoholic products were frequently found to link alcohol consumption with images of having fun with friends, relaxation and with humour. These attributes were especially prevalent in television advertising and somewhat less so in magazine advertising (Atkin & Block, 1981; Finn & Strickland, 1982).

Following social learning theory (Bandura, 1977), advertisements may be especially likely to have a profound impact when consumers identify with actors and models in the commercial messages. The use of characters who matched the target consumer groups in terms of demographic profile was particularly notable of magazine alcohol advertisements (Strickland & Finn, 1984). A recent Australian study of magazine alcohol advertising (Donovan et al., 2007) in magazines popular with adolescents and young people found alcohol advertisements and promotions to be prominent, with two thirds of magazines containing at least one alcohol advertisement or promotion. The study also sought to assess whether alcohol advertisements and promotions were compliant with the Australian Alcoholic Beverages Advertising Code. The authors found that 52 per cent of magazine alcohol advertisements/promotions appeared to contravene at least one section of the Code, with the two major apparent breaches being in relation to the Code's 'section B – the items having a strong appeal to adolescents (34%) and to section C – promoting positive social, sexual and psychological expectancies of consumption (28%)' (p. 73).

Television advertising

Television has, for many years, been the most prevalent and widely used mass medium in developed countries and a significant proportion of developing countries around the world. Despite the emergence of the Internet, it remains the dominant advertising medium in the UK and across the rest of Europe. Television is a platform that has been regularly used by alcohol advertisers to promote their products. It is pertinent therefore to consider the nature of televised advertising of alcoholic drinks to consider whether it is characterised by features likely to hold special appeal to young people and to establish how compliant such advertising is with established codes of practice.

The importance of television as an advertising medium for the alcohol sector was underpinned by data indicating growth in alcohol advertisements on US television between 2001 and 2003, with particularly strong growth in advertising for distilled spirits on cable television channels (CAMY, 2004). While most television alcohol advertising was devoted to beer products, advertising of alcopops represented the second biggest area of expenditure among alcohol advertisers (CAMY, 2004).

In an attempt to establish the extent to which alcohol advertising was promoted on television in the UK, Barton and Godfrey (1988) analysed 1258 television advertisements over a 10-week period covering the Christmas and New Year holidays. All advertising was recorded from ITV and Channel 4. In all, they found 156 advertisements (12% of the total sample) that promoted alcoholic drinks. More often than not (56% of the time) alcohol advertisements occurred in first position in advertising breaks and tended to be longer than other product commercials. Alcohol advertisements were equally likely to occur before and after the 9 pm watershed, but occurred with greatest intensity between 6 pm and 7 pm in the evening. This meant that they could have been seen by large numbers of children.

Neuendorf's (1986, 1987) research on magazine advertising, discussed in the preceding section, found that teenage audiences frequently misinterpreted advertised alcoholic products as non-alcoholic because of their close association with food in the commercial message. The association between alcohol and food was also found in a recent study of changes in food advertising during prime-time television from 1991 to 2006 in the UK and Canada (Adams et al., 2009), which showed that '[t]he "TV diet" in the UK in 1991 was high in fat, sodium, sugar and alcohol and low in fibre compared to current recommendations. By 2006, the UK "TV diet" was high in sodium, sugar and alcohol and low in fibre' (p. 584).

Fielder, Donovan & Ouschan (2009), in a study of alcohol advertising on Australian metropolitan free-to-air television, examined exposure levels for all alcohol advertisements screened from November 2005 to October 2006 in each capital city market for: children 0–12 years; underage teens 13–17 years; young adults 18–24 years; and mature adults 25+ years. The study found that overall children were exposed to one-third the level of mature adults, but there were considerable variations between markets. In two markets, underage teens thus had higher rates of exposure than young adults. The study also found that the '30 highest exposed advertisements contained at least one element known to appeal to children and underage youth, with 23 containing two or more such elements' (p. 1157). On the basis of these findings, the authors argue that the self-regulating system governing alcohol advertising in Australia 'does not protect children and youth from exposure to alcohol advertising, much of which contains elements appealing to these groups'.

Analysis of televised alcohol advertisements in New Zealand showed that much of this advertising is characterised by masculinity themes that revolve around spending time with 'your mates', following or taking part in sport, having a good time and (for men) success with the opposite sex (Trottman, Wyllie & Casswell, 1994).

Research in Brazil found that alcohol advertising on television was greater than that for tobacco, non-alcoholic drinks and medicines, but less than that for foods and other fast-moving consumer goods. The most frequent themes in alcohol advertising were relaxation, national symbolism, conformity, camaraderie and humour. Human rather than animated actors were depicted in most alcohol advertisements. There were no messages present within televised alcohol advertising that advised people to drink moderately, but a small proportion of advertisements (7%) contained appeals that promoted excessive drinking (Pinsky & Silva, 1999).

Research from the US found that the most common themes associated with alcohol advertising broadcast within televised sports programmes were humour, friendship, surreal fantasy and love/sex/romance. Less common themes were escape/adventure and success/achievement. Few advertisements still focused on product quality and very few exhibited moderate drinking themes (Zwarun & Farrar, 2005). A recent study in the UK of children's interpretation of television alcohol advertisements (Nash, Pine & Messer, 2009) adds further weight to the importance of considering the type and format of imagery and connotations used alcohol advertising. The research showed that children of all ages liked the alcohol advertisements in the study and perceived them as effective. There was also clear evidence that 'advertising styles affected popularity with humour, cartoon format or the inclusion of an animal, or character increasing the appeal of an advertisement' (p. 85).

New forms of alcohol promotion

Regulations for alcohol advertising can be found in many countries and cover all the longer-established advertising media – television, radio, cinema and print media. One new medium to which advertisers have increasingly turned is the Internet. This has proven to be more resistant to regulatory controls. The promotion of alcohol on this platform occurs not only in the form of advertising, but also web sites that draw visitors in with more generalised entertainment and information content. Many of these sites are operated by major alcohol companies. Evidence has already emerged that commercial alcohol-related web sites are accessible to and accessed by children and teenagers (see Grube & Walters, 2005). These web sites are often produced or sponsored by alcohol manufacturers and link alcohol brands with interactive games, music and online social networks designed to have special appeal to the youth market (see Anderson, 2007).

In Australia, Roberts (2002) found a number of web sites that contained features that would have appeal for young people. These features included games, videos and music content. Roberts examined 28 web sites in total, all of which were maintained by alcohol companies in 2002. These sites did not originate only in Australia. The analysis coded a number of attributes that included references to music and sport, slogans, competitions and games, use of animation, video material and download options, and the use of language and colour.

Many, though not all of these, web sites contained age disclaimers that required visitors to register that they were old enough to drink. Some sites depended upon the honesty of users to self-disclose that they were old enough to visit the site, and others required the visitor to provide their date of birth before they could proceed into the depths of the site.

These Internet sites were found to utilise a number of attributes that could be expected to have youth appeal. Colour schemes, music, video material, download options and interactive games featured among other attributes as core elements. Some sites even offered visitors free alcohol. The general concern here was that controls over entry to the site were minimal and could be easily circumvented by underage users. Furthermore, it was clear that the sites frequently used production techniques that are known to play well with young consumers.

One of the concerns about the effects of alcohol advertising is that it may represent depictions of alcohol consumption from which social learning can take place. Thus, young consumers, who are still under the legal drinking age, observe attractive drinking scenarios and role models consuming alcohol and they wish to emulate that behaviour. This effect does not invariably occur following mere exposure, however. It is well-established that children and teenagers develop a growing cynicism about advertising as they grow older and their consumer and media literacy develops (Young, 2003).

Further research into the potential role played by Internet promotions for alcohol has been carried out in New Zealand. Groups of teenagers, aged between 14 and 18 years, were interviewed about their experiences with alcohol advertising in different media. Special attention was paid to web sites concerned with alcoholic beverages (Borell, Gregory & Kaiwai, 2005). Although not technically targeted at underage drinkers, web sites associated with alcohol brands contain many features likely to appeal to this age group and do little to deter them from entering such sites. Most of these sites ask visitors to enter their date of birth. This has been found to be an ineffective barrier in the case of users under 18 years. Given the prominence of competitions many of which had sexual and sporting themes, it was not surprising that these sites would attract the attention of users not yet old enough legally to buy alcoholic beverages. A number of campaigns depicted young attractive females. In some instances, these models were depicted at or in association with sports events. These alcoholic brand web sites often formed part of a mixed media marketing strategy that embraced a wide range of marketing devices that included advertising in mass media, sponsorship of (usually sporting) events and merchandising.

The positioning of alcohol advertisements

While the content and format of advertisements can be manipulated in an attempt to influence the nature of the meanings presented to consumers about alcohol, the placement of advertisements in different media is another significant aspect of the way alcohol is presented to the public by marketers. Controls and codes of practice linked to advertising of alcohol often make references to placement issues in the context of restricting exposure to such advertising of young people.

Alcohol marketers have been accused of singling out specific target groups for advertising purposes. This happens regardless of the platform being used for advertising. Beer advertisers may buy advertising space on television in and around major sports broadcasts in the knowledge that large numbers of potential beer drinkers (e.g., males) will be watching. Similarly, wine manufacturers may advertise in glossy supplements of broadsheet Sunday newspapers knowing that the readership has a healthy representation of wine drinkers.

There is research from the US that has indicated that alcohol advertisers target specific demographic communities through billboard advertising. Alcohol billboards were found to be located disproportionately in black and poorer parts of urban areas. Such areas averaged 38 such billboards compared to seven in predominantly white and more affluent community districts (Hackbarth, Silvestri & Cosper, 1995).

An analysis of alcoholic beverage advertisements in magazines in 2001 found that a significant proportion of expenditure on that advertising was devoted to magazines with primary readerships aged 12–16 years (CAMY, 2002). The same organisation reported a marked increase in the number of alcohol advertisements on US television between 2001 and 2003. CAMY figures showed that there were 298,054 alcohol advertisements on US television in 2003, up from 289, 381 in 2002 and 208, 909 in 2001. The most dramatic growth occurred in respect of advertisements for distilled spirits which increased from just 513 in 2001 to 33, 126 in 2003. A more critical set of figures concerned so-called over-exposed underage youth. This audience category is likely to be overexposed when alcohol advertisements are placed in programmes for which the percentage of 12- to 20-year olds in the audience exceed the percentage of people aged 21+. Thus, the number of alcohol advertisements that carried the risk of over-exposing youth to alcohol promotions increased to 69,054 in 2003, from 66,218 in 2002 and 51,084 in 2001 (CAMY, 2004).

Winter, Donovan & Fielder (2008), in a comprehensive study of exposure of children and adolescents to alcohol advertising on television in Australia, found that while adults aged 25 years and older received the highest exposure (660 Target Audience Rating Points – TARPs – per week), underage teenagers (13–17 years) and young adults (18–24 years) received exposures of 426 and 429 TARPs per week respectively. Children (0–12 years) were exposed to approximately one in every three alcohol advertisements seen on average by mature adults (25 years and older). These findings lead the authors to conclude 'that Australian children and teenagers below the legal drinking age currently are exposed to unacceptably high levels of alcohol advertising on television' (p. 676).

Another popular location for alcohol advertising is their placement within televised sports events. One analysis of these broadcasts in the US between 1990 and 1992, for instance, has shown that more advertisements appear for alcoholic beverages than for any other product category in televised sports events. Commercial messages for beers were especially prevalent. Advertising through commercials in programme breaks were further reinforced by the sponsorship of stadium signs and onsite promotions that also appeared on camera (Madden & Grube, 1994).

In view of the popularity of sports programmes on television among alcohol advertisers (Grube & Wallack, 1994), research has been conducted in the US to examine the nature of alcohol advertising in these programmes and to determine whether such advertising breaches industry codes of practice. While this research found virtually no literal breaches of advertising codes, a number of ambiguous cases were revealed in which some alcohol advertisements challenged the 'spirit' of a code (Zwarun & Farrar, 2005).

Across a sample of 103 hours of network television sports programming containing 144 alcohol advertisements broadcast between 1994 and 1997 and 1999 and 2002, no advertisements were found that showed anyone intoxicated, below the legal drinking age or engaging in potentially hazardous pursuits after or during drinking. However, three out of four alcohol advertisements (75%) broadcast between 1999 and 2002 and six out of ten (59%) broadcast between 1994 and 1997 were ambiguous about whether drinking had taken place. A small proportion of the advertisements coded (2% in 1999–2002 and 9% in 1994–7) suggested that drinking to excess had taken place. One example here was an advertisement for Foster's Lager that depicted a man conveying his friends who had passed out, presumably from drinking too much, in a wheelbarrow. In addition, one in ten (11%) alcohol advertisements broadcast between 1999 and 2002 and nearly one in five (19%) of those broadcast between 1994 and 1997 hinted at excessive alcohol consumption. While none of the advertisements depicted underage people, nearly half (49%) overall depicted characters judged to be between 21 and 29 years of age. Hence, a significant proportion of these advertisements were apparently targeted at the young adult market. If alcohol advertisements could potentially appeal to 21-year olds (legal drinkers), the question arises as to whether they might also have appeal to 20-year olds (underage drinkers) (Zwarun & Farrar, 2005).

Summary and conclusions

In summary, studies from the last 30 years have provided significant evidence regarding the extent and nature of alcohol advertising across a broad range of media, including print media, broadcast media and – more recently – the Internet. They have shown that alcohol advertising images deploy a range of attractive and popular images – not surprisingly, given their promotional objective – associating alcohol and drinking with fun, humour, celebration, pleasant socialising and with gender stereotypes as well as with sexual and other (e.g., sports) prowess. By contrast, alcohol advertisements have been found to contain little or insufficiently clear information about alcohol strength or related nutritional information.

As some audience studies have demonstrated, alcohol advertising not only contains attributes that might hold some appeal for young people, they are also placed in media locations that attract large numbers of children and teenagers below the legal alcohol drinking age. A key finding of a number of relatively recent studies (in the US, Australia and elsewhere) is the finding that much alcohol advertising, ostensibly aimed at adult audiences, reaches significant and sizeable underage audiences, to the extent that the effectiveness of voluntary or self-regulatory codes aimed at protecting younger audiences from this kind of promotion must be questioned. Although as we will see later in this book, advertising regulators have revised codes of practice to tackle this issue, the expansion of the Internet has opened up new opportunities for alcohol product marketers over which regulators have little or not control. Further, while traditional forms of advertising in the older mainstream media such as television, radio, cinema and print can face more restrictions, newer and more subtle forms of promotions embedded within non-advertising content in online environments can circumvent these restrictions and provide a much bigger challenge not simply to regulators but also to media consumers in distinguishing advertising from non-advertising content. The latter distinction is critical if consumers are to be able to consciously recognise when they are being confronted with advertising messages. These issues turn our examination of alcohol advertising towards the audience. The next three chapters review research literature on alcohol advertising and consumers, exploring how consumers individually and collectively might be influenced by promotional messages for alcohol products. Chapter 3 starts this journey with an analysis of the role played by advertising of alcohol on macro-levels of consumption in national and regional markets.

3
Advertising and Alcohol Consumption in Society

Introduction

Alcohol manufacturers and retailers have been placed under increased pressure by medical and health lobbies over the promotional activities they use to encourage consumers to purchase their products. In a report published by the British Medical Association, Hastings and Angus (2009) remind their readers that alcohol consumption in the UK has increased over time, especially among young people, giving the UK one of the worst records in Europe for alcohol abuse, and also that marketing communications have powerful effects upon triggering the onset of drinking, affecting how much is consumed. While it is conceded that other factors including price, availability, personal and social influences that embrace individuals' personality characteristics as well as parental, sibling and peer-group attitudes have proved pivotal in driving consumption, the case for the role played by marketing activities is regarded as proven.

Other writers have noted that drinks promotions can influence excessive drinking habits by providing incentives, usually associated with price offers, for volume purchases or intensive drinking bouts. These promotions have been aimed at young adult markets where the alcohol consumption scene shifted in the 1990s from pubs to dance clubs. Alcohol consumption became socially branded as one among a range of substances used to achieve altered mental states that were deemed to be a critical aspect of having a good time in such settings (Measham, Aldridge & Parker, 2001).

Hasting and Angus (2009) did not pull any punches. They regarded the effects of marketing factors as so serious in this context that they recommended more far-reaching and stringent controls over all forms of alcohol promotion that were currently in place. They identified controls over price levels, sales practices and the density of alcohol outlets as critical and advocated increased taxation on alcohol products and a comprehensive ban on all alcohol advertising. These steps were believed to be justified given the growing social costs of alcohol misuse and abuse, which is particularly prevalent among young people. There are immediate or short-term costs of excessive consumption on anti-social behaviour and longer-term health implications of persistent over-indulgence.

One source of evidence cited in support of the significance of alcohol advertising was the overall amount that was spent on it each year by the industry. Citing figures from Ofcom/ASA, Hasting and Angus reported that expenditure of alcohol advertising across television, radio, the pres, outdoors and cinemas increased from £167m in 2002 to £221m in 2005 before settling back at £194m in 2006. Most of the fall between 2005 and 2006 was accounted for by a reduction in televised advertising. Even so, television remained the main advertising medium for the drinks industry and alcohol advertising incurred greater expenditure than most other product categories. Despite the decrease in expenditure on alcohol advertising on television between 2005 and 2006, the numbers of televised advertising spots actually increased across these two years from 412, 000 to 442, 000 (Hastings & Angus, 2009). These authors then cited econometric evidence based on studies of societal-level links between volumes of alcohol advertising or expenditure on such advertising and levels of alcohol consumption in specific markets as further support for the role played by advertising and marketing in shaping drinking behaviour.

The role played by advertising and other forms of marketing (e.g., price promotions, event sponsorship, branded merchandising) in relation to commodities such as alcohol has been empirically investigated over several decades and is still a matter of much debate, especially with regard to its potential to increase consumption among young people. The review of research evidence presented in the remainder of this book will underline this point. The presumption on the part of professional bodies such as the British Medical Association that the debate about advertising and marketing influences is over because it has been empirically settled may be a premature assertion that still bears closer analysis. Indeed, even some world authorities that have expressed serious concerns about the spread of alcohol misuse among young people, recognising also that alcohol marketing is highly visible in many parts of the world, still express caution about the evidence for the role played by advertising and marketing in shaping alcohol consumption and associated behaviours.

According to the International Center for Alcohol Policy (ICAP) and as reported in 2003 to a World Health Organisation (WHO) meeting, no compelling evidence exists to support an association between advertising and drinking patterns among young people. It was stated that

> The industry does not condone promotion and advertising of beverage alcohol to those under the legal minimum purchase age. Yet it should be acknowledged that young people are inevitably exposed to beverage alcohol advertising, as they are to advertising for any other consumer product. They are aware of it, and are able to identify and distinguish between alcohol brands, just as they are able to discern brands of other consumer goods. However, the evidence does not support the notion that such awareness increases consumption by young people.
>
> (point 30: 9)

This observation, however, contradicts the work of health care researchers and workers who have suggested that there are associations between exposure to alcohol advertising and drinking behaviour (see BMA, 2008). A number of cross-sectional surveys have managed to demonstrate that an increased awareness of alcohol messages among young people might lead to earlier onset of and higher consumption. Alongside these studies, evidence from which will be discussed in the next chapter, a number of macro-level analyses have compared advertising coverage with drinking consumption, in an effort to offer insight in the potential role of alcohol advertising and levels of consumption. Such analyses have also been employed in the study of advertising bans and their effectiveness in reducing alcohol use and abuse.

Further doubt has been cast on the influence of alcohol advertising and other marketing by a major international study that explored factors that underpin the onset of alcohol consumption and patterns of drinking among young people. Focus group interviews with teenagers and young adults aged between 16 and 25 years questioned participants about their use of alcohol. Data were collected in seven countries: Brazil, China, Italy, Nigeria, Russia, South Africa and Scotland (Martinic & Measham, 2008b).

Alcohol consumption was widely associated with socialising with friend and peer groups, as well as with family members. Alcohol was also consumed during times of celebration. Drinking helped people to bond and for some individuals it boosted their self confidence. Typical drinking experiences did vary however not only between countries but also with the life stage and everyday living circumstances of group participants. Those living with a long-term relationship, for instance, might enjoy a quiet drink at home with their partner, while young adults still living at home with their parents would more often drink out of the home with their friends.

What was perhaps most significant in the context of discussion about the role of advertising and other forms of marketing in triggering alcohol consumption is that many of the young people interviewed in this study reported that they were introduced to alcohol by their parents often in the context of family celebrations and parties. Afterwards, peer groups had a longer-term influence on drinking patterns once they had taken that first step. There were cultural variations in whether going out to get drunk was purposive or not. In many countries, drunkenness was an unintentional effect of having a good time when out with friends. This was true of most youth drinking in Brazil and Italy. However, going out with the deliberate intention of getting drunk was reported by interviewees from Nigeria, Russia, Scotland and South Africa. In China, there were often strict social, generally family-based, controls over alcohol consumption. Advertising and marketing were rarely mentioned at all and when they did emerge in group discussions, they were seen as peripheral factors linked to alcohol consumption habits of the young people being interviewed (Martinic & Measham, 2008b).

As the present chapter will demonstrate, the findings from macro-level analyses should be treated with caution. Although such studies offer some evidence of the role that advertising plays in shaping consumption, especially among young people, they still suffer from limitations as they do not offer compelling evidence regarding the role of advertising in the onset of drinking or the direct effect of advertising on alcohol consumption levels.

Advertising and alcohol consumption through macro-level analyses

Traditionally, 'macro analysis' is employed for the investigation of consumption experiences *across* products rather than the experience of a single product; and as Holbrook (1986) explains,

> This macroview looks for general patterns of consumption behavior and thereby extends beyond the typical but somewhat parochial pre-occupation with a single brand in some product category.
>
> (Holbrook, 1986: 43)

The macro analysis method is used widely in the field of advertising research, where the units of observation are the advertisements rather than individuals (Stewart and Furse, 1986; Holbrook and Batra, 1987; Olney et al., 1991; Chaudhuri and Buck, 1995, in Chaudhuri, 1998: 160). In the area of alcohol advertising, macro-level analyses mostly refer to the investigation of the relationships between overall volumes of advertising or amounts of expenditure on advertising and consumption levels, producing findings that have been of interest to alcohol manu-facturers who seek to maximise their market shares and need to be able to measure the effectiveness of advertising campaigns.

A notable aspect of the relationship between advertising and alcohol consumption is that increased consumption does not always translate in a gradual increase in sales. An interesting finding was revealed by a US study that covered all forms of advertising for beer by the four larg-est breweries. While advertising appeared to stimulate immediate sales of alcohol, it also resulted in consumers building up their own stocks which then had a negative effect on future sales volumes (Peles, 1971a, 1971b). Apart from the fact that causal relationships cannot be directly inferred from studies based on secondary statistical analysis of aggre-gated data sets, these studies do not assess how advertising might influ-ence specific drinking patterns or plays a part in the onset of drinking among alcohol consumers. It is important when examining aggregated data sets to check that any correspondence between alcohol advertising volumes and alcohol consumption volumes is correctly interpreted as an effect of advertising. This has been attempted by a number of stud-ies focusing on issues of advertising expenditure, type of alcohol and product brand.

Alcohol consumption and advertising expenditure

The assessment of advertising expenditure has been widely used as a method of analysis of advertising effects on consumption habits. Critics of alcohol advertising highlight the importance of expenditure because of the significant amounts it can reach, especially in developed countries such as the UK, and also because it indicates the potential for exposure to alcohol advertising in different media (Hastings & Angus, 2009). Of course, expenditure on advertising can be a misleading proxy for measurement of the actual amount of such advertising. For example, while commercial advertising spots on television for alcoholic beverages increased in the UK between 2004 and 2006, expenditure on televised advertising declined over this period (Ofcom, 2007).

Early research on the overall impact of advertising on alcohol sales indicated that the amount of expenditure on advertising offers no guarantee of enhanced product sales (Simon, 1969). In this research, data focused on sales of spirits in 17 states in the USA over the 1953–63 period; and evidence showed that advertising expenditure data were limited to advertising in magazines and newspapers. In certain cases advertising is even found to respond to rather than trigger consumption levels, with increases in alcohol consumption triggering greater expenditure on advertising (Fisher, 1993).

This was confirmed by another US study, which was not limited to alcohol product sales only and demonstrated that although advertising volumes were associated with sales levels, including for alcohol, sales led advertising rather than the other way around. Sales figures and consumption levels tended to be influenced by price as much as any economic factor (Grabowski, 1976). Along similar lines, an analysis of quarterly data covering the 1956–75 period in the US investigated the relationship between advertising volumes and total consumption of alcoholic beverages. Yet, it provided no evidence that advertising impacted upon alcohol consumption. If anything, the authors concluded, advertising expenditure was triggered by product demand (Ashley, Granger & Schmalensee, 1980).

The strength of associative links between advertising expenditure and alcohol consumption can also be affected by normal levels of consumption in particular markets. In markets where drinking levels are fairly low, a boost to advertising expenditure might be associated with a clear uplift in volume of consumption. Where consumption levels are already high, and where competition between brands is fierce, additional advertising expenditure might be linked to changes in brand market shares but does not necessarily produce an increase in overall alcohol consumption. In fact, in competitive markets, advertising may serve to maintain market share of established brands, but little else. In these kinds of markets, additional advertising expenditure may therefore yield only marginal returns (Hastings et al., 2005; Saffer & Dave, 2002a).

Last, in a study that departed from the usual econometric approach and analysed advertising expenditure in connection to motor vehicle fatalities in the USA, Saffer (1997b) found that advertising could potentially influence consumption. After building in various control variables, this analysis showed that advertising volume was related to motor deaths on the road, but once again pricing effects proved a more significant variable, which could also reduce fatalities.

Role of alcohol type and brand in advertising effects: macro-level analyses

In assessing potential effects of advertising on alcohol consumption, the alcohol type in question may matter too. Barnes and Bourgeois (1977) conducted research on advertising and per capita consumption of alcohol in Canada covering the 1951–74 period. Overall alcohol consumption was significantly linked to neither broadcast nor print advertising volumes. Some evidence did emerge, however, that print advertising was predictive of increased beer consumption and decreased spirits consumption. These data suggest that it is not simply the impact of advertising *per se* upon alcohol consumption that is important, but also the possibility that any changes in levels of consumption of type of alcohol (e.g., in this case, beer) could have an impact upon consumption levels for a different type of alcohol (e.g., spirits).

A further investigation confirmed the advertising–alcohol consumption relationship of the previous study (Bourgeois & Barnes, 1979). Barnes (1984) extended this Canadian research further and included data up to 1981. Few significant relationships emerged between advertising and different types of alcohol consumption (i.e., for beer, wine and spirits) and these relationships tended to be negative. This relationship was consistent with the explanation that while consumption levels had increased over the period examined, advertising expenditure levels had not increased in line with consumption.

Finally, research conducted in Ireland examined beer consumption in relation to income, unemployment figures, product prices and advertising volumes and found a small, but statistically significant and positive relationship between beer consumption and advertising between 1967 and 1977. This finding indicated that advertising could have contributed towards per capita beer consumption during that period (Walsh, 1980).

Brand should also be taken into consideration as other studies have found that advertising can affect consumption of the brand being advertised but has no impact on consumption of other brands within the same alcohol product category (Gius, 1995). There is also evidence that advertising of one type of alcohol (spirits or wine) might enhance consumption of that product category and at the same time reduce consumption of other product categories, suggesting some kind of displacement effect (Nelson & Moran, 1995). Comanor and Wilson (1974) reported that advertising volumes were associated with increased wine consumption and a smaller demand increase for spirits, but no effect was apparent in respect of malt liquor. These researchers concluded that the primary effect of advertising was to drive market shares among broad drinks categories and brands.

Macro-level analysis of advertising and alcohol consumption in the UK

Research in the UK has largely echoed the findings from the US, though once again the evidence suffers from the limitations embodied in analyses conducted at a macro level. Hence, research conducted in the UK has been unable to offer meaningful findings about factors that might shape alcohol consumption at the level of the individual drinker. Moreover, analyses that have been conducted about the strength of any associations between annual expenditure on advertising and overall consumption have mostly failed to reflect the way advertising campaigns operate in practice. Because campaigns usually run for limited periods, are then discontinued, only to be relaunched later, their impact on consumption may therefore be manifest in 'pulses' around the campaigns themselves. Consequently, annualised averaging of relationships between advertising expenditure and consumption can fail to represent these pulsing effects.

These research weaknesses were reflected in the study of Waterson (1989) who reported that the amount of money spent on advertising does not always equate to greater consumption of a product category. Data for 1978–87 showed that while beer advertising in the UK increased by 80 per cent, consumption fell by 14 per cent. Expenditure on spirits advertising across the same period rose by 70 per cent but consumption fell four per cent. In contrast, advertising expenditure on wine fell by 26 per cent and sales rose by 65 per cent.

What research in the UK has demonstrated is a distinction between the potential advertising effects on specific alcoholic drinks and on overall consumption. For instance, over the late 1950s, 1960s and early 1970s, although wine and beer advertising was found to exhibit no relationship with consumption (see Calfee & Scheraga, 1994), a small positive effect was found in the case of spirits advertising, (McGuiness, 1980, 1983). Further research that covered a period (1963–79) during which alcohol consumption doubled in volume found that advertising exerted a weak effect on beer and spirits consumption, but had no clear impact on wine consumption (Duffy, 1980).

In a second publication, Duffy (1982) asserted that there was no compelling evidence that total alcohol consumption was affected by advertising, but in the case of beer the data are equivocal. It was therefore not possible at that time to conclude that alcohol advertising had no impact whatsoever on any aspect of alcohol consumption. Moreover, it should be noted that this study omitted advertising at the cinema and on posters and radio, and so failed to represent a complete account of advertising expenditure for alcoholic products.

In a third paper, Duffy (1985) reconfirmed the possibility of advertising effects on the consumption of certain alcohol types by concluding that there could be a small effect upon the way drinking is distributed across beer, wine and spirits consumption, even if the overall effect of advertising on aggregate consumption of alcohol was unclear.

The data originally collated by Duffy and McGuiness were used for further analysis that offered more extensive evidence of the role of different alcoholic types in shaping advertising effects on consumption. It was also found that advertising for one type of alcoholic beverage could reduce demand for a different type of drink, and spirits advertising appeared to reduce demand for wine (Godfrey, 1988). Such research indicated that overall quantities of alcohol consumption may not be affected by alcohol advertising, but the market shares of different types of alcoholic beverage can be affected. Consequently, price proved to be a more defining factor in shaping alcohol consumption than was advertising volume.

Limitations in macro-level studies of alcohol advertising effects

Overall, it appears that a significant segment of the research addressing the relationship between advertising and alcohol consumption stems from econometric analyses using aggregated data to examine relationships over time between the volume of advertising and quantity of alcohol consumption in specific markets (Bourgeois & Barnes, 1979; Duffy, 1987, 1991; Franke & Wilcox, 1987; Nelson, 1999; Nelson & Moran, 1995; Saffer, 1997a; Selvanathan, 1989). The data produced by such analyses, however, suffer from specific limitations. They cannot offer evidence regarding the role of advertising in the onset of drinking, nor can they indicate anything about direct effects of advertising volumes or expenditure on advertising upon individuals' alcohol consumption levels. Even if advertising is shown to play a part in shaping consumption among young people, whether it serves as an initial trigger point for drinking onset or a force that maintains consumption or directly affects level of consumption is less certain. This has also led a number of writers to question whether alcohol advertising does influence consumption or can be legitimately cited as a causal variable in relation to alcohol-related behaviour and health problems (Fisher, 1999; Fisher & Cook, 1995; Young, 1993).

Interestingly, the absence of compelling evidence regarding causal links between advertising and the overall level of alcohol consumption has often been utilised by alcohol and advertising industries to argue against alcohol advertising bans; but at the same time, it is this same absence of compelling data emerging from macro-level analyses that has led to some econometric studies seeking to assess potential advertising effects through the effectiveness of advertising bans. There are extensive debates regarding the effectiveness of placing restrictions on or even removing alcohol advertisements. These debates are mostly centred on two counterarguments, the view of health experts and that of the industry. While the former emphasise the association of advertising with alcohol-related deaths and see a potential ban as an effective prevention measure, the latter argue that, as any other legal product, alcohol should be possible to advertise. However, as discussed in the following sections, even in the study of advertising bans, researchers have been unable to demonstrate adequate evidence of effectiveness of advertising restrictions.

Advertising bans and restrictions

Opinions regarding the effectiveness of banning alcohol advertising, either partially or comprehensively, are divided. Those who support bans have argued that removal of advertising would take out constant reminders about drinking alcohol along with the distorted lifestyle messages, frequently associated with drinking, by alcohol advertisers (Horgan, 1986). These reminders are believed to be particularly dangerous for children, upon which advertising can be very influential. In contrast, those who oppose restrictions have not simply argued that they have no effect, but that any effect they do have could be positive as well as negative. This argument is made on the basis that depictions that show moderate drinking as the norm and which promote sensible use of alcohol could actually enhance non-harmful consumption (Horgan, 1986). Questions regarding the effectiveness of a ban on alcohol advertising have triggered further investigations that have looked at the effects of advertising when advertising itself is restricted or removed altogether from a market environment. However, no conclusive answers have been provided so far.

The effectiveness of bans on alcohol advertising is often assessed through research on advertising that uses aggregated data sets, and which often seeks to provide a rationale for such bans. For instance, drawing on data from Organisation for Economic Co-operation and Development (OECD) countries, Saffer and Dave (2002b) suggested that advertising bans could lead to significant reductions in alcohol consumption, after finding a linkage between total expenditure on alcohol advertising and high levels of consumption.

A further macro-level investigation conducted by the two researchers sought to provide evidence of the effectiveness of bans through an assessment of the effects of alcohol advertising on youth drinking behaviours. This was based on a comparison of federally reported levels of youth drinking with detailed reports on alcohol advertising in local markets. It was found that markets with higher advertising expenditure on alcohol products contained the heavier drinking survey respondents and that higher prices for alcohol products in certain markets were associated with lower levels of consumption. These findings prompted the analysts to suggest that a complete ban on alcohol advertising could result in reductions to the monthly levels of youth drinking and binge drinking (Saffer & Dave, 2003).

Such analyses have been used to suggest that any sustained downturns in alcohol consumption have been attributed to existing bans, hence highlighting the effectiveness of such advertising restrictions. Another version of this type of study is one that investigates the effects on macro-level alcohol consumption of partial or complete advertising bans in specific markets or communities (Calfee & Scheraga, 1994; Coulson, Moran & Nelson, 2001; Duffy, 1995, 2001; Lariviere, Larue & Chalfant, 2000; Lee & Tremblay, 1992; Nelson, 1999; Smart & Cutler, 1976; Ogborne & Smart, 1980; Makowsky & Whitehead, 1991). These macro-level studies can indicate broad changes in alcohol consumption levels that occur alongside changes in levels of advertising and infer that the two are causally connected. The legitimacy of the causal agency of advertising is strengthened if changes in alcohol consumption levels follow changes in the amount of advertising.

Restrictions on advertising can be applied on a partial or total level. Partial restrictions may apply to specific media or specific alcoholic products. Hence, there may be limits placed on where spirits advertisers are permitted to advertise that do not apply to beer or wine advertisers. Alternatively, there may be restrictions placed on advertising of alcohol on television that do not apply to advertising in print media. Total restrictions apply when there is a complete ban on all forms of alcohol advertising covering all major advertising media.

Partial restrictions are considered ineffective as they lead to other forms of marketing that aim to replace the enforced restriction. This is mostly because selective bans cannot rule out the possibility of substitution towards non-banned media.

In an investigation conducted by Seldon & Jung (1993), the authors estimated the substitution flexibility among messages in broadcast, print and other media. The study showed that although broadcast advertising was the most effective type of medium, bans of advertising on this medium did not reduce rates of alcohol consumption. Moreover, partial bans that apply to only some types of media can always stimulate advertising initiatives within the non-banned media. Hence, even if advertising controls on traditional media such as broadcasting and print may show some effectiveness, controlling advertising on broadband cable and satellite television remains a challenging task (Harrison & Godfrey, 1989).

Overall, the total amount of advertising and the extent of young consumers' potential exposure to any alcohol promotional campaigns may not change, as one form of advertising substitutes for another. For this reason, it is widely believed that only through comprehensive bans on all forms of advertising can alcohol use be reduced. One argument is that complete bans should work because they lower the degree of competition between brands in the industry. Such competition is important because it can cause prices to be driven down in order to ensure that they remain competitive in the marketplace. If this level of competition is diminished, prices may rise and discourage consumption (Tremblay & Okuyama, 2001).

A useful method for measuring the effect of a ban on alcohol advertising is with the use of international data. As Farley and Lehmann (1994) explained, data from one country may be less useful since changes in alcohol advertising bans within countries are rare and the imposition of a ban may require an extended period for consumption to adjust. On the contrary, the variation that exists in the use of advertising bans across countries, can offer a better insight into the effectiveness of such bans. Many countries have imposed restrictions on alcohol advertising in the broadcast media, which have been particularly stringent in respect of advertising for distilled spirits. They include time of day restrictions, content guidelines and outright bans. In some countries, voluntary codes have been operated by the alcohol industry in respect of advertising and marketing. Chapter 7 examines advertising and marketing codes for the UK in more detail. In the US, however, spirits manufacturers voluntarily withdrew advertising from radio in 1936 and from television in 1948. Bans on broadcast advertising of spirits have been implemented in many other countries, including Canada, Denmark, Finland, France, Ireland, Norway, Spain, Sweden and the UK.

Restrictions on alcohol advertising are often employed to protect children from exposure to potentially influential messages. Across Canada and the US, policies have been introduced to prohibit or restrict the use of alcohol advertising in or near locations or areas frequented by young people under the legal drinking age. Any events, whether staged indoors or outdoors, that are targeted at children and teenagers are therefore deemed to be out of bounds for alcohol advertising. In some states, such restrictions are applied to alcohol advertising that might occur in the vicinity of schools. Some observers, however, have questioned the vigilance with which such restrictions tend to be implemented and enforced (Hovius & Solomon, 2001). In the US, the alcohol industry has placed voluntary bans on advertising on platforms where there is likely to be an audience of more than 30 per cent who are minors. This restriction has been referred to as the 30 per cent cap (CAMY, 2005a), but there are doubts about whether this 'cap' has had the desired effect in practice. One lobby group has called for a tighter restriction whereby no alcohol advertising occurs anywhere where more than 15 per cent of the audience consists of people who are too young legally to buy alcohol (Hass, 2005), but this recommendation has not been acted upon so far.

Last, it is worth noting that advertising bans can be a fairly cost-effective public health intervention, as shown in CHOICE, a World Health Organisation work programme implemented in WHO regions. The programme evaluated a number of policies including alcohol tax, drink driving legislation and random breath-testing, reduced hours of sale, a comprehensive advertising ban and brief advice intervention in primary health care. Using scenarios over 100 years, it compared the cost and effectiveness of each policy with the impact and cost of taking no action over 10 years. Although alcohol tax proved the most effective policy in six sub regions with high prevalence of heavy drinkers, advertising bans proved to be more effective at less cost when compared to the remaining types of intervention (Chisholm et al., 2004).

Are alcohol advertising bans effective?

Most developed countries have introduced controls over alcohol advertising that have been enacted through legislation and associated regulatory codes of practice. In some cases, these controls have taken the form of comprehensive advertising bans covering all or most advertising media, while others have only partially restricted alcohol advertising in specific media. Furthermore, advertising bans may apply to all alcoholic products or just to some. Do these restrictions have any impact upon the alcohol consumption? Does the nature and extent of a restriction have a critical bearing on whether advertising restrictions are effective at all?

Research on the effectiveness of alcohol advertising bans follows similar work that has been conducted for tobacco advertising and, unsurprisingly, has yielded parallel findings too. Research conducted on the effectiveness of tobacco advertising bans – which have generally been more extensive than those imposed upon alcohol advertising – has shown that bans implemented in just one or two media tend to be relatively ineffective in terms of their overall impact upon societal levels of tobacco consumption (Saffer & Chaloupka, 2000). A distinction was made here in terms of the extent to which advertising restrictions or bans were imposed across seven specified advertising media: television, radio, print (newspapers or magazines), outdoor advertising (e.g., billboards and posters), cinema advertising, point of sale advertising and sponsorship (Saffer & Chaloupka, 2000). In this context, three types of bans have been differentiated: Weak Bans (advertising restrictions covering one or two media), Limited Bans (advertising restrictions in three or four media), and Comprehensive Bans (restrictions across five to seven media). Other research has indicated that even when comprehensive bans have been imposed in different national markets, this has not invariably led to a drop in consumption (Lancaster & Lancaster, 2003).

The ineffectiveness of selective bans in the area of alcohol advertising has been confirmed empirically. In an update of Saffer's (1991) study, Saffer and Dave (2002b) examined alcohol consumption data from 20 countries over 26 years in relation to alcohol advertising bans. They found that a new ban could reduce consumption by up to eight per cent if it covered all alcohol advertising in a specific medium. In contrast, if a new ban on alcohol advertising within a specific medium only covered a specific category of alcoholic product (e.g., beer or spirits or wine) but not all categories, consumption of the banned product type might reduce by around five per cent. Although, partial bans could have some influence on subsequent levels of alcohol consumption, often this was only marginal and complete bans were always found to be more effective.

The effectiveness of alcohol advertising bans in US

A significant number of studies have been conducted in the US where bans are underpinned by statutes implemented in relation to billboard advertising; as well as cross-media bans in relation to price advertising of spirits. The latter bans cover billboards, newspapers and visible store displays (Nelson, 2004). Such restrictions represent a form of partial advertising ban, leaving open the possibility of substitution whereby advertising investment in banned media is switched to non-banned media. This phenomenon has been observed in relation to bans on cigarette advertising, for example, which are more far-reaching than any bans on alcohol advertising (Nelson, 2004).

A number of studies have also investigated the effectiveness of alcohol advertising restrictions on a state-level and in selected media such as billboards. Interestingly, such studies were still unable to provide evidence that advertising bans could significantly reduce alcohol consumption or alcohol abuse. In a study that examined per-capita consumption for distilled spirits every five years from 1955 to 1980 across 48 states, Hoadley et al. (1984) analysed the effects of state regulations and controls. These controls included the ban of billboard advertising, restrictions on exterior advertising and restrictions of price advertising of any kind. Regressions analyses showed that the aforementioned restrictions were insignificant predictors of alcohol consumption. Especially in the case of billboard advertising, results showed a consistent and fairly large effect in the wrong direction. On the contrary, alcohol prices, income, tourism, religion and state monopoly control proved more significant predictors of consumption.

The effectiveness of restrictions on price advertising in billboards was examined by Ornstein and Hanssens (1985) who studied the potential influence of advertising bans on the consumption of beer and spirits across 50 states and the District of Columbia, from 1974 to 1978. Along with bans on price advertising, bans of billboard advertising were also examined. The authors found a somewhat contradictory result in relation to spirits. Although allowing price advertising on billboards increased consumption of spirits, suggesting that a ban could be effective in this case, allowing billboard advertising was found to decrease spirits consumption. Along similar lines, allowing beer price advertising on billboards had a small positive effect on beer consumption. The authors concluded that, despite the impact that control laws related to price can have on consumption, consumers' overall attitudes towards drinking is mostly shaped by socio-demographic and economic variables.

The findings were confirmed through later studies conducted by Nelson (1990a, 1990b), who examined the effects of price advertising bans on per-capita consumption of beer, wine and spirits. The study included 48 continental states and the District of Columbia and found no effect on consumption of advertising bans. Alcohol prices, income, tourism, number of outlets and the minimum legal age proved more significant determinants of alcohol consumption in this case.

In a further analysis of data from the US, the 51 states were classified in terms of their level of restriction on alcohol advertising. Mostly, these restrictions applied to print media and varied in how stringent and extensive they were. Three levels of restrictiveness were identified and these scores (0, 1 or 2 for least to most restrictive) were entered into regression analyses along with availability of alcohol, per capita income and percentage of population living in an urban environment. These variables were regressed on per capita consumption of beer, wine and spirits. The results indicated that advertising restrictions were not related to any form of alcohol consumption.

The effectiveness of alcohol bans has also been investigated through measuring alcohol consumption in relation to the time in which a ban was introduced. Ogborne and Smart (1980) examined the effects of alcohol advertising restrictions in Manitoba, Canada and in the US by analysing alcohol consumption data before and after bans had been introduced. In Manitoba, beer advertising was banned from all electronic and print media, while wine and spirits advertising was still permitted in print media and some television advertising for wine was approved. The ban, however, only applied to broadcast and print media originating inside the Province. The data on per capita beer consumption, which were analysed over the 1970–8 period, offered little evidence of an effect of the advertising ban on beer consumption levels.

An assessment of alcohol advertising bans on an international level

Comparative analyses between countries that banned alcohol advertising and countries in which such advertising was permitted seem to reinforce the above findings. In a study of alcohol consumption across 17 OECD countries, Saffer (1991) examined the cross-national effects of laws that ban broadcast advertising of alcoholic beverages, over the period 1970–83. Saffer examined the effectiveness of advertising bans for all beverages and bans of broadcast advertising of spirits in connection to other variables including price, income, alcohol sentiment and tourism. He also examined these bans in relation to alcohol abuse outcomes such as motor vehicle fatality rates and liver cirrhosis mortality rates. The findings showed that countries with bans on beer and wine advertising had lower alcohol consumption than countries without any bans or with bans only on spirits advertising. However, Saffer drew attention to the difficulty in capturing the cultural differences among the various countries, which could have led to biased estimates.

The same OECD data was also used by Nelson and Young (2001), who assessed advertising bans in relation to additional explanatory variables such as age distribution, and unemployment, which were omitted by Saffer. Using data for 1977–95, the authors found that bans of broadcast advertising resulted in greater alcohol consumption and even higher rates of motor vehicle fatalities, with the latter being statistically correlated with the youth variable. Moreover, during the period for which data were analysed, five countries (Denmark, Finland, France, Norway and Sweden) introduced bans on all broadcast advertising of alcohol, but these total bans had no effect on alcohol consumption in those countries relative to countries where broadcast advertising of alcohol was still permitted.

In another study, Calfee and Scheraga (1994) examined the alcoholic beverage markets in France, Germany, Netherlands, Sweden and the UK, between 1970 and 1990. In this case, Sweden was used as the control case, since it was the country that banned all alcohol advertising in 1979. For the four other countries, the explanatory variable was advertising expenditure while variables such as price, income and a time trend were also included. The findings showed no significant differences in the regression results between Sweden and the other four countries, while an alcohol consumption decline was reported in all five countries during that period. The authors explained the decline as the outcome of social forces, other than prices and income, which alcohol advertising was not significant enough to prevent.

Alcohol advertising bans and young people

Questions regarding the effectiveness of alcohol bans have also emerged from research that has focused on alcohol consumption among young people, in particular. Data collected by the ESPAD survey (European School Survey Project on Alcohol and other Drugs) indicated variations between countries in the extent to which young people consume alcohol (Hibbell et al., 2000). Across these countries, some had imposed partial or complete bans on alcohol advertising, while others relied on industry self-regulation. Interestingly, while Denmark had imposed a ban on broadcast advertising of alcohol, ESPAD revealed it exhibited one of the highest levels of alcohol consumption among young people in Europe. In contrast, one of the lowest levels of alcohol consumption among young people occurred in Italy where alcohol advertising was governed by self-regulatory practices of industry. However, it also needs to be mentioned that the ESPAD survey demonstrated some level of ban effectiveness. It was found that in countries, such as Romania, where alcohol advertising was comprehensively banned, alcohol intoxication levels were low.

Moreover, it needs to be noted than when compared to other public health interventions, advertising bans may prove more effective than other policies employed to contain alcohol consumption. A recent US study sought to estimate the effect of public health interventions, including advertising bans, to decrease harmful drinking among young people. The study involved the use of life table methods to estimate the years of life lost by age 80, due to alcohol-related reasons, among 4 million aged 20 in 2000, and national survey data on transitions in drinking habits by age. It was found that, along with tax increases, advertising bans were the most effective interventions. Hence, although it was estimated that around 555 alcohol-attributable deaths over the lifetime of the cohort would take place if there were no interventions, deaths from harmful drinking could be reduced by 7609 (16.4% decrease in alcohol related life-years lost) with a complete advertising ban. However, partial bans did not prove equally effective as they were estimated to produce only a 4-per cent reduction (Hollingworth and Ebel, 2006).

To ban or not to ban?

As the evidence from econometric studies of advertising bans demonstrates, this method is not capable of producing any notable change in levels of alcohol consumption in specific markets (Smart & Cutler, 1976). Even when no advertising is present in a national market, alcohol sales may still flourish (Treml, 1975). This is a finding that reinforces the observation that alcohol consumption is not dependent upon advertising. In comparisons between nations that have imposed varying degrees of alcohol advertising ban, ranging from no ban to a ban reaching across most major mass media, no evidence emerged that advertising bans made any difference to alcohol consumption levels (Simpson et al., 1985). It is important in studies of this kind, however, that adequate statistical controls are implemented for general levels of alcohol consumption before as well as after advertising bans were introduced (Smart, 1988).

Admittedly, the empirical evidence on the efficacy of alcohol advertising bans is equivocal. In this respect, the literature has matched that on tobacco advertising bans, where similar analyses have failed to produce consistent evidence about the effectiveness of advertising bans. What has emerged in the latter field is that advertising bans must be total or very close to it before any significant impact upon consumption levels occurs (Saffer & Chaloupka, 2000). Even with comprehensive bans on advertising of tobacco, however, consumption did not invariably fall. This evidence begs the following questions: what are the underlying reasons for this phenomenon? Could advertising bans cause greater harm than benefit to consumers and society, as a whole? Seeing advertising bans in a wider social context could shed some light on the roots of their relative ineffectiveness.

One aspect of advertising that should not be overlooked is that it represents a form of expression as well. As such, it has inevitably been affected by the debates regarding free speech. Drawing on the informational role of advertising, arguments against bans proposed that they represent curtailment of freedom of speech on the part of advertisers. They deny consumers' access to important information about product availability and brand characteristics that they use to make brand choices. In the US, this issue has sparked debates over whether 'commercial speech' should be protected by the First Amendment in a similar way as personal and political forms of expression.

Unsurprisingly, the industry has consistently maintained that the regulation of advertising should be treated as a form of censorship. So far, it seems that, despite the legal battles that have sprung from this controversy, the Supreme Court has largely upheld the right of advertisers to produce their advertisements with few regulations (Advertising Educational Foundation, 2005). In addition, advertising constitutes a mechanism for manufacturers to introduce new products into the market and let consumers know about them. In response to those supporters of advertising bans who argue that advertising plays a part in encouraging youngsters to start drinking is the counter-argument that advertising operates upon the 'mature' market and its primary purpose is to establish brand share among existing drinkers.

Moreover, one should not neglect the fact that advertising bans carry an implicit message of prohibition of types or aspects of certain behaviour, which can often lead to an increase, rather than a decrease, of the harmful behaviour and its effects. In essence, prohibiting certain behaviour can prove counterproductive, in a broader sense. For instance, attempts to prohibit the consumption of alcohol, such as the Eighteenth (Prohibition) Amendment of the US Constitution managed to reduce overall alcohol consumption among teenagers, but this reduction came at a cost and was followed by significant costs of enforcement, in money, corruption, crime and alcohol (Duke and Gross, 1993: 86). In the case of alcohol advertising, the net effect of bans could be the opposite of the one intended, and there may be psychological reasons for this. According to the theory of psychological reactance, rendering products hidden via bans could render them even more attractive and enticing to consumers. Restricting the visibility or availability of commodities turns them into 'forbidden fruit' and this can represent an especially powerful reaction among young people.

The forbidden fruit hypothesis has been tested in relation to restrictions that may be placed on media content. For example, cinema films and television programmes may be classified as being inappropriate for particular age groups or as containing content that may be likely to upset or cause harm to some viewers. If such messages or warnings are perceived by viewers as overly restrictive or as attempts at censorship, then such labels can render those films or programmes more appealing. Research with young people has indicated that creating 'forbidden fruits' out of films and programmes through restrictive labelling can motivate viewers to want to watch them all the more. This effect is particularly acute among individuals whose personality profiles lead them to reject authority and messages designed to restrict their behavioural choices that derive from authority sources (Bushman & Stack, 1996). Restrictive age-related ratings or advisory labels for television programmes can also render them more attractive to younger children and lead to greater disagreements with parents over what they should watch. Furthermore, in the absence of parental control, children would be more likely to choose a programme to watch if it had been labelled as age inappropriate for them than when presented without any such advance labelling (Kracmar & Cantor, 1997).

Evidence indicative of a possible 'forbidden fruit' effect of advertising bans, has emerged from Australia where tighter restrictions on tobacco advertising produced general downturns in prevalence of smoking, but this effect was not universal. Young adults, aged 18–24 years, exhibited increased smoking prevalence in those states where tighter tobacco advertising restrictions were introduced for the first time. One interpretation of this finding was that young adult smokers were effectively rejecting the advertising restrictions which they also regarded as a restriction on their freedom to choose what to consume. Although these findings apply to tobacco consumption, the principles, in respect of the role played by advertising, may be transferable to the alcohol consumption context too. If they are, then the tobacco findings imply that overt restrictions on advertising, where interpreted as part of a wider campaign to control youth drinking, could produce a boomerang effect among young drinkers.

Summary and conclusion: From macro to micro

As the review of evidence in this chapter has described, macro-level analyses attempt to find relationships between overall quantities of advertising and consumption of specific products. In the case of alcohol, there is mixed evidence as to whether the overall volume of advertising affects overall volumes of consumption. Macro-level measures of advertising volumes can be crude. Where they depend upon levels of expenditure on advertising, such measures do not always equate with the overall volume of advertising placed in different media environments. Although on the surface, the introduction of restrictions or bans on alcohol advertising seem to offer opportunities to conduct field experiments on the impact of advertising, advertisers may react to restrictions imposed in their use of one medium, by placing greater investment in another medium. Overall, then, partial bans may have little impact on total volumes of alcohol beverage sales and consumption.

Perhaps the most important missing link with aggregated, macro-level data is that they do not indicate what happens at the level of the individual. We know little or nothing, from macro-level econometric analyses, about levels of exposure to advertising on the part of individuals who are drinkers or non-drinkers. It is important therefore to dig down at the micro level to uncover the factors that are related to and may even predict the onset of drinking and the amount that people drink.

Large data sets at the macro level also do not provide consistent patterns of relationships between alcohol advertising volumes and alcohol consumption volumes. Between 2001 and 2005 in the US, for example, it was calculated that youth exposure to alcohol advertising on television had increased by 41 per cent. There was, in particular, a significant increase in the numbers of advertisements for distilled spirits on television. In 2001, a total of 1973 spirits advertisements were found and by 2005, this figure had risen dramatically to 46,854 advertisements (CAMY, 2006a). Further analysis by the same source reported that alcohol advertising in magazines decreased by 31 per cent between 2001 and 2004. Nonetheless, in 2004, more than half of youth exposure to alcohol advertisements in magazines was contributed by 22 brands most of which used advertising campaigns with youth-oriented themes (CAMY, 2006b). The youth orientation of alcohol advertising was reinforced further by the finding that most radio alcohol advertising for the 25 leading brands was placed in programmes with audiences that had above average representation of listeners aged 12–20 years (Jernigan & Ostrom, 2006).

In the UK, research published by Ofcom (2007) indicated a 21 per cent drop in expenditure on alcohol advertising on television between 2005 and 2006 that occurred after changes of alcohol advertising codes of practice that restricted the nature of appeals alcohol advertisers were permitted to use. Over the same period, however, there was a seven-per cent increase in the volume of televised advertising spots for alcoholic products. The overall changes in amount of alcohol advertising disguised differing movements in the volumes of televised advertising for different types of alcoholic drink. The amounts of spot advertising for beer, lager, stout, whisky, rum and alcopops fell between 2005 and 2006, while the amounts of spot advertising for cider, vodka and wine increased. Upon tracking alcohol advertising impacts upon young adults (aged 16–24 years) and children (10–15 years), a decline in impacts occurred for both age groups (6% and 15.5% respectively) from 2005 to 2006. Hence, there is no guarantee that changes in expenditure on alcohol advertising is directly correlated with amount of alcohol advertising shown or that either of these two measures is, in turn, correlated with exposure to alcohol advertising among young consumers.

The overall volume of alcohol advertising can therefore change quite dramatically over relatively short periods of time, but not always in the same direction in different media. This is an important observation, but when examined at a more micro level, with data obtained from individuals, measures of reported exposure to media that carry advertising do not consistently predict whether alcohol consumption will be increased or decreased or remain unaffected by the experience. Even within the same medium, such as magazines for example, reported exposure to different genres of magazine can exhibit varying relationships with reported volumes of alcohol consumption (Thomsen & Rekve, 2004). Furthermore, within the same medium such as television, whether there is a relationship between reported advertising exposure and reported alcohol consumption can vary between categories of alcoholic product. Exposure to alcohol advertisement-containing programmes can influence uplifts in drinking of beers, wines and spirits to differing degrees (Stacy et al., 2004).

Evidence provided by macro-level analyses, as presented in this chapter, can offer insights in the changes of overall volume of alcohol advertising. This provides a broader context within which such changes would need to be examined more closely in connection to individual consumption habits. The collection and assessment of data on individual drinking is not a straightforward procedure either. Evaluating the potential impact of alcohol advertising on an individual level offers a more focused approach, but is also contingent on a range of interconnected and often conflicting variables. These include psychological, social and environmental factors, personal preferences and other idiosyncratic characteristics that are often difficult to capture fully. The complexity of assessing the role of alcohol advertising on this level requires the employment and combination of different quantitative and qualitative methods. The evidence presented in the next chapter is an attempt to provide a more rounded picture of the role that alcohol advertising plays in the lives of children and young people through an evaluation of research findings collected with experiments, surveys and interviews. Inevitably, each methodological approach suffers from weaknesses. It is based on the combination of the respective findings that more conclusive answers can be drawn.

4
Alcohol Advertising and Youth Drinking Behaviour

Introduction

Assessing the influence of alcohol advertising on people's drinking habits is admittedly a challenging task. Nelson and Moran (1995) describe alcohol as a 'mature' product category, which consumers are already aware of. Inevitably, this would limit the potential effects that alcohol advertising could have on increasing overall consumption and induce advertisers to focus on creating an appealing brand rather than increasing the total market for the product. However, if new consumers are not advertisers' prime target, can we really neglect the power of alcohol advertising campaigns to shape consumption habits? Attention has also been drawn to the rate at which alcohol-related TV commercials are transmitted during prime time TV with some scholars suggesting that alcohol is more likely to be portrayed during TV programmes than during commercials (Madden and Grube, 1991). Once again, questions may arise regarding the influential power of alcohol advertising, and one of the greatest challenges lies in identifying the impact of advertising independent from other influential factors.

This chapter will focus on studies that have sought to assess potential advertising effects in isolation from exposure to surrounding media content, offering evidence for relationships between exposure to media advertising for alcoholic beverages and alcohol consumption among young people. Chapter 7 will examine evidence for the possible impact of alcohol consumption representations in non-advertising media content. While many investigations have been interested in this type of link, consumer measures have often focused on attitudes towards alcohol or alcohol brands or towards alcohol advertising rather than on actual consumption behaviour. Attitudes and beliefs about alcohol or alcohol advertising are not irrelevant to understanding how advertising might influence consumption. Such psychological measures may represent important orienting responses or priming mechanisms that encourage young consumers to consume alcohol. Nevertheless, they must not be treated as valid proxies for behaviour measurement. A young consumer's liking of a beer advertisement, for example, does not automatically translate into beer consumption. Even if they do drink beer, a measure of liking of a beer advertisement does not itself measure consumption – even though it might be correlated with such consumption.

Advertising and the wider social and psychological context of drinking

In considering whether advertising has an impact upon young people's alcohol consumption, it is important to remember that the onset of drinking alcohol can be influenced by a range of psychological, social and environmental factors (Martinic & Measham, 2008a). Parental, sibling and peer group influences can be highly significant in this context (Adlaf & Kohn, 1989; Fisher & Cook, 1995; Milgram, 2001). These social groups can provide behavioural role models and establish a positive attitudinal climate towards drinking. There is also evidence that the media influences on young people's alcohol consumption extend beyond those emanating from advertising (Stockdale, 2001). Although the present research is concerned principally with the effects of advertising and marketing of alcoholic beverages on young people's alcohol consumption, it is worth taking a summary look at other factors associated with the onset and nature of alcohol-related behaviour. Such evidence provides a broader context in which to consider the impact of alcohol advertising and marketing activities which do not take place in a social vacuum.

A number of survey studies of teenagers and young adults have indicated that alcohol consumption is often significantly related to parental and peer-group influences. Whether a young person's friends drink alcohol has been found to be a particularly powerful predictor of their own drinking behaviour. Research has demonstrated that adolescents may be especially likely to consume alcohol themselves when their best friend also drank (Wilks, Callan & Austin, 1989; Kuther & Higgins-D'Alessandro, 2003). In a study conducted among college students from California State University, the quantity and frequency of drinking of the respondents was assessed in connection to the respondents' perception of the same aspects of each parent's drinking. The study showed a small but significant correlation of male participants' drinking scores with their fathers' frequency and quantity of alcohol consumption. However, neither mothers' nor fathers' drinking was found to be significantly related to the drinking level among the female participants (Jung, 1995). Hence, the nature of apparent parental influences on adolescent drinking can vary between boys and girls (Wilks, Callan & Austin, 1989). The authors demonstrated that teenage males' perceptions of themselves as drinkers were related to both their fathers' and mothers' alcohol consumption habits, while for teenage girls, it was the fathers' drinking alone that emerged as a potential influence.

It has also been found that male teenagers were more likely to perceive themselves as drinkers if their best friends drank. Female teenagers were also more likely to consume alcoholic beverages if they believed their best friend was a drinker (Wilks, Callan & Austin, 1989). Similar findings emerged in a study conducted with young people aged 17–21 years in central England, highlighting the significance of the social context within which alcohol consumption occurs. Through a self-completion survey, it was shown that the lifetime and yearly alcohol consumption was strongly related to the influence of family and friends. The role of friends proved particularly influential as heavier alcohol consumption was closely related to the frequency with which respondents met with their friends in places that served alcohol and the number of friends who reportedly drank alcohol (Gunter, Hansen and Touri, 2009).

The respective influences of parents and peer groups over teenagers' drinking of alcoholic beverages vary not only with the age of the young drinker but also with the social setting in which drinking takes place. Research among under-age drinkers aged 15 in New Zealand found that the presence of peers could encourage these teenagers to drink more in a session provided alcohol was consumed away from their own home. The amount consumed by these underage drinkers was also related to whether their friends approved or disapproved of alcohol. Hence, boys whose girlfriends frowned upon drinking drank less, while those with girlfriends who endorsed drinking drank more (Connolly et al., 1992).

Both parental and peer-group influences can have important effects on the onset of alcohol consumption among teenagers, but they also represent social forces that can pull in different directions. Parental rules about drinking can come into conflict with peer-group norms. Family rules about alcohol may exert quite a powerful influence over teenagers expressed intentions to drink alcohol in the future, perhaps weakening those intentions. Such effects, however, may be limited to young people who have so far not felt any social pressures to drink from their peer group. Teenagers with friends who drink may be more likely to reject family rules and restrictions on alcohol consumption. They may also question the veracity of these rules if their own experiences or those of their friends lead to positive expectancies about alcohol (Thomsen & Rekve, 2006). As we will see in the next section, peer-group influences may also determine the extent to which media role models of alcohol consumption are likely to influence teenagers' beliefs about drinking and intentions to drink in the future. However, it needs to be noted that despite parental and peer-group influences in shaping young people's alcohol consumption, further evidence has indicated that drinking onset is not simply a matter of copycat behaviour. Adolescent drinkers weigh up the different (positive and negative) consequences of drinking as well as making assessments of relevant groups norms and beliefs linked to drinking.

The role of advertising: Assessing methodological evidence

A significant amount of empirical evidence has accumulated on the way young drinkers respond to advertising. Some of this research has explored young people's attitudes towards alcohol advertising, while other work has investigated links between exposure to alcohol advertising and consumption. In this chapter, we focus on cause-effect relationships that have been investigated primarily through statistical links between reported exposure to alcohol advertising and reported consumption of alcohol. The findings from more qualitative approaches, such as interviews, will be discussed as well. A more comprehensive picture of the role of advertising in alcohol consumption among young people will be offered in the following chapter, which turns attention to research that has considered how young people respond to alcohol advertising in terms of their perceptions of advertising messages and the general appeal of this advertising.

According to the World Health Organisation, alcohol advertising can influence positive perceptions of drinking and pro-drinking attitudes that may, in turn, increase the probability that young people will consume alcoholic beverages (Babor et al., 2003). There are two specific aspects to the role believed to be played by advertising. The first of these is that exposure to alcohol advertising over time can lead young people to perceive drinking as a normative behaviour and therefore understandably as an activity in which they would wish to partake. The second aspect of alcohol advertising is that it may reach children and early teenagers and encourage alcohol consumption well before they are legally old enough to purchase alcoholic drinks for themselves.

There is, however, mixed empirical research evidence on whether children are influenced by televised advertising of alcoholic beverages in terms of their own consumption behaviour. Early research with teen-agers concluded there was little evidence of an effect (Strickland, 1982; Adlaf & Kohn, 1989). Later evidence indicated that any effect there might be was indirect rather than direct in nature and that exposure to televised advertising could raise brand awareness, which in turn was linked to future drinking (Austin & Nach Ferguson, 1995; Lipsitz et al., 1993). Other writers have argued that the influences of alcohol adver-tising can be subtle rather than open and direct. Exposure to alcohol advertising may operate at the level of priming thoughts about alcohol through association with other attributes that have significance for young people. If young people think about drinking more often, there is an increased likelihood that they will eventually consume alcoholic drinks (Krank & Kreklewetz, 2003; Krank et al., 2003). Other review-ers have indicated that through raising young people's awareness and familiarity with alcohol, advertising is a contributor towards their deci-sion eventually to take up drinking (Hastings et al., 2005).

Interestingly, children themselves have been found to believe that alco-hol advertising can cause alcohol consumption (Lieberman & Orlandi, 1987; Wyllie Casswell & Stewart, 1989; Wyllie, Zhang, & Casswell, 1998), while American evidence has demonstrated that even mere awareness of alcohol advertisements could be linked to positive beliefs about alco-hol, which is in turn associated with future intention to drink (Grube & Wallack, 1994). In this context, it comes as no surprise that liking of alcohol advertisements has also emerged as a significant factor in under-standing potential effects. Liking has been linked to drinking alcohol among young adults in multivariate statistical tests that took into account other potential causal factors such as parent and peer variables (Wyllie, Zhang, & Casswell, 1998).

In determining what the evidence really shows about the impact of alcohol advertising on actual consumption, the research evidence can be organised by methodology. Some studies have attempted to address the issue of a direct cause-effect relationship through interventionist methodologies in which young people are exposed to alcohol advertis-ing or media portrayals of alcohol consumption under controlled con-ditions. Subsequent measures are then implemented to assess whether alcohol consumption behaviour has been primed in a particular way by the earlier media exposure. Most of the research that has attempted to demonstrate relationships between alcohol advertising exposure and consumption has been conducted in the 'field' among large samples of young people and has been dependent upon their self-reports about their behaviour. Such studies use survey methodology to determine whether reported exposure to alcohol advertising is correlated with or predictive of alcohol consumption. Some studies have surveyed samples of young people on one occasion only, while others have surveyed them more than once over time. It is helpful therefore in constructing a critique of the research literature to conduct a review of the evidence that is organised by methodology. In each case, there are specific strengths and weaknesses associated with particular methodologies that need to be borne in mind when interpreting their findings.

Experiments

Experiments are interventionist studies in which researchers attempt to control the level of exposure to stimulus materials (in this context, media advertising of alcoholic beverages) and construct conditions in which consumption behaviour can be precisely measured. Experiments are designed to enable researchers to test cause-effect hypotheses. Their use helps examine whether individuals who have deliberately been placed in different advertising exposure conditions behave differently subsequently in controlled conditions in which their alcohol consumption behaviour is measured.

The strengths of experiments are found in their ability to exert close control over the conditions in which individuals' behaviours are monitored. They can ensure that advertising exposure conditions are also arranged such that there is a clear view of how and to what extent individuals were exposed to advertising messages. This type of tight control over the circumstances of alcohol advertising exposure and alcohol consumption does not exist in respect of their occurrence in the real world. However, this degree of control over experimental procedures comes at a certain price. The inherent weakness of the experimental methodology is that it creates an artificial environment that may depart in critical ways from natural behavioural environments. An important question therefore is whether experiments can and do effectively 'model' real-world behaviour. In addition, participant samples in experimental studies tend to be small and non-representative in nature. While participants can be randomly allocated to experimental conditions to ensure that any intrinsic differences among them are evened out between experimental groups or conditions, the general sampling in the first place tends more often than not to have a 'convenience' nature. The critical limitation of experiments therefore is how far one can effectively and legitimately generalise from their results to produce meaningful theories and explanation of human behaviour in natural environments. This limitation is frequently labelled as a matter of 'ecological validity'

The ecological validity of experiments can be enhanced by taking them outside the laboratory. Field experiments entail researchers constructing interventions in real-world environments to then monitor whether such social manipulations produce behavioural differences in participants later on. An example of a field experiment of this kind is reviewed below in which the researchers recruited shoppers in a large mall to engage in a task of advertisement evaluation, and then created a condition in which they could measure naturally occurring alcohol consumption behaviour (Kohn, Smart & Ogborne, 1984). The problem with field experiments is that because they study people in natural environments the researchers sacrifice a degree of control over factors that might influence participants' behaviours.

Questionnaire-based surveys

Survey studies examine patterns of relationships among 'real-world' behaviours and the personal characteristics of respondents. However, they are dependent upon post-hoc self-reports about behaviour usually recorded by respondents on questionnaire forms and researchers have no control over respondents' behaviours or the environments in which they exist. Survey studies generally use larger and often more representative samples than do experiments. This means that their findings can be generalised to wider populations from which the survey samples are drawn. Their major weakness resides in the reliability and validity of the self-report evidence they gather from respondents. Verbal reports about behaviour do not always provide accurate representations of actual behaviour. Furthermore, analytically all that the best survey studies can manage is to demonstrate correlations between variables. These coefficients alone do not prove causality.

Surveys can also be criticised for the quality of their question formats. The use of multiple-choice responding, for example, to promote consistency of reference frames across respondents and ease of data processing, can place artificial constraints on respondents in terms of the range and quality of answers they can give. This framing of questions can further reduce the validity of the data because respondents may not be permitted to give their preferred answers.

Qualitative research and the use of interviews

The constraints that quantitative methods like surveys often pose have prompted researchers to champion more qualitative approaches in the study of media content effects. The general belief that the search for cause-effect relationships is futile and that human behaviour is best understood by observing it in the social context in which it occurs, accounts for several attempts to explore the role of advertising through the use of in-depth interviewing. Such techniques give individuals an opportunity to express themselves more comprehensively than questionnaires. In a group interview context, a special social dynamic can be established between participants that models real-world conversations and hence the normal way in which individuals would naturally communicate with each other about their behaviours.

Qualitative studies collect data from small samples and use depth interview techniques with small groups, dyads or single interviewees. They allow respondents to reply to questions in their own terms and at length. Such studies can yield rich data from individual participants both about their drinking behaviour and their interpretation of advertisements. While questionnaire surveys supply ready-made answers, which may not necessarily represent the full range of responses respondents might wish to articulate, qualitative interviews allow participants to express themselves fully in any way they wish. This type of research has been used to investigate how teenagers interpret alcohol advertisements and the importance of alcohol consumption in their social environment. Such studies have indicated that young people may be sensitive to the appeals of alcohol advertising (Dring & Hope, 2001), that young drinkers have greater brand awareness than non-drinkers (Aitken, 1989) and that designer drinks and alcopops have special appeal to youngsters because of their taste (Cragg, 2004). One focus-group study with teenagers and young adults conducted across seven countries found, however, that when talking about their alcohol-related habits, advertising rarely surfaced as a factor that had any perceived influence over their drinking (Martinic & Measham, 2008).

The following sections in this chapter will present an overview of the studies that have been conducted internationally with the employment of the above methodologies, in an effort to delineate the influential power of alcohol advertising in consumption among young people.

Experimental approaches to the study of alcohol advertising

Experiments are widely used in the social sciences and in studies that seek to identify potential media influences on human behaviour. Experimental studies allocate participants, usually at random, to different intervention conditions controlled by the researcher. Although data are collected from individuals, analyses focus on group-level differences. In research related to alcohol advertising, such studies may demonstrate the ability of advertisements to create a short-term interest in alcohol consumption or to shape a preference for one type of drink over another, but they do not indicate anything about the role advertising might play in the genesis of alcohol consumption in individuals (McCarty & Ewing, 1983; Kohn & Smart, 1984; Sobell et al., 1986). In these experiments, alcohol advertising and consumption was tested in various contexts including group discussions and gatherings, shopping and watching sport. However, the most frequently used condition was the direct exposure of participants to televised alcohol advertisements and/or alcohol scenes. Overall, it could be argued that the findings produced by such experiments have not been compelling enough to offer adequate evidence of advertising effects on alcohol consumption.

One of the earliest laboratory experiments invited participants to evaluate the spirit and mix content of vodka and tonic drinks and as part of the procedure they were shown print advertisements for alcohol and tobacco products. The findings indicated that those who witnessed the alcohol advertisements drank more vodka, which the researcher interpreted as evidence for an effect of advertising on consumption volume (Brown, 1978). Since this experiment was conducted, a number of experimental studies have followed with each study adding to our knowledge about the role of alcohol advertising on drinking habits and about the precision of the findings produced by experiments.

Hence, a subsequent experiment was conducted by Kohn and Smart (1984) who showed a videotaped recording of an indoor soccer match and another of the 1982 NFL Super Bowl to 125 male college students. Different versions of the programme were produced that included zero, four or nine beer advertisements. The participants were told at the outset that the purpose of the study was to evaluate the potential fan appeal of a televised soccer game. Refreshments would be available and among the drinks, participants could choose between soft drinks or beer. Half the participants were given immediate access to beer which they could consume throughout the session, while the other half were told that because of a mix-up the beer would be late arriving. In the event, beer was made available to the second group about 30 minutes after initial instructions were given.

Beer consumption occurred throughout where beer was available and in the case of the second group, delayed availability of beer resulted in compensatory behaviour whereby the men who had been made to wait for beer to become available drank more once it had arrived. It was found that the occurrence of advertising produced a temporary upward shift in beer consumption, but over time, consumption dropped away in all conditions. Thus, the results here indicated that televised alcohol advertising is capable of triggering a short-term effect on beer consumption. Furthermore, in conditions where consumption was tailing off over time, a first-time appearance of a beer advertisement could temporarily boost consumption again.

A replication of this study was reported by Kohn and Smart (1987), which was conducted among female college students who viewed and were asked to evaluate videotaped programmes with wine advertisements (or not) embedded within them. Under different conditions, the programming contained zero, three or nine wine advertisements. This study featured a key difference since a debriefing session was added to the end of the procedure that not only revealed the true purpose of the study but also checked whether any participants had been suspicious about its real nature anyway.

Overall, it was found that women in the condition with nine alcohol advertisements drank more than those shown three alcohol advertisements, but those in the zero alcohol advertisements condition did not differ from the other two groups in their respective alcohol consumption levels. However, an interesting finding was that 12 out of 66 participants were suspicious about the purpose of the study and when these women were removed from the analysis, all intergroup difference disappeared. What this experiment underlined was the need to include controls for 'second-guessing' the objective of the respective study, which is an element that could possibly result in participants complying with the experimental hypothesis.

Another laboratory-based experimental study combined an analysis of the potential effects of both televised alcohol advertising and scenes of alcohol consumption within a programme (Sobell et al., 1986). Ninety-six male college students watched a videotape of a television programme with or without alcohol scenes and embedded either with advertisements for alcohol drinks, non-alcoholic drinks or food products. Participants were asked to give personal evaluations of the programme to indicate their current and likely future interest in viewing it, and afterwards they were introduced to an additional procedure that they were led to believe was unrelated to the television viewing task. This procedure was designed to provide measures of alcohol consumption, during which, participants could drink as much or little beer as they liked and were asked to rate the taste qualities of light beers.

The study provided no evidence that either the presence of alcohol advertising or drinking scenes within a programme caused enhanced alcohol consumption to occur afterwards. The authors pointed out, however, that they had not used a random or representative sample and television viewing took place in isolation rather than in a social context and in an artificial environment. Alcohol consumption was measured immediately after exposure to television programming and so no measures of possible delayed effects of alcohol advertising or drinking scenes were included.

A further study by these researchers several years later indicated that televised advertising and non-advertising images of alcohol consumption did affect the perceived ability of males with a drink problem. Once again, an experimental design was used in which alcohol or non-alcohol advertisements were embedded in programming that contained or did not contain scenes of alcohol consumption. In this study, questionnaire measures of drinking behaviour and related matters were obtained before and after viewing. The key results indicated that very heavy drinkers showed a decrease in confidence of being able to resist drinking heavily again after exposure to alcohol drinking scenes in a television programme and alcohol advertising (Sobell et al., 1993).

Two other experiments were conducted in different contexts, but similar to the previous examples, offered little evidence of potential advertising effects. In a creative but problematic study, McCarty and Ewing (1983) invited groups of participants to take part in an investigation described to them as examining the effect of alcohol consumption on group discussions. At the outset some groups consumed alcoholic drinks and others did not and while some of them witnessed alcohol advertisements, others did not. During an interval, all participants had the opportunity to prepare and consume alcoholic drinks. The researchers measured the total amount of alcohol consumed by the different groups and found no differences in overall amount of consumption, but breath tests indicated a greater presence of alcohol in the blood of those who had seen the alcohol advertisements. Unfortunately, breath test results can be affected by individual tolerance for alcohol and not just by amount consumed. Moreover, the results were taken for groups rather than for individuals and there was some evidence that group results could have been affected by particularly heavy drinkers.

In a different experimental context, Kohn, Smart and Ogborne (1984) conducted research with shoppers in a mall who were asked to view and evaluate print alcohol or non-alcohol (control) advertisements. Participants were given a $5 restaurant voucher for their help. Details were then collected from the restaurant on the alcoholic beverages ordered by voucher holders. Finally, all participants were contacted by telephone six to 12 weeks later. Once again, there was no evidence that exposure to alcohol advertisements in this controlled context had any impact on alcohol consumption within the mall that day or later.

A number of experimental studies, primarily in the US, have also sought to address potential alcohol advertising effects on children. One of the earlier studies was conducted by Rychtari et al. (1983) who examined the extent to which exposure to a television programme with alcohol scenes could prompt the children to choose an alcoholic beverage as an appropriate drink for adults. The experiment involved 75 children of eight- to 11-years old, who were exposed to one of three conditions. The first condition comprised five minutes of a television programme with alcohol scenes, in the second condition the same five minutes of a programme had the alcohol scenes cut and the third condition involved no exposure to television at all. Following their exposure to one of these three conditions, the children were shown pictured scenes with adults and children in which they were asked to choose whether to serve an alcoholic drink (whiskey) or water to either the adult or child depicted.

As the findings demonstrated, exposure to alcohol scenes on television made children more likely to offer the alcoholic drink to a pictured adult compared to the children who were not exposed to television at all. Although this study did not use alcohol advertising as stimulus material, it offers evidence that television depictions of alcohol consumption can prime children, immediately afterwards, to show a preference for an alcoholic over a non-alcoholic beverage in specific settings.

A similar experiment was conducted by Kotch, Coulter & Lipsitz (1986), who exposed 43 fifth- and sixth-grade children to two types of videos in order to examine their attitudes about alcohol. While the first video showed the main characters consuming alcohol, the second video included no alcohol scenes at all. Having watched the two videos, children of each group were asked to identify the possible good and bad things that might result from alcohol consumption and think which of the two, the good or the bad, were more important to them. Some effects on attitude were found among the group of boys who watched the video with the alcohol scenes and who found the good things about alcohol being more important than the bad things.

In a more recent study, Lipsitz et al. (1993) conducted experimental studies with children aged 10–11 years and teenagers aged 13 years. Participants viewed 40 television advertisements, which included five beer advertisements, five soft drinks advertisements and five beer advertisements plus two anti-drinking messages. A questionnaire was used to measure future drinking expectancies, and the general finding among all three age groups was that no effect of alcohol advertising exposure emerged.

In brief, it could be said that evidence emerging from such experiments suggests limited advertising influence on alcohol consumption as any demonstrated effects can be best described as short-term or tentative. In some instances, interpreting certain attitudes towards alcohol as an indicator for potential consumption becomes problematic. As it was mentioned earlier, experiments suffer from a number of methodological limitations that could eventually compromise the ability to generalise their findings beyond the laboratory setting in which they occurred. Perhaps, a more accurate interpretation of these findings could be achieved through a combined evaluation with findings from different methodological approaches.

Use of self-reports on advertising exposure and alcohol consumption

The survey is the most commonly used method in measuring alcohol advertising effects with most of the relevant evidence stemming from self-reported data on alcohol consumption and advertising exposure. Survey studies obtain data from individuals about both their alcohol consumption habits and preferences and their exposure to alcohol advertising. These data are often combined with information about family background, peer groups, attitudes and beliefs, which can also be collected through surveys.

The surveys used in alcohol-and-advertising research can be distinguished into two types: cross-sectional and longitudinal surveys. Cross-sectional surveys collect data from a sample of respondents at one point in time and have indicated significant statistical associations between reported alcohol advertising exposure and alcohol consumption (Atkin & Block, 1984a; Atkin, Neuendorf & McDermott, 1983; Robinson et al., 1998) or between liking of alcohol advertisements and alcohol consumption (Wyllie, Zhang & Casswell, 1998). Longitudinal surveys collect data at two or more points in time and have also indicated links between self-reports of advertising exposure and alcohol consumption among young people (Connolly et al., 1994; Ellickson et al., 2005).

Cross-sectional surveys

One of the first major survey-based studies of relationships between exposure to alcohol advertising and young consumption of alcohol in the US found that among 12- to 18-year olds, those who were found to be highly exposed to alcohol advertising drank more frequently and heavily (Atkin and Block, 1981). Six different studies were completed and published in a series of reports and papers (Atkin, Neuendorf & McDermott, 1983; Atkin & Block, 1984; Atkin, Hocking & Block, 1984); but in the main technical report, the authors advised caution in the interpretation of their data and in particular underlined the fact that correlation coefficients do not demonstrate causal relationships. The studies approached alcohol consumption from a number of angles. Hence, in one analysis emphasis was placed on brands and comparisons were made between youngsters in terms of whether they were more likely to report having tried a number of brands of beer if they also reported heavy exposure to alcohol advertising. In this case, a greater percentage of 'high alcohol advertisement exposure' (52%) than of 'low alcohol advertisement exposure' respondents (37%) claimed to have tried any of six brands of beer (Atkin & Block, 1984b).

The frequency and nature of drinking was also addressed as Atkin and colleagues (1983) reported that young people with heavy exposure to alcohol advertising were much more likely to engage in heavy episodic drinking at least once a week. Reported problem drinking among the teenagers in this sample was associated with regular exposure to alcohol advertising. Moreover, among older teenagers, those who had heavy exposure to alcohol advertising were much more likely to report driving after drinking than those with local alcohol advertising exposure. After surveying a sample of 1227 respondents between 12 and 22 years, the researchers examined the connection between variables including brand awareness, alcohol knowledge, images of drinkers, brand preferences, attitude towards drinking and personal patterns of drinking.

The relationship they found between the day-to-day exposure to beer, wine and liquor advertising and excessive alcohol consumption or drinking in hazardous contexts, such as driving, was described as moderate; but they also explained that advertising may even have an impact by producing a more accepting attitude towards hazardous consumption. A more interesting finding was the observation of a reverse flow of influence, in the sense that heavy drinkers may have the tendency to look for advertisements to reinforce their personal practices

The Atkin and Block research was strongly criticised by Strickland (1984) who was concerned about non-representative sampling of respondents. Strickland observed that the dependence upon college students on communications courses meant that the samples were probably not representative of the general student population let alone the general consumer population. Another sampling problem was that there seemed to be a strong bias towards drinkers, while non-drinkers were underrepresented. Strickland also articulated concerns about some of the measures of media exposure, most notably those used to measure television viewing and magazine reading. What needs to be borne in mind is that the correlation-based nature of the analyses also opens up the possibility of a reverse causal hypothesis that drinkers are more attuned to alcohol advertising.

Strickland (1982) later conducted his own research into alcohol advertising and alcohol consumption among young people, in which a self-completion questionnaire assessed the habits of 1650 American 12- to 18-year olds. These habits included the participants' alcohol consumption, advertising exposure and orientations to advertising and it was reported that exposure to alcohol advertising was correlated with alcohol consumption. Other important influences also included age and peer-group factors (Strickland, 1981, 1982, 1983).

This survey used a more robust sampling approach, but as it focused on a younger sample, its eventual recruitment was limited by parental consent issues. The alcohol consumption measure comprised a self-report of quantity and frequency of drinking in terms of ounces of alcohol per day; and advertising exposure was calculated by getting respondents to indicate how often they had watched programmes from a supplied list over the previous month in the case of weekly programmes or previous week in the case of daily programmes. Attitudes towards advertising were measured with statements that explore the reasons why respondents would want to watch commercials. The reasons included finding out what certain products are about or about the kinds of people who might use them. The presence of alcohol advertisements within these programmes was identified through the use of television station logs and a formula was then used to compute the level of alcohol advertising exposure from these sets of data.

Focusing on respondents who classified themselves as drinkers (75% of sample) Strickland found no significant relationships between his advertising exposure measure and total consumption of alcohol. Moreover, age was significantly and positively related to alcohol consumption and negatively related to advertising exposure. These findings may signal the fact that as they advance into middle and later adolescent years, young people drink more and watch television less often. Similarly ethnic differences emerged, in that blacks watched more television than whites, but drank less alcohol.

Although there was no link found between advertising exposure and alcohol consumption across the sample as a whole, some significant relationships did emerge for one sub-category of young people. In particular, one advertising orientation emerged as a possible mediator of such a link. Teenagers who said they watched advertisements for social comparison purposes displayed a significant statistical relationship between reported alcohol consumption and measured advertising exposure. Watching advertising to have something to talk about did not make any difference to the link between advertising exposure and alcohol consumption.

Measuring alcohol advertising effects in conjunction with contextual factors and social influences

Potential advertising effects, especially in the case of alcohol, are often assessed in connection with the evaluation of other social factors and influences, such as the role of the family and of peer groups. Further research conducted over time among over 3000 American youth aged 12–15 years in which they were asked questions designed to track their alcohol consumption behaviour, found that exposure to different kinds of alcohol advertising and other social factors were both linked to drinking. This panel of youngsters was surveyed three times over three years. The initial survey established whether they had yet started to drink alcohol or not, the second survey focused more on reported exposure to alcohol advertising and the third survey returned to focus its analysis on drinking behaviour again (Ellickson, et al., 2005).

At the outset, among youth in grade seven in the US school system, around six in ten had tried alcohol (61%), while the remainder (39%) said they had not yet done so. By the time they had reached ninth grade, around half of grade seven non-drinkers had started to drink while over three in four grade seven drinkers were still drinking in the ninth grade. Perhaps the most significant finding, however, was that the heavier their reported exposure to alcohol advertising in grade eight, the more likely it was that grade seven drinkers or non-drinkers would drink in grade nine. The advertising 'effect' persisted even after statistical controls for other social factors such as peer and parental influences on alcohol consumption. Furthermore, reported exposure to point-of-sale and magazine advertising exhibited stronger relationships to later drinking than did other forms of alcohol advertising.

In contrast, the role of family and peers proved more prominent in a survey-based study that sought to investigate the role of alcohol advertising in the consumption habits of young people in central-east England (Gunter, Hansen and Touri, 2009). The study examined a wider range of alcohol-related consumption and alcohol advertising exposure behaviours and aimed to understand alcohol consumption in relation to family and peer-group drinking habits as well. Using a convenience sample of 298 university and secondary school students aged 17–21 years, the study measured alcohol consumption via a self-completion questionnaire survey which explored respondents' own consumption of alcoholic beverages; reports of the alcohol consumption habits of people known to them; and reported exposure to advertising for alcoholic drinks.

Through a series of multiple regression analyses, the study found that respondents' alcohol consumption was predicted by parental drinking (especially by the male parent or guardian), having friends who drink and spending time drinking with friends. These factors proved more important than exposure to alcohol advertising in underpinning how often the young people in this sample reported consumption of alcohol. In terms of the role of advertising, alcohol advertising on television (though not in any other media) and point-of-sale attention to alcohol proved to be among the key predictors. Moreover, as the specific study indicated, it was specific types of alcohol the consumption of which is likely to have occurred under the influence of advertising. Hence, exposure to alcohol advertising predicted reported consumption mostly of cider and alcopop and not beer, wine or spirits.

Longitudinal surveys

Longitudinal surveys obtain self-report data from the same respondents on more than one occasion over time. These surveys comprise two or more separate waves of data collection and can therefore not simply examine relationships between measured variables at one point in time but also over different points in time. This enables researchers to investigate behaviour patterns that may develop gradually over time. One of the problems associated with this type of research is that the original sample of respondents can become significantly eroded over time as respondents refuse to take part in later survey waves or move home and can no longer be contacted.

Anderson et al. (2009) reviewed longitudinal studies of associations between reported exposure to alcohol advertising, depictions of alcohol consumption in the media and alcohol consumption by respondents. They restricted their review to studies carried out with individuals aged 18 or younger and searched a number of major research databases for work published between 1990 and 2008. Out of an initial discovered sample of 810 titles, 16 publications met the selection criteria covering 13 studies that were conducted mostly in the US. One study was also conducted in Belgium, in Germany and in New Zealand respectively.

Five of these studies measured reported other media content that contained portrayals of alcohol consumption. Two others studies measured brand recognition and recall or liking of alcohol advertising. Eight studies examined initiation of alcohol consumption among respondents and finally six studies used random selection methods to construct their samples either at the respondent level (three studies) or at the school level (three studies).

Anderson et al. concluded that the body of research they reviewed produced evidence that the onset of alcohol consumption among teenage non-drinkers could be triggered by exposure to alcohol advertising and promotions. In addition, exposure to these messages could encourage existing youth drinkers to consume large quantities of alcohol over time. However, weighing up all this cited evidence, the conclusions reached by the authors, that there is a collective body of compelling evidence that exposure to alcohol advertising and promotions triggers the onset of alcohol consumption among young people or influences the magnitude of that behaviour, do not seem to be so powerfully supported by that evidence. A closer inspection of the studies reviewed reveals that most studies featured a relatively weak relationship between exposure and drinking or suffered from methodological weaknesses that restricted direct measurement of exposure. It is worth looking at the key studies reviewed here and in the following sections (many of which have already been examined earlier in this chapter).

An American study with 12- to 13-year olds conducted over one year reportedly indicated a link between exposure to television advertising of alcohol and onset of alcohol consumption, but the measure of 'exposure' to advertising was based on claims of watching listed titles of TV shows identified separately by the researchers as containing alcohol advertising. In other words, there was no direct measurement of exposure to TV alcohol advertising (Stacy et al., 2004).

Further US research referenced by Anderson and colleagues that had been conducted by Ellickson et al. (2005) reportedly examined relationships between a number of different forms of alcohol advertising and drinking among 12- to 13-year olds. However, no significant relationships emerged between self-reported exposure to television advertisements, magazine advertisements or in-store advertisements and drinking onset over time. The only significant relationship to emerge was between exposure to beer concession stands at music and sports events.

A further cited study by Fisher et al. (2007) examined the impact of ownership of or willingness to use an alcohol promotional item on initiation of alcohol consumption among young non-drinkers or levels of drinking among early established drinkers. Ownership of or willingness to use these items were reportedly related to drinking onset and drinking levels among teenage girls and boys. However, these variables again do not serve as valid proxies for exposure to alcohol advertising. Furthermore, it is possible that ownership of such items may have arisen as a result of them being gifted by family members who drank. It is not clear whether such factors, known to be important causal elements in youth drinking onset, were adequately controlled. Another cited study by Pasch et al. (2007) found no evidence that the presence of alcohol advertisements in outdoor locations close to schools predicted drinking levels among teenagers in those schools, although this variable was associated with adolescents' intentions to drink. Actual exposure to alcohol advertising on the part of survey respondents was not directly measured again here. Instead, the extent to which there was outdoor alcohol advertising in the vicinity of schools was used as a proxy for exposure.

In additional evidence allegedly supportive of the influence of alcohol advertising on alcohol consumption among young people, Anderson and colleagues cited research by Collins et al. (2007) who reported higher likelihood of teenage alcohol consumption onset among those who watched a TV sports channel, reportedly saw sports advertisements featuring beer or beer advertisements, as well as reported exposure to in-store product displays, concession stands at events and other beer promotions. Collectively these variables reportedly predicted drinking onset.

Measuring alcohol advertising effects through advertising recall and appeal

The potential impact of alcohol advertising on consumption habits has been measured through assessments of advertising recall among audiences. In this case, longitudinal survey research has offered some interesting findings. In particular, a survey conducted in New Zealand among young people aged from 13- to 18-years old, has examined the connection among a number of variables including the respondent's recall of alcohol-related mass media, the number of hours spent watching TV, drinking patterns, peer approval of drinking, living situation and occupation as well as the difference between male and female drinking. The research sought to identify the relation between exposure to alcohol advertising and advertisement recall at the ages of 13 and 15 years with alcohol consumption at the age of 18 years.

It was found that the more male teenagers were able to recall beer advertisements at the age of 15 years, the more they drank at 18 years.

However, this finding occurred only for beer drinking and not for consumption of wine or spirits, while even in the case of beer drinking, the advertising recall effect only had a modest effect. In the case of female participants, a positive association emerged between the frequency and quantity of wine and spirits consumed by 18-year-old women with the hours spent watching television at ages 13 and 15 years. Data from the female cohort also revealed two unexpected negative relationships. The number of commercial advertisements recalled at age 13 was weakly and inversely related to the frequency of beer drinking at age 18 and the number of portrayals of alcohol in the entertainment media recalled at age 13 was weakly inversely related to the maximum quantity at age 18 (Connolly et al., 1994).

Another study that sought to investigate connections between alcohol advertising recall and alcohol consumption was conducted in Los Angeles by Stacy et al. (2004). The study involved a sample of 2998 children of 12 years of age and examined the relation between drinking, recall of alcohol advertisements and the viewing of particular television programmes on the one hand; and alcohol consumption that took place 12 months later, on the other. The study showed it was mostly the viewing and recall of television programmes with alcohol advertisements that was associated with an excess risk of beer use (44%), wine/liquor use (34%) and three-drink episodes (26%) that took place a year later. It was beer consumption in particular that was predicted by viewing programmes with alcohol advertisements or sports coverage with higher levels of alcohol advertising.

In New Zealand, evidence produced by Connolly et al. (1994) indicated some connection of modest magnitude between young girls' and boys' recall of alcohol advertisements and beer consumption. This result, however, does not demonstrate a direct link between alcohol advertising exposure (which was not measured) and alcohol consumption. Henriksen et al. (2008) also reported that brand recall, brand recognition and high receptivity to alcohol marketing predicted alcohol consumption onset. As Anderson et al. (2009) noted however, this study did not measure alcohol advertising exposure effects.

Along with recall of advertising messages, whether – in the case of televised advertisements – viewers like the commercial messages may also make a difference to links between advertising exposure and alcohol consumption. The role of alcohol advertising appeal was investigated in further longitudinal research that followed through 18-year olds until the age of 21 years which found that earlier liking of televised alcohol advertisements and associated brand allegiance were associated with greater volume of beer consumption later on. The study used a sample of 630 beer-drinking participants and examined the effect of televised alcohol advertising and allegiance to specific brands of beer not only on subsequent beer consumption, but also on self-reports of aggressive behaviour linked with drinking (Casswell & Zhang, 1998). Along with the positive impact of liking alcohol advertisements and brand allegiance at age 18 on the volume of beer consumed at age 21, this approach found self-reports of alcohol-related aggressive behaviour as well.

Further data from New Zealand from among young people aged 18–29 years indicated that liking for beer advertisements on television was associated with being a heavier drinker and a greater likelihood of admitting to drink-related problems such as work performance being adversely affected or getting involved in drink-fuelled fights (Wyllie, Zhang & Casswell, 1998). As the authors on this occasion themselves cautioned, however, the data reported here could not demonstrate causal connections between any of the measured variables. Again in New Zealand researchers found links between reported 'liking' of alcohol advertisements and alcohol consumption both at one point in time (Casswell & Zhang, 1998) and over time (Casswell, Pledger & Pratap, 2002). The measure of 'liking' of alcohol advertisements used here represents a very blunt indicator of exposure.

The impact of alcohol advertising appeal was examined in a survey of Californian teenagers as well. This assessed exposure to a variety of types of alcohol advertising and alcohol consumption and found that liking of alcohol advertisements and other media exposure variables were significantly associated with reported alcohol use. Measures included general television viewing, frequency of viewing televised sports, perceived frequency of exposure to alcohol advertising, ability to recognise alcohol advertisements and recall brand names, receptivity of alcohol marketing and liking of alcohol advertisements.

These variables were related to reported use of or intention to consume alcohol through the use of multivariate statistical analyses and as the results indicated, liking of advertisements, brand recall and receptivity to alcohol marketing predicted alcohol use. The findings suggested that exposure to alcohol advertising could produce favourable opinions about alcohol among young people and that this may in turn increase their likelihood of future consumption (Unger et al., 2003).

The same research group conducted a longitudinal survey of American teenagers aged 13–14 years, which focused on the impact of televised alcohol advertisements on youngsters' likelihood of drinking alcohol. In this case, results indicated that increased exposure to alcohol advertisements on television in the first year of the study was associated with greater likelihood of consuming beer or wine a year later (Stacey et al., 2004).

Measuring alcohol advertising effects through market expenditure

Some researchers have explored links between the volumes of alcohol advertising and promotion that occurs in particular markets and young people's drinking habits. However, it needs to be noted that market expenditure levels cannot serve as valid proxies for individual consumer levels of exposure to advertising.

One such study found that the amount of money spent on beer advertising could predict young people's brand awareness, brand preferences and alcohol consumption. Those brands on which the most advertising revenue was spent were also the more popular and were most likely to be among the brands adolescent respondents said they would most like to drink (Gentile et al., 2001).

A further study cited by Anderson et al. (2009) in support of the alcohol advertising exposure to consumption link was that carried out by Snyder et al. (2006). This investigation examined the impact of alcohol advertising expenditure on consumption levels among young people aged 15–26 years in 24 Nielsen local geographical media markets. Larger amounts of expenditure on alcohol advertising were found to be associated with higher consumption levels. However, Anderson et al. (2009) argued that the latter study was severely critiqued by Schultz (2006) and Smart (2006) for sample attrition over time and for confusing correlation with causality.

Another longitudinal panel study in the US combined self-report data about alcohol advertising exposure and advertising expenditure data in different regional US markets to investigate the impact of advertising on alcohol consumption among teenagers and young adults aged between 15 and 26 years. Four survey waves were carried out over a period of more than two years. The initial survey sample comprised nearly 1900 respondents which were eroded to fewer than 600 respondents by the fourth survey wave. Respondents were sampled from 24 regional markets for which alcohol industry advertising expenditure data were obtained and combined with the survey data.

Self-reported alcohol advertising exposure was related to reported alcohol consumption, while market advertising expenditures per capita were also related to drinking levels and to growth in drinking over time. As the results showed, for every additional dollar per capita spent on advertising in the market, individuals consumed three per cent more alcoholic beverages per month. Moreover, young people who lived in markets with lower alcohol advertising expenditure consumed less alcohol and exhibited declining consumption over time (Snyder, Milici, Slater, Sun & Strizhakova, 2006).

The potential impact of market expenditure has also been investigated through the use of alcohol-related merchandise, or alcohol-branded merchandise (ABM). Following evidence of a causal relationship between cigarette-branded merchandise and the initiation of smoking among youth, McClure et al. (2006) conducted a cross-sectional study among middle-school adolescents in northern New England in order to examine the prevalence of ownership of such items and its relationship with alcohol use. The study used a combination of initial and follow-up surveys. This aimed to identify those students who, in the first instance, had never had any alcoholic drink and to establish whether they had commenced drinking during the one- to two-year period before the follow-up survey. Ownership of an ABM item was also evaluated at follow-up.

More than 10 per cent of the sample was reported to own an ABM, and this was found to be associated with initiation of alcohol use. Initiation of drinking was linked to other factors too including male gender, poorer school performance, rebelliousness, smoking and peer drinking. To identify the role of ABM alone, the researchers controlled these covariates and found that ABM ownership was an independent risk factor for initiation of alcohol use. However, the limitation of this design was clarified as it could not establish the causal direction; and whether onset of drinking preceded or followed ABM ownership, remained unclear.

Understanding alcohol consumption and the role of advertising via interviews

As the previous section demonstrated, surveys have produced a significant portion of our knowledge regarding causal relationships between alcohol advertising and consumption. The employment of in-depth interviews in the same context is less common owing mostly to the unsuitability of the said method for the examination and identification of cause-effects relationships. Nevertheless, depth interviewing can provide a more comprehensive and profound understanding of human behaviour. This can shed light on the role of advertising in drinking habits from a different angle, rounding out the knowledge from surveys.

An attempt to offer an understanding of children's attitudes towards drinking was made by Grube and Wallack (1994) who suggested that awareness of alcohol advertising could shape children's drinking knowledge and influence their future. The authors employed a combined

method comprising a self-completion survey and face-to-face interviews. This enabled them to collect data on sensitive questions, such
as those addressing drinking intentions, through a self-administered
instrument, while questions addressing television viewing were discussed through a face-to-face interview. The authors used a sample of
468 fifth- and sixth-grade students from public schools in Northern
California and measured their viewing habits, awareness of beer advertising, knowledge of beer brands and slogans, beliefs about the positive
and negative effects of drinking, intentions to drink as an adult and
parental and peer drinking.

Interestingly, the study demonstrated that intentions to drink in the
future were stronger among those children who had a better knowledge
of television alcohol advertising, brands and slogans. With regard to the
use of interviews as a method for understanding potential influences of
advertising on alcohol consumption, it could be argued that the specific study did not necessarily offer the in-depth understanding of the
children's behaviour that would be expected from the employment of a
qualitative method. The authors used structured interviews for measuring television viewing, awareness of beer advertising and beer brands
and slogans; but these elements were assessed through standardised
interview questions that were integrated in the survey and were not
treated as purely qualitative data.

In another original study, McCreanor et al. (2008) used group interviews to investigate the meaning-making practices of Maori and Pakeha
young people in New Zealand in response to alcohol marketing. The
main objective of the study was to obtain an understanding of the ways
in which young people experienced socialising and drinking in a range
of youth events, and more specifically, how young people engaged
with marketing promotions and industry-given knowledge. The sample
comprised 24 groups of three–six friends (male and female), aged 14–17
years, who were interviewed three times at approximately eight-month
intervals.

The findings demonstrated that in Aotearoa, New Zealand, rising
expenditure, sophistication and diversity in alcohol marketing are
closely related to increasing alcohol consumption among young people
and growth of alcohol-related harms. This relationship emerges primarily from the positive messages about alcohol, which are transmitted
through peers in social networks. Social interactions among friends
during social events proved a pivotal factor in increasing the scope of
alcohol marketing and in making the choice of alcohol intoxication the
easy choice. According to the study, this is primarily due to the so-called

intoxigenic social environments that marketing creates and which young people tend to incorporate in their interactions and discourses.

These findings may suggest an indirect and subtle influence of alcohol advertising, which could also imply that it is within certain contexts and in combination with other factors that such advertising can shape drinking habits among young people. In a way, this observation can be reinforced by a study conducted in areas of Southern, Central and Northern England, Wales and Scotland by Cragg (2004). He also conducted group discussions among young people seeking a deeper understanding of their attitudes towards alcohol advertising and consumption. The study included 18 extended small group discussions with both male and female respondents of aged 11–17 years.

Cragg examined issues of advertising recall and appeal, which will be examined in greater detail in the next chapter; but more importantly he demonstrated a close association between recall and/or appeal of advertisements of a certain type of alcohol (alcopop) and consumption of the same types of alcohol. Hence, respondents' recall of advertising was consistent with alcoholic drinks and brands they already consumed.

Those who regularly drank Bacardi Breezer, for example, were able to recall a number of Bacardi commercials. However, what could perhaps be a more significant finding was the fact that respondents' liking of the style of alcohol advertising did not necessarily translate into liking or buying the product or even feeling persuaded to drink.

In essence, the use of qualitative methods in the study of alcohol advertising can offer insight in the connection between alcohol advertising and consumption among people, but such findings should be treated with caution and not be automatically translated into cause-effect relationships. In contrast, what these depth interviews and discussions seem to highlight is the significance of other contextual and social factors in understanding the role of advertising in alcohol consumption.

Summary and conclusion: alcohol advertising: From exposure to orientation

In this chapter we have reviewed research evidence concerning the possible role played by exposure to alcohol advertising in triggering the onset of alcohol consumption among young people. Most of this research can be divided into two broad types: studies of relationships between verbally reported advertising exposure and drinking behaviour and studies that have used interventionist designs to observe the immediate reactions of observers following exposure to alcohol advertising. In both cases, the limitations of these methodological approaches were outlined as a reminder that the empirical evidence in this body of work should not be taken at face value.

With the exception of a few studies that have taken a more qualitative approach, therefore most of our knowledge regarding alcohol advertising exposure and alcohol consumption originates from experiments and statistical analyses of self-report data. The evidence presented in this chapter suggests that experiments have demonstrated mostly short-term effects of alcohol advertising on consumption or perceptions of it.

Alcohol advertisements may have the power to impress consumers, but whether and to what extent they can be held accountable for drinking habits remains unclear in these studies. Admittedly, questionnaire-based surveys have provided considerable variation in the investigation of cause-effect relationships between exposure to alcohol advertising and consumption. The statistical analyses from these studies produced some evidence of potential advertising effects, but at the same time, it highlighted the significance of contextual factors, such as parental and peer influences or social comparison, that yields inconclusive answers. Another interesting finding that emerged from these studies was the association of current alcohol consumption with the level of recall and appeal of related advertisements. The relevance of advertising recall and appeal was reinforced through the qualitative studies as well, creating scope for a closer inspection of the reasons that increase the liking of alcohol advertising among young people.

In effect, these studies offer mixed evidence with regard to the direct links that exist between exposure to alcohol advertising and alcohol drinking onset or quantity of consumption among young people. This raises questions about the sufficiency of these types of analysis for understanding young people's attitudes towards advertising and drinking. A key factor that can illuminate the role of alcohol advertising in shaping drinking habits among young people lies in the adolescents' awareness of alcohol-related advertisements and in the appeal of these commercial messages. It has been known for many years that young people pay attention to alcohol advertising and that the best liked alcohol advertisements may be among children's and teenagers' overall favourite advertisements for any product (Greenberg, Fazal & Wober, 1986).

Research has also emerged that indicates that young people's attitudinal or perceptual responses to advertisements for alcohol might also mediate their impact on drinking-related beliefs and behaviour. Hence, it has been found that teenagers who held positive attitudes towards alcohol advertisements were also more likely to hold positive beliefs about drinking. In this case, it was feelings about the advertisements rather than extent of reported exposure to them that mediated favourable views about alcohol and its consumption. Furthermore, these findings occurred among teenagers but were not repeated among people in their twenties (Fleming, Thorson & Atkin, 2004).

The investigation of young people's attitudes towards alcohol advertisements can reveal another dimension of the interrelation between advertising and alcohol consumption, which although more subtle than the reported alcohol consumption, can still shed light on the potential influences that such advertisements can exert on drinking habits. A useful example can be found in the longitudinal research conducted with a panel of nine- to 16-year olds in California. The study investigated whether exposure to alcohol advertisements could influence beliefs about drinking and drinking behaviour. Respondents were asked for their opinions about alcohol advertisements and about programmes that contained examples of drinking. On this occasion, opinions about alcohol advertisements were unrelated to reported alcohol consumption. However, the attractiveness of televised portrayals of drinking that triggered identification with on-screen characters and drinking occasions were related to positive views about drinking (Austin, Chen, & Grube, 2006). It is the role of such opinions that needs to be looked at more closely and whether and to what extent they may translate into consumption.

It is apparent therefore that we must look beyond simple statistical relationships between reported alcohol advertising exposure or other media exposure and reported alcohol consumption. Alcohol advertisements can trigger reactions in young consumers who may be positive or negative, but more often than not they tend to be positive. Enjoyment of alcohol advertisements might cultivate a generally positive disposition towards alcohol consumption because advertisements that give pleasure can create a halo effect around not just the advertised brand but alcohol and its consumption more generally. Even if, as discussed earlier, enjoyment of alcohol advertising does not automatically translate into drinking, one should not overlook the positive orientation it can produce about alcohol products and consumption. Such positive orientations are of course shaped by contextual and socio-psychological factors such as the ones discussed in this chapter. However, the content of advertising *per se* should also be given due attention as it manifests advertisers' attempts to incorporate consumers' preferences and likings in their promotional messages. As discussed in the next chapter, the power of themes and images that children and young people reportedly find appealing can render certain alcohol brands particularly attractive. Can these 'orientations' towards alcohol advertisements cause equally powerful effects on consumption habits? Do the opinions and perceptions young people formulate about promotional messages translate into drinking? As we have showed so far, drawing such conclusive answers is not an easy task. However, one should not neglect the role that positive dispositions to alcohol advertising can play in increasing consumers' interest in drinking. Even if appeal of advertisements cannot necessarily suggest causality, it does not cease to be a cause for concern.

5
Orientations towards Alcohol Advertisements

Introduction

This chapter will examine evidence for the role played by advertising in shaping young people's attitudes and beliefs concerning alcohol and alcohol brands. Initial investigations of the impact of alcohol advertising on young people's drinking habits worked on the principle that influence almost directly followed exposure. Over time, theoretical and empirical advances in research in this area have indicated that the relationship between advertising exposure and alcohol consumption is not that straightforward. Behavioural effects, for instance, are increasingly believed to be mediated by cognitive-level responses that embrace brand perceptions, enjoyment of advertising and expectations about alcohol consumption and personal image (see Grube & Walters, 2005).

The importance of psychological factors in understanding and even predicting drinking behaviour among young people should not be underestimated. Such factors can mediate potential advertising effects and account for the problematic nature of the relationship between advertising exposure and alcohol consumption. The role of this type of 'mediating' factor was illustrated in a study conducted by Fleming et al. (2004), that examined the impact of alcohol advertising exposure on intentions to drink and actual consumption.

The authors focused on cognitive responses to advertising messages and positive expectancies about alcohol use as mediating factors that could shape potential advertising influences. In this case, expectancies reflect the process of linking 'experiences regarding alcohol use obtained at one point in life with a later point when the actual decision to drink is made and when alcohol-related behaviours are emitted'

(Christiansen et al., 1989: 98 in Fleming et al., 2004). They conducted a survey on two age cohorts, 15–20 years and 21–9 years, in which they employed the so-called Message Interpretation Process (MIP) model (Austin & Johnson, 1997; Austin & Knaus, 2000). The model underlines the importance of factors such as children's beliefs about media images and media models' desirability in the development of expectancies about alcohol drinking. In other words, accepting or rejecting an advertising stimulus is a dynamic process which involves the processing of information other than just the content of the message.

The findings in the study showed that greater exposure to alcohol advertising did shape the attitudes in both age groups, but the positive responses to alcohol advertising led to positive expectancies about alcohol drinking only for the 15- to 20-year-olds. Most importantly, alcohol advertising did not emerge as the determining factor that predicted the young adults' alcohol consumption or intentions to drink in the future. Instead, their consumption and drinking intentions were mostly predicted by their positive expectancies regarding alcohol, demonstrating the key role of psychological factors. Of course, the role of such psychological factors in defining young people's attitude towards drinking does not negate the potential influence of advertising, especially when one considers that the principles of advertising are largely based on cognitive psychology. The significance of psychological factors in perceiving and responding to stimuli is of course entrenched in advertising and an illustrative example can be found in the case of branding.

Branding in alcohol advertising

The recognition of brand names is one of the aspects of advertising that carries considerable weight for consumers' perceptions of the quality of a given product. Empirical research has demonstrated that strong brand names stabilise the quality perceptions of a branded product (Della Bitta, Monroe and McGinnis, 1981 and Dodds et al., 1991 in Grewal et al., 1998: 335). Consumers' positive perceptions of brands are mostly dependent on brand familiarity, which grows with the frequent exposure to various media advertisements for the brand, exposure to the brand in a store and purchase or usage of the brand (Alba and Hutchinson, (1987) in Park and Stoel, 2005: 150). Brand familiarity is even thought to increase consumer confidence eliminating their perception of risk in purchasing a given product (Laroche et al., 1996).

Considering the importance of brand recognition and familiarity, it comes as no surprise that efforts are increasingly made for the establishment of brand names in the alcohol market as well. In large national and international markets, major alcoholic drinks manufacturers have come to dominate. They have established well-known brands that have been widely promoted. The alcoholic beverage market is therefore highly competitive and consumers have an extensive range of brands to choose from within a number of different product categories. Advertising plays a critical part in the establishment of brand identities, brand prominence and market share. Alcohol advertisers strive through their promotional campaigns to associate their brands with appealing attributes that will set them apart from their competitors. Although marketing campaigns are conducted via all the major mass media, many brands of alcoholic beverage are targeted at specific groups of consumers. This may also mean that advertising media are used selectively with advertisement positioned in locations designed to achieve maximum exposure among target group members.

Effectively, establishing brand identities is no longer confined to advertising only but can also include such marketing efforts as sales promotions, branded merchandising, field sales exercises and events sponsorship. These efforts have been further facilitated by the use of technologies such as the Internet and the adoption of more diverse cultural themes. Hence, the branding is often done by combining a commercial trademark with a subcultural motif the consumers can identify themselves with. In this case, the brand works as the linking point between culture and marketing. This can prove a successful recipe for the promotion of youth brands. Such an example is the promotion of energy drinks, like the premixed vodka and energy drink called 'Vodka Kick' introduced by a UK company called GBL International. With caffeine being one of the main ingredients of such drinks, advertisers promote the product in association to the 'all-night clubbing' culture (Jernigan and O'Hara, 2004). Moreover, as shown by research conducted in New Zealand, alcohol brand images and lifestyle marketing provide young people with commercialised identities to take up, along with the alcoholic products (McCreanor et al., 2005).

This technique works particularly well with adolescents since according to Solomon's (1983, 1992 in Pechmann et al., 2005) symbolic interactionism theory, their self-consciousness and social anxiety make them more receptive to heavily advertised brands. In this case, it is theorised that consumers often buy products for their value as consumption symbols, which can enhance perceptions of self-worth. As teenagers find themselves in a period of transition often characterised by uncertainty about their ability to attain a desired role, their reliance on consumption symbols intensifies.

In understanding the role that advertising plays in youth alcohol consumption, we need to examine the significance of branding. To what extent do young people become aware of brands? Research may suggest that exposure to alcohol advertising over time may increase brand awareness among some teenagers and pre-teenagers. One American study found that small minorities of nine-year-olds (14 per cent) and 13-year-olds (20 per cent) were able to correctly identify beer brands in advertisements where the brand was hidden in at least three out of four cases. One very popular brand, Budweiser, however, was identified by overwhelming majorities of nine-year-olds (75 per cent) and 13-year-olds (87 per cent) (Collins et al., 2005). However, does brand awareness signal a propensity to drink alcohol? To what extent also do they respond favourably to alcohol advertising? Are there particular kinds of attributes that can enhance young consumers' attitudes towards brands and the way they are advertised?

As with research into advertising and consumer behaviour, studies that have utilised non-behavioural measures or verbal measures that report on psychological dispositions rather than actual behavioural consumption can be differentiated by methodology. Most of the research derives from surveys with convenience or representative samples of young people. Some research has adopted an interventionist approach to test cause-effect relationships, and other studies have used more qualitative approaches and relied on unconstrained answers to open-ended questions in an interview format.

Rather than dividing the research by methodology, however, this chapter examines different measures of 'orientation' towards alcohol and alcohol advertising and considers the relevant evidence from different methodologies under each heading. In particular, it examines what is known about children's and teenagers' liking of alcohol advertisements, the reasons for liking and their attitudes towards these advertisements and their memory for alcohol advertising. It has been known for some years that children and adolescents, though not necessarily the targets of alcohol advertising, nevertheless have extensive awareness of brands and of advertising for them, particularly when that advertising occurs on television (Aitken, 1989). It is important though to understand what factors might underpin this awareness. What aspects of alcohol advertising underpin its appeal to youth? In order to address this question, the chapter will also examine key themes and images in alcohol advertising that have proved particularly appealing to young consumers.

Alcohol images and representations in contemporary advertising

Alcohol advertising is admittedly a significant source of information for consumers about related products and, most importantly, about alcohol brands. At the same time, advertising is central to the product itself. The advertising and promotion of alcohol products has seen significant changes in the last two decades. There has been an obvious shift from alcohol being marketed based on the quality, purity and price of the product, to being promoted based on the identity of the brand and the consumers' desires and dreams (Casswell, 1995; Jernigan and O'Hara, 2004). In effect, there is an increasing emphasis on packaging alcohol products with attractive images and lifestyles, which are associated with wealth, power or social approval (Gerbner, 1995; Wallack et al., 1990).

Among the most common lifestyle images are the portrayals of young, attractive and elegant people that enable the association of alcohol products and brands with mostly positive and appealing ideas. The effectiveness of such practices lies in embedding brands in the lives and lifestyles of consumers and creating an intimate relationship between a given brand and the user, to the point that 'the brand becomes an extension or an integral part of the self' (Aaker, 1996: 156 in Jernigan and O'Hara, 2004: 631). In this case, it is not just an alcohol product that is being sold, but a whole set of values.

This association of alcohol brands with widely desired and admired lifestyles is commonly achieved through the employment of specific techniques that, as we will see later in this chapter, can invoke positive perceptions about drinking among young people. One of the most widely used techniques is the use of celebrity characters that lend their support to a particular brand of alcohol, prompting consumers to do the same. Another one is the implicit suggestion that if everyone in the advertisement is doing something, you should too and in most cases this refers to the consumption of the advertised brand. Jim Beam is a useful example of a campaign that employs this technique. One of their recent advertisements shows a group of young men making silly poses in front of a camera while the tag line reads 'You can count on them to never ask you to "Get in touch with your feminine side". Real friends. Real bourbon.' A possible interpretation of this advertisement could imply that your real male friends drink Jim Beam and you should do the same.

Moreover, on many occasions, alcohol advertisements feature ambiguous words that aim to invoke positive emotions in the consumer. The use of terms such as 'magic', 'pride' and 'power' often succeeds in making implicit promises for the capacity of the advertised brand to deliver desired lifestyles (Wechsler, 2001).

In terms of the potential effect that such techniques might have on consumers, adolescents and young adults are generally believed to be more vulnerable for the simple fact that they normally get greater exposure to alcohol advertising than do older adults (Atkin & Block, 1981; Atkin et al., 1984; Wyllie et al., 1998). However, as the use of appealing images increase and efforts to associate alcohol brands with attractive characters and lifestyles can intensify, advertisers increasingly seek to create a unique experience, which for many products is essentially a youth experience. This approach may inevitably increase the potential influence of alcohol advertising on young people's drinking habits.

The influential power of such images and themes can stem from the strong impressions they leave on children and young people's minds, rendering certain advertisements memorable and recognisable even when the product or brand name has been disguised. This was found in a study conducted in South Dakota were a number of masked television advertisements for beer were shown to children between the ages of nine and 13 years, the majority of whom could recognise most of the advertisements and the advertised brand as well. (Collins et al., 2005).

What needs to be clarified is that awareness of alcohol advertising is not unconditional and as the above study also demonstrated, it was those children with greater exposure to alcohol advertisements in magazines, at sporting and music events and on television and those who knew adults who drank that exhibited greater knowledge of the selected advertisements. Gender played a role too, as advertisement awareness was higher among boys. Among the conditions that render certain advertisements more memorable and recognisable are the features and themes used in alcohol advertising that contribute in creating a unique and appealing life experience for young consumers.

Awareness and appeal of alcohol advertisements

The significance of 'liking' as a youth response to alcohol advertisements and the degree of attention paid to such advertising has already been confirmed by research. Interestingly, evidence has emerged that alcohol advertisements have an appeal for children, even before they have begun drinking, especially those portrayed on television (see Aitken et al., 1988b; Aitken, Leathar & Scott, 1988a; Waiters, Treno & Grube, 2001; Wyllie, Zhang & Caswell, 1998). Indeed, research has demonstrated that alcohol advertisements feature among children's favourite commercials (Nash, Pine & Messer, 2009). Children and teenagers from the age of 10 years show signs of familiarity with and liking of alcohol brands and such appreciation continues to grow with age. Although research evidence based on open-ended discussions does not prove a causal link between advertising exposure and alcohol consumption, advertising may help to reinforce a positive attitudinal climate around drinking (Aitken, 1989).

In one study conducted in USA, early teenagers (aged 13–16 years) were shown a series of videotaped advertisements for beer, wine and soft drinks that had originally been broadcast on television. Respondents indicated whether they had seen these advertisements before, how much the advertisements had attracted their attention and then provided a number of evaluative ratings for each commercial message. They were also asked how much they drank alcoholic beverages and how often they got drunk. The findings indicated that respondents who claimed to pay attention to alcohol advertisements also drank more and enjoyed the advertisements more as well. The researchers reasoned that if liking of these advertisements motivated attention that was, in turn, linked to propensity to drink, advertisers could provide a useful social function by making their alcohol advertisements less attractive to young people (Grube, Madden, & Fries, 1996).

The role of contextual factors

Contextual factors have proved to play a significant role in the case of advertising appeal as well, since in most cases whether and how much young people like alcohol advertisements depends on a number of parameters. One such parameter is the drinking experience of young people as awareness, attention and liking of alcohol advertisements appears to relate to whether young people are alcohol consumers.

A group of studies by Aitken and his colleagues explored children's and teenagers' orientations towards alcohol advertising in terms of liking for advertisements and brand awareness, and how these measures differed between youngsters who drank and those who were still teetotal. Aitken, Leathar & Scott (1988a) interviewed 150 children in focus groups – aged 10–16 years, while a follow-up study comprised face-to-face interviews with 433 children aged 10–17 years and involved respondents in identifying still photographs from television advertisements (Aitken et al., 1988b). It was found that the degree of attention to alcohol advertisements depended upon whether the youngsters were already alcohol consumers themselves. Hence, those who drank exhibited greater appreciation of alcohol advertisements than did those who did not drink (Aitken, 1989). In another controlled experimental study of liking for alcohol (and tobacco) advertisements, Unger, Johnson & Rohrbach (1995) examined the degree to which liking for the advertisement for a product type is related to susceptibility to consume it. A sample of 386 13–14-year-olds was recruited to take part in this investigation in southern California with the sample being slightly more heavily weighted towards females (54 per cent). All participants were presented with two booklets that contained print advertisements for alcohol and tobacco products from male and female-oriented magazines. Brand names and verbal references to the product were digitally removed in each case and each advertisement was evaluated in turn using a common set of rating scales. Participants were asked to identify the (missing) brand name, to say how much they liked the advertisement and rate the degree to which it made them want to buy the product. Their alcohol consumption status was also rated. Participants were divided into non-susceptible non-drinkers who did not drink and were unlikely to try; susceptible non-drinkers, who did not drink but might try in the future; and drinkers who had tried alcohol at some point.

Alcohol users were more likely than non-susceptible non-users to recognise alcohol brands, but this difference did not quite achieve statistical significance. Alcohol consumption was a significant predictor of liking for alcohol brands in the case of three out of six alcohol brands that were evaluated. In the case of just one brand, liking was greater among susceptible non-drinkers than non-susceptible non-drinkers. Hence, some evidence emerged that liking for alcohol advertisements was enhanced by being a drinker already. Among non-drinkers, those who thought they might drink in the future were more likely than committed non-drinkers to like alcohol advertising. These results, however, revealed nothing directly about any possible effects of alcohol advertising on the onset of alcohol consumption among young people.

Evidence that has found connection between liking of alcohol advertisements and consumption suggests that such effects were manifest over time. Research with pre-teenagers and teenagers in the United States revealed that liking of these advertisements, as distinct from mere exposure to them, was related to having positive expectations about alcohol and to the belief that more of their peer group drank. These beliefs, in turn, were related to onset of alcohol consumption three years later (Chen & Grube, 2004).

Age has emerged as one of those factors that shape alcohol advertising appeal. As the study of Aitken, Leathar and Scott (1988a) demonstrated, although pre-teenage children were found to enjoy some television advertisements for alcoholic products, liking for these advertisements can change with age. Research conducted in the UK has also shown that televised alcohol advertisements that are popular among 10-year olds are less so among 12-year olds (Aitken et al., 1988b). Even so, most pre-teens and teenage respondents in this UK study expressed some degree of liking for alcohol advertisements (Hastings, MacKintosh & Aitken, 1992).

Young people's critical approaches to alcohol advertising

An interesting finding that has emerged from the above studies is the ability of young people to approach alcohol advertisements critically. Although significant proportions of these youngsters said they 'liked' alcohol advertisements on television, many were also able to articulate some awareness that these messages were targeted at adults and not at them (Young, 2003). Nor do young people express an appeal to alcohol advertising unconditionally.

In a study by Waiters et al. (2001) the authors conducted focus group interviews with nine- to 15-year olds in California in which they assessed respondents' opinions to six television advertisements for beer. This young sample displayed widespread enjoyment of beer advertisements in terms of their production attributes, but some reacted negatively to the fact that they were for a beer. Disliked elements in advertising included the way they portrayed women and their encouragement to drink. Moreover, it had emerged from in-depth interviews with pre-teenage children and those in their early teens that some vocalise negative opinions about drinking alcohol and the effects it can have on the drinker. Where the advertising messages did not reflect on or represent those kinds of issues, youngsters could experience difficulties interpreting what message the advertiser was trying to convey (Waiters et al., 2001). Once in their teens, however, and presumably at a stage when they were beginning to think about becoming alcohol consumers themselves, advertising messages that projected images of lifestyle and social success in association with drinking hold greater appeal (Lieberman & Orlandi, 1987; Waiters et al., 2001).

Does liking lead to advertising effects?

Associating the appeal of advertising with potential effects may seem a logical observation. Nevertheless, whether the research literature on this subject demonstrates a causal connection between exposure to alcohol advertising and its consumption is debatable (Young, 2003). It has been argued that 'liked' commercials may be more persuasive and influential, leading to alcohol consumption (see Covell, 1992; Kelly & Edwards, 1998; Waiters et al., 2001). One finding that has reinforced this position is that teenagers who drink alcohol tend to appreciate alcohol advertisements more than their teetotal peers (Aitken et al., 1988a).

We must observe caution, however, in the way such data are interpreted, given that neither causation nor direction of causation can be proven by these kinds of self-report evidence. What we also need to unravel is whether the alcohol consumption came first or whether it was followed by enjoyment of advertising, which is a more difficult issue to clarify. What does seem apparent from early British research is that once a youngster has become an underage drinker, he or she will become more aware of and more attuned to advertising for alcohol. It is possible also that the youngster might identify with these commercial messages more because they feature other drinkers – a community of which they now regard themselves as members. Overall, alcohol advertisements tend to be appreciated by drinkers to a greater extent than by non-drinkers. It was particularly the humour of alcohol advertisements that adolescents who had become underage consumers of alcohol and others who were experimenting with alcohol enjoyed more than other children and teenagers (Aitken, 1989).

Determining whether, to what extent and in what ways young people like or dislike alcohol advertisement can require subtle lines of questioning as some children may say they like everything about an advertisement except that it is selling an alcoholic beverage. Hence liking of an advertisement and a product could be quite separate thought processes (see Nash, 2002; Waiters et al., 2001). In fact, children may recognise that alcohol advertisements are not meant for their age group, anyhow. Hence, while alcohol consumption might be projected as 'cool' by some advertisements though not by others, either message may carry little direct relevance for pre-teenagers who have not yet begun to think about drinking.

Attributes of appeal in alcohol advertising

'Liking' as a response is rather non-specific. What does it really tell us about the way young consumers are responding to alcohol advertisements? Identifying the appeal that alcohol advertisements may have for children is an important step towards the drawing of more conclusive answers regarding the extent to which children's drinking habits may also be shaped by such advertising. What we also need to know is which attributes or features of the advertising drive that appeal. So far, there has been some considerable consensus among studies across the world about those attributes that appear to be more appealing to young consumers. Such attributes include animated characters, human characters, humour, music and same-age role models. These attributes emerged as the most influential in terms of driving liking of alcohol advertisements and being most closely related to alcohol consumption among Californian children and teenagers aged between 10 and 17 years. It needs to be mentioned though that humour emerged as a more important factor than the rest (Chen et al., 2005).

The same finding occurred in a study among pre-teenage and teenage children in Scotland, who were drawn to alcohol advertising primarily by humour. Other attributes included bright and colourful features, and a production format that had pace and action (Aitken, 1989; Hastings, MacKintosh & Aitken, 1992). The following sections will present a description and assessment of some of the key themes that render alcohol advertising appealing to children and young people.

Humour

Humour has emerged as one important ingredient in this context (Preston, 2000). In the US, young consumers aged 10–14 years often justified their choice of favourite advertisement in terms of its humour content (Neuendorf, 1985). In the UK, when children and teenagers nominated their favourite advertisements, messages with humour have also tended often to come out on top (Aitken et al., 1988a; Aitken et al., 1988b; Nash, Pine & Lutz, 2002). Again, British children as young as 10 years have been found to nominate alcohol advertisements on TV as their favourites.

Later qualitative research found that children and teenagers respond differently to humour in advertisements depending upon how sophisticated it is. For young children, the humour has to be simple while for older children more complex forms of humour work well (Waiters et al., 2001). Some high-profile campaigns are successful because they are founded upon a specific buzzword or phrase which enters popular public consciousness especially among young people. The Budweiser 'Whassup' is perhaps one of the best examples of this phenomenon. The campaign depicts a group of friends speaking on the phone and exchanging the term 'Whassup' (a similar advertisement depicted another group of men exchanging the foreign version of 'Whassup' – 'Ya Hey Der'), demonstrating how the use of certain linguistic devices can render advertisements appealing to young consumers. The potential appeal of catch phrases lies in the degree of familiarity or resonance that the specific language has with the life experiences of young people (ASA, 2005: 46).

A category of humour found in alcohol advertisements that is believed to be popular among children and teenagers is the so-called kidult humour, a strategy that harnesses the values and attitudes of childhood/youth for marketing adult products. While the 'kidult' theme is ostensibly aimed at adults, it blurs the fixed lines between adults and children with 'kidults laying claim to childhood or youth' (ASA, 2005). An example of an alcohol campaign featuring this strategy was the Smirnoff Ice campaign featuring Uri, a character adopting a comical behaviour that that can be perceived as a juvenile behaviour, and therefore quite appealing to young people, and could fall under the 'kidult' concept. Interestingly, in September 2006 the campaign was eventually banned in UK by the Advertising Standards Authority (ASA) on the grounds of using themes that blur the lines between adult and children behaviour.

Unlike the examples of Budweiser and Smirnoff Ice, a more sophisticated type of humour can be found in the Famous Grouse campaign. The campaign is known for the Grouse icon, which represents the brand image and a registered trademark, and has often been used to create a series of humorous spots based on the personification of the grouse. In this case, meaning is drawn from the various activities the grouse was involved in, such as ice-skating, walking on a red carpet or playing golf. The humorous use of animation technology with the grouse seen in a series of relevant social situations is among the attributes that would appeal mostly to older children.

Celebrities and sports personalities

Atkin and Block (1981) reported that young consumers seemed to be attracted to advertisements with celebrities endorsing the brands, with young people featured as consumers and with sexual themes. The appeal of young endorsers and celebrity figures including sports personalities was further underlined by research showing that these features were often well recognised and recalled (Lieberman & Orlandi, 1987).

It needs to be noted that recognition and recall of advertisements featuring celebrities does not automatically translate into appeal of these advertisements. In a pilot study to explore the potential effects of alcohol advertising shown during sporting broadcasts on children in Australia, Phillipson and Jones (2007) examined brand recognition and likeability of alcohol advertisements that appeared on public broadcast television during the three One-Day Cricket finals between Australia and Sri Lanka during the months of January and February of 2006. The authors conducted group interviews with children and found considerable variation in their recall and recognition of advertisements depending on the appeal of the product and the appeal of the actual advertisement. Interestingly, although advertisements were evaluated as appealing due to the presence of features such as humour and the use of mascots, the use of sports celebrities alone did not prove sufficient to make an advertisement appealing.

The use of celebrities is often aimed at creating an identification of the advertised alcohol product with features of the respective celebrity. In this case, although the use of a celebrity in an adult context not particularly appealing to children would not increase children's liking of the advertisement, the association of a celebrity with other appealing features, such as humour, can reinforce the influential power of the advertisement.

A useful example can be found in the campaign for the John Smith's beer that was broadcast in UK from 2002–4 and featured comedian Peter Kay in a number of comical everyday life situations. The campaign was entirely character-driven and built on the element of entertainment. Therefore, it did not communicate a product-related image, but became attractive and memorable due to the hilarious/funny advertisements it comprised. With the use of the 'No nonsense' slogan it communicated a certain profile of the John Smiths brand, which was associated with the profile of its celebrity character.

Considering the strong appeal that this kind of humour and comedy is likely to have on young people, the use of the specific celebrity character could have enhanced the liking of the advertisement and the possible effect it could have on young consumers. Moreover, the use of celebrities can receive a mixed reception depending upon whether their presence is regarded as central to the sales message and production treatment of the advertisement (Waiters et al., 2001; Wyllie, Casswell & Stewart, 1989).

Animated characters

The use of animated characters has been identified as a feature that can attract the attention of youngsters. Support for this observation derives from an American study in which nine-year-old children and teenagers aged 14–15 years were shown photographs taken from televised beer commercials from which brand or producer names were removed. One beer advertisement featured an animated ferret and lizards while three other beer advertisements contained more adult themes. There was a fairly low level of awareness of the beer advertisements with adult themes, but a high level of awareness of advertisement that featured animation. In fact, around eight out of ten 14- to 15-year-olds and a third of nine-year-olds could recognise the latter advertisement and the brand it advertised, while only around one in ten youngsters recognised the other beer brands (Collins et al., 2005).

Further evidence offered from qualitative research with children, however, related again to the Budweiser commercials (Waiters et al., 2001). One difficulty here is separating out the effects of this variable and those of the humour of this advertising campaign, both of which make the campaign particularly appealing to children. The employment of animated characters relies largely on the technique of personification and the attribution of human qualities to them. The Budweiser commercial that featured two lizards impersonating the 'Bud-weis-er' frogs and discussing the race for 'President of Beers' is a well-known example. Nevertheless, animated characters are often used in more adult-orientated contexts. For instance, although Miller employed animal characters for the 'Miller Auditions' campaign, these characters were portrayed in an innovative way as they were shown auditioning about an advertisement in a human-like voice and manner. These spots tended to be deeper in emotion and funny in their own right. Looking past the animals the viewer can see that the message (and joke) is mostly about advertisers who use animals. They can therefore be described as subtle parodies, employing the animals in a way that is quite unlikely to be particularly appealing to the young consumers. Along similar lines, the Famous Grouse campaign was built on the personification of the Grouse icon and meaning was drawn from the various activities the grouse was involved in, such as walking on a red carpet, or playing golf. In this case, the campaign used the animated grouse in a humorous context to promote the quality and tradition of the brand as 'Scotland's favourite whiskey' rather than to attract the attention of youngsters.

Aspirational lifestyles and young characters

Advertisements that play on lifestyles that are attractive to young people can command greater attention and liking. Such features include attractive, sophisticated young people, behaviour that could be described as 'cool', images of young people partying and having fun and elements that carry connotations of a contemporary culture. These elements hold a special appeal to young people who have reached a stage of development at which they are seeking to establish a self-identity (Donohew, 1990).

Such images were often present in the Bacardi commercials, where attractive, young people were portrayed having a good time. For example, the advertisement titled 'Peep holes' featured a young woman hosting a party and looking through the door peephole to ensure her guests carried Bacardi drinks before she invited them in. The advertisement included scenes of attractive, well-dressed people in a party, conjuring up notions of what it would be like to be with beautiful people in a carefree, confident environment (ASA, 2005: pp. 45).

The use of visual imagery that plays on lifestyle fashions can prove especially effective in enhancing the appeal of an advertisement to young people (Covell, 1992; Kelly & Edwards, 1998). Preferences for image advertisements have been found to be related to intentions to drink in the future among teenagers aged 13–16 years (Kelly & Edwards, 1998). Image advertisements have also been found to work well in promoting alcoholic beverages (Slater et al., 1996). In a comparison of imagery and tombstone versions of advertisements for selected brands of alcoholic drink, advertisements that featured only the brand name (tombstone) were rated as much less attractive and resulted in the advertised product being perceived as much less socially desirable by young consumers aged 12–16 years. The format used in the advertising, however, made no difference to perceptions of risks associated with alcohol consumption (Kelly, Slater & Karan, 2002).

The portrayal of young role models contributes in the creation of such aspirational images too. Young people's attention to and liking of alcohol advertisements can be influenced by the presence of young role models. This effect, however, does not occur equally among all young people. One study found that the perception that alcohol advertisements featured underage characters associated with alcohol was associated with self-reported use of alcohol among teenage respondents. However, while this relationship emerged among 15- to 16-year olds, it was not replicated among 17- to 18-year olds. Thus, similar-age role models in alcohol advertisements may have an impact among young people who have reached a stage where they are thinking about whether they should drink or not, but are less influential among slightly older adolescents who have already decided what to do (Slater et al., 1996).

Sport

The use of sport is another particularly appealing element. In fact, TV beer advertisements with sports content have proved to be consistently preferred by male teenagers in the US while liking for these advertisements has also been found to predict current drinking and future drinking intentions (Slater et al., 1996, 1997). Sport contributes in the creation of the aspirational lifestyle images that young people find appealing. Moreover, like celebrities, sports personalities, are particularly endorsed by young consumers (Lieberman & Orlandi, 1987; Hastings, MacKintosh & Aitken, 1992, ASA, 2005). Considering that identification is an important aspect of social modelling (Bandura, 1994) and especially male adolescents tend to identify with persons involved with athletic activity, sports content is likely to make alcohol advertisements better accepted and more appealing. In an experiment that examined the reactions of American male adolescents to TV beer advertisement including sports content, Slater et al. (1996) sought to identify the potential effect of sports-related content on perceptions and liking of beer advertisements.

The study focused on young people between 13 and 16 years of age who were shown a number or videos featuring beer advertisements with sports content, beer advertisements without sports content and non-beer advertisements from sports programming and entertainment programming. After viewing the relevant videos, participants were given an opportunity to respond in writing describing the thoughts and feelings they had while watching the commercials. Although no inferences were made regarding potential effects of such advertisements on consumption of beer, one clear-cut finding was the more positive response of the participants to beer advertisements with sports content than to beer advertisements without sports content. A more positive response was also found to non-beer advertisements during sports programming than those during entertainment programming, reinforcing assumptions about sport being an appealing element. Interestingly, but not surprisingly, the authors found that positive responses to beer advertisements with sports content were correlated with the degree in which respondents were involved with sports.

Given the popularity of sport-related TV and advertising content, it comes as no surprise that a number of alcohol advertising campaigns have invested on sport images and personalities. One of the most representative examples is the Budweiser campaign that, over the last few years, has sought to promote sport and beer consumption as an attractive and relaxing lifestyle. Spots such as the 'Picture Phone', 'True' and 'Ya Hey Der (Whassup)' promoted the 'chill-out' image of the Budweiser drinker who enjoyed watching the game and having a Bud. However, it needs to be noted that sport is not invariably portrayed in a way that appeals to young people. A somewhat different depiction of sport in relation to alcohol was found in the Guinness campaign where football was used as theme for the promotion of values and ideas such as the Irish tradition in the advertisement 'The Backpacker'. The advertisement portrayed a backpacker in Asia walking in the rain and entering a house in which people were watching a football game on TV, while the camera focused on their T-shirts that featured Ireland's colours. In another campaign of the same brand, an advertisement titled 'Believe' portrayed football in association with ethnic equality. The advertisement featured Subuteo pieces that showed the first black football player to play for England. The values, with which the brand was associated through football in this case, addressed an adult audience and cannot be seen as particularly appealing to young people.

Variation of appeal

Apart from the general consensus found in studies regarding the attributes of appeal, attention has also been drawn on the significant variation of liking for different alcohol advertisements and the fact that specific categories of attributes of appeal could vary greatly in terms of how much consumers enjoy them in different televised alcohol advertisements.

An example of this type of variation is found in a study conducted by Chen et al. (2005), where the most-liked beer advertisement of all was for Budweiser, preferred by 92 per cent of respondents, while the least liked, for Busch, was rated positively by just 16 per cent. An interesting variation emerged within the groups of fans of both these brands. Hence, the Budweiser advertisement was thought to be funny by 97 per cent of respondents, with the same percentage liking the animal characters of the advertisement; but although 93 per cent liked the music, a smaller group of 84 per cent admitted liking the storyline. With the Busch advertisement, just two per cent thought it was funny, 26 per cent liked the characters, 25 per cent liked the music and 18 per cent liked the story. The same authors reported that the more specific alcohol advertisements were liked, the more influential they were perceived to be by their child and adolescent respondents. 'Influence' in this case was operationally defined in terms of respondents saying they would be likely to buy the advertised brand.

A variation in the appeal of these attributes has emerged also in relation to age and gender. It has been found that older children tended to like alcohol advertisements more than did younger children (Aitken, 1989). In general, all these attributes were more frequently named by 14- to 17-year olds than by 10- to 13-year olds. Moreover, while some features such as humour may appeal equally to both sexes, there are other attributes of alcohol advertising that seem to be more gender-specific in their appeal. Hence, girls have demonstrated evidence of being particularly drawn to alcohol brands that use advertising with feminine themes (Aitken, 1989).

Another element that contributes in the creation of appealing advertisements for young people is the use of strong imagery. However, the imagery can be so powerful that it overrides the product in terms of giving the advertisement an identity. Thus, whether such powerful advertising is effective in terms of enhancing brand image and strength of appeal of the product (rather than the commercial message) remains an open question. Hence, advertisements that contain images that are designed to link the product with a specific social status or lifestyle or which suggest that through consumption, the consumer's personal image will be boosted can drive message appeal among young consumers. However, the appealing power of imagery works best among teenagers than among pre-teenagers, (Covell, 1992; Kelly & Edwards, 1998).

Memory for alcohol advertisements

Whether an advertising message ultimately has an impact upon consumers after exposure will depend upon whether its essential ingredients are remembered. Memory can be measured in different ways. Individuals can be asked to recall details of messages to which they have been exposed. Alternatively, they can be tested with prompts to see if they recognise aspects of messages previously shown to them. Researchers have found that a majority of pre-teenage children (aged 10–12 years) can accurately recognise images taken from televised advertisements for alcoholic products (Aitken et al., 1988b; Wyllie, et al., 1998). Verbal descriptions of advertisements are even more widely recognised (Wyllie, Casswell & Stewart, 1989). Among nine- to 10-year olds, however, accurate recognition of still photos taken from alcohol advertisements was less widespread than recognition of stills taken from advertisements for non-alcoholic products (Nash et al., 2002). Across the 10- to 16-years age span, alcohol brand recognition has been found to increase with age (Aitken, 1989).

Alcohol brand names have been found to be widely recognised by pre-teenage children (Wyllie, Zhang & Casswell, 1998). Furthermore, children can recall brand names when asked to do so in an open-ended and minimally prompted free recall test (Aitken et al., 1988b). Children can also recognise advertisements for alcoholic brands even when the product was not shown to them as a prompt. Thus, particular advertisement productions are learnt by children even when precise recollection of brand names fails (Wyllie, Casswell & Stewart, 1989).

Pre-teenage children's attention to alcohol advertising has been confirmed by research showing that they can identify brands from attribute prompts within such advertising (Leiber, 1998). When shown still photographs depicting animated characters from television, a clear majority of nine- to 11-year-old children were able to recall the Budweiser brand (81%) and slogan (73% recalled the 'Bud-weis-er' slogan) when shown a picture of the Budweiser frogs. In fact, recall of the Budweiser slogan was more widespread than that of the Tony the Tiger slogan for Kellogg's Frosties (57% for 'They're grrreat') or the Mighty Morphin Power Rangers (39% for 'It's morphin' time'). Only Bug's Bunny's catchphrase was more widely recalled (80% for 'Eh, what's up doc?').

Memory of advertisements is also closely associated with appeal and current alcohol consumption. In the study mentioned in Chapter 4, conducted by Cragg (2004), recall of advertisement endlines was more evident and frequent for popular alcopop brands like Smirnoff Ice, Bacardi Breezer and WKD. The advertisements for the specific alcohol drink and brands included elements such as humour and rebellious behaviour that children and young people find appealing. The respondents were also able to remember those advertisements that promoted brands they were already consuming.

While memory for advertisements is a critical component of their overall impact upon consumers, the ability to remember exposure to an advertisement for alcohol does not demonstrate causal agency in respect of drinking onset among youngsters. Suggestive evidence for such a link has emerged from research in which pre-teenagers (aged 11–12 years) who exhibited greater self-reported exposure to alcohol advertisements and higher levels of alcohol brand recognition also displayed firmer expectations that they would eventually consume alcohol one day (Wallack, Cassady & Grube, 1990). Children's knowledge of alcohol brands has been associated with their awareness of televised alcohol advertising and slogans associated with brands (for beer). This awareness in turn was correlated with how much television they watch and with their intention to drink as adults (Grube & Wallack, 1994).

Advertising, attitudes and beliefs about drinking

There is mounting evidence that young people get information about alcohol from advertising and that this can shape their attitude and beliefs about alcohol. Essentially this evidence has indicated that exposure to alcohol advertising, especially on television, may cultivate more favourable orientations towards alcohol consumption. It would be a mistake, however, to treat all young people aged under 18 as a homogeneous population. When it comes to their attitudes towards alcohol, they are not. Pre-teenagers have been found to take the moral high ground and judge drinking alcohol in terms of whether it is good or bad. While their personal consumption experiences may be limited or non-existent, children may exhibit awareness that alcohol can cause people to behave oddly or differently from usual and that is not always a good thing.

As they enter adolescence, young people adopt a different orientation that is strongly driven by their aspirational needs to be viewed as more grown up. They are more sensitive to lifestyle appeals and judge alcohol advertisements not in terms of the worthiness of the product itself, but by the way it is promoted. The more a promotional campaign uses attractive role models or depicts lifestyles associated with alcohol that they desire, the more young people identify with advertisements and enjoy them (Austin & Knauss, 2000).

One early American survey of young people aged–22 years found that those who exhibited high exposure to televised alcohol advertising also held more positive views about getting drunk (Atkin & Block, 1981). A subsequent American survey with 10- to 14-year olds suggested that exposure to alcohol advertising and other media representations of drinking might promote perceptions that people who drink tend to be happy and have fun. In this case, the key measure of exposure was overall weight of television viewing which may provide only a very generalised representation of exposure to alcohol advertising on that medium (Neuendorf, 1985).

Wallack, Cassady & Grube (1990) interviewed 11- and 12-year olds about their attitudes and beliefs towards beer drinking. Further questions probed for information about their television viewing habits and exposure to beer advertisements. Photographs from beer advertisements were shown to the children who were asked whether they recognised the advertisements. Children who were skilled at recognising the beer advertisements were more likely than others to think that drinking beer is 'cool' or 'macho'. The researchers also noted relationships between reported viewing of televised sports events embedded with beer advertisements and the expectation among these young respondents that they would drink alcohol as adults.

Focus groups have also been considered as an appropriate methodology to explore complex issues such as adolescents' perceptions of alcohol use and media messages. In a study published by the Irish Department of Health and Children, Dring and Hope (2001) used focus groups to explore the impact of alcohol advertising on teenagers in Ireland. For this study, 20 focus groups were selected with ten boys' groups and ten girls' groups. Half of the groups comprised students of 12- to 14-years of age and half comprised students of 15–17 years. A total number of 180 participants took part in the research. Prior to the group discussions, data was collected about the participants' exposure to alcohol advertising, with the use of a short questionnaire. It was found that for most of the respondents television was the main source of exposure with billboards in second place. Moreover, girls reported that alcohol-branded products, such as hats, T- Shirts, key chains and computer screen savers, were a common source of exposure.

The discussions were based on the content of a sample of alcohol advertisements that students had the chance to watch and then express their views on. The study aimed at making observations regarding the potential role of advertising on alcohol consumption among the selected teenagers, based on the knowledge and beliefs, awareness and appeal of advertising, as well as perceptions of specific advertisements viewed during the session.

The findings that are of most immediate relevance from this study relate to the alcohol beliefs of the participants and the observations that the authors made regarding the anticipated influence that alcohol advertising would have on teenagers' drinking habits. Hence, it emerged that both the older and younger groups of the participants held some positive beliefs regarding alcohol consumption. It was found that 'having fun' emerged as the most common belief and key benefit of alcohol consumption, especially among older girls. Other beliefs were mostly concerned with mood such as 'feel happy', 'feel relaxed' and 'feel more confident'. Some negative beliefs were also expressed by the younger participants and included 'getting a hangover', 'feeling sick to your stomach' and 'doing something you'd regret'.

The authors concluded that there were specific views held by the younger group of participants and the 15–17 year old girls. These views made them more vulnerable and likely to be influenced by alcohol advertising. Apart from associating alcohol consumption with having fun, these groups perceived the advertising messages as an indication that alcohol can help them have fun, make friends and become popular, while they felt that those that don't drink are missing out. They also perceived alcohol advertisements as widening their knowledge of alcohol use, normalising it and portraying it as a safe activity. Alcohol consumption was also seen as a way to increase self-confidence, especially among the female participants.

Similar findings emerged from group discussions with children and teenagers in England, Scotland and Wales (Cragg, 2004) where participants identified a connection between alcohol consumption and having a good time through their recall of advertisements about alcopop drinks, in particular. This association was triggered by the commonly depicted images of attractive young people that were enjoying themselves.

Further experimental research has been deployed to explore whether exposure to media depictions of alcohol can exert a direct influence on young people's opinions about alcohol. In this instance, a small sample (n = 43) of 11- and 12-year-old boys were shown videotaped television programmes in which main characters were depicted drinking or in which such scenes were edited out. Afterwards, the boys were asked to think about good things and bad things that could happen to you if you drink alcohol and then to determine whether the good things are more important than the bad things. Watching a programme that contained characters drinking alcohol led to a more positive disposition towards alcohol consumption (Kotch, Coulter & Lipsitz, 1986).

A combined quantitative and qualitative study in New Zealand has indicated that pre-teens and young teens report relying on advertisements for information about alcoholic drinks (Wyllie, Zhang & Casswell, 1998). This apparent dependence on advertising for information about drinking, however, was more prevalent from 10- to 13-year-old boys (51%) and girls (39%) than among 14- to 17-year-old boys (27%) and girls (20%). This study has also been challenged for the effectiveness of its measures of advertising exposure and alcohol consumption (Young, 2003). Other research has shown that children obtain brand information from alcohol advertisements and that brand knowledge often outstrips general knowledge about alcohol (Austin & Nach Ferguson, 1995).

Summary and conclusion

As the research reviewed in this chapter has indicated, alcohol advertising techniques that relate into the content and themes used in popular advertising campaigns can lead to varied responses by young people to alcohol advertising. Attitudes towards advertisements and perceptions of their messages can sometimes represent important variables that can mediate post-exposure impact of advertisements. Young people may notice and recognise alcohol advertisements and the brands they promote long before they start drinking alcoholic beverages themselves, owing to the appealing images and messages employed by advertisers in their campaigns. Whether noticing alcohol advertisements *per se* is enough to render them powerful triggers to the onset of alcohol consumption remains an open question that the evidence review here has not fully answered.

One understandable concern of critics of alcohol advertising is that their young people's attention to advertisements for alcohol could create favourable dispositions towards drinking. This could in turn create a positively disposed behavioural intention to consume alcohol, ultimately leading to actual consumption. Much of the evidence that has focused on the appeal of alcohol advertisements to children and teenagers has not established whether liking of alcohol advertisements triggers early consumption. While greater advertisement and brand awareness among young people might differentiate them in terms of whether they are drinkers or not, this evidence on its own is not enough to prove any kind of causality. It is quite logical to expect young people who already drink alcohol to know more about available brands than non-drinkers. To what extent this awareness triggered onset of drinking alcohol or drives the frequency with which young drinkers consume alcohol or how much they consume remains contentious.

Evidence has emerged that exposure to alcohol advertising over time can result in the internalisation of meanings about alcohol that might at some future point influence alcohol consumption. Repeated exposure to alcohol-related messages on television, including those found in advertising, can enhance young people's interest in alcohol and cultivate a range of positive expectations associated with its consumption (Austin & Knaus, 2000). What is clear though is that alcohol advertisers have often used techniques or themes that have special appeal to young consumers, whether or not the youth marketed is deliberately targeted. Children and teenagers often enjoy the humour used in these advertisements.

In the past, the association between alcohol consumption and having a good time has also struck a chord with young people. The codes of advertising or marketing practice adopted by media regulators, trade organisations and specific companies place mandated or voluntary restrictions on the types of promotional appeals that may be used in connection with alcohol products. Many of these restrictions recognise the potency of specific attributes of appeal revealed by research among young alcohol consumers, including underage consumers. What we need to establish though is whether advertisements for alcohol in mainstream media continue to utilise attributes or themes that are likely to appeal strongly to young drinkers.

The power of appeal is not confined to mainstream media advertising, which is the area we have concentrated so far. Product display and packaging can prove equally powerful instruments in rendering certain alcohol brands particularly attractive to children and young people. Point-of-sale marketing, which focuses on making products look attractive and is extensively discussed in the next chapter, has a significant role to play in the promotion of alcohol brands It includes the use of advertising at shopping outlets, both on their exteriors and interiors, the use of price offer notices and the design and layout of product displays. There is a growing concern about the impact of these promotional techniques because they are used in environments that young people are often to be found and where there may be no restrictions of the exposure of children and teenagers to the products themselves. Being a marketing technique with proven effects on adult consumers, the influence of point-of-sale on children and young people is where we turn our attention to in the next chapter.

6
Alcohol Representation at Point of Sale

Advertising at the point of sale has been acknowledged to have potentially powerful effects on consumers. With some product categories, such as tobacco, the spread of increasingly comprehensive restrictions on advertising have meant that promotions at the point of sale are the only options left. Quite apart from their role in promoting products, points of sale represent sites of access to alcohol for young people. Ultimately, control over consumption comes down to how easily accessible alcohol is to obtain and that control must be exerted at the point of sale.

The availability of alcohol in the local environment of young people has been identified as one important factor related to underage drinking (Wagenaar & Perry, 1994; Scribner et al., 2008). One study in the US reported that the numbers of on-premise and off-premise alcohol-selling outlets within a three-mile radius of 32 college campuses were correlated with general levels of alcohol consumption and propensity to drink a lot when partying (Scribner et al., 2008). Reducing this availability and creating an environment in which alcohol is perceived by young people as difficult to obtain, especially if they are under the legal drinking age, may represent one of the most significant steps that can be taken to tackle the problems of youth alcohol consumption (Edwards et al., 1994). Yet, in the US, for example, most young people believe that alcohol can be readily obtained, whether the purchaser is underage or not (Johnston et al., 2004). This belief is not surprising in the light of other research showing that illegal alcohol sales to minors were widespread in the US (Forster et al., 1994, 1995). Furthermore such purchases were easier to achieve in retail stores than in bars or clubs (Forster et al., 1995; Wolfson et al., 1996a).

The need to examine the role played by point-of-sale factors in the consumption of alcohol by young people is underlined by findings that not only is drunkenness linked to alcohol abuse (Engineer et al., 2003), but that around half of underage drinking derives from alcohol purchases they make from retail off-licence premises (Bradshaw, 2003).

The significance of marketing in retail outlets where products are purchased by consumers has been championed by the Point-of-Purchase Advertising Institute (POPAI) in the US and in other parts of the world. Point-of-sale advertising comprises a range of different marketing and promotional devices that are used by advertisers on the insides or exteriors of retail outlets to enhance consumer awareness of their brands and to trigger purchases (Pegler, 1995). Such devices include banners, checkout displays, counter-top unit, illuminated signs, posters, shelf signs, wall units and window displays. In some larger retail outlets (e.g., supermarkets) product advertising can even be carried on shopping baskets and trolleys.

The purpose of these devices is to attract consumer attention in retail environments, then to encourage purchase through interest and desire. Thus, point-of-sale promotions and product displays represent important marketing devices. By making the product look attractive, point-of-sale factors have a part to play in promoting brand image (Pollay, 2007). Their role can be critical given that they occur at the site of purchase and if they can appeal to the consumer, their impact will be immediate. This effect can be especially acute if point-of-sale promotions cause a brand to stand out from the rest. In this way, point-of-sale effects have been cited as having an important role in the establishment of brand share (Lavack & Toth, 2006). In the context of alcohol sales, retail site promotions have been found to influence the drink choices of young people who frequent those shops (Brain & Parker, 1997). Some writers have argued that point-of-sale promotions have effects that go beyond the manipulation of market share; they can drive overall growth in the market by encouraging new consumption among those who do not yet consume particular products (Pollay, 2007).

Advertisers will often coordinate the use of point-of-sale advertising devices with advertising campaigns in other media. Manufacturers may offer incentives to retailers to display point-of-sale promotions such as providing discounts, direct monetary incentives and promises to buy back unsold merchandise. They may also pay for the cost of creating on-site advertising displays in retail outlets. The point-of-sale environment represent the one occasion when product promotions, products and consumers all come together in the same place at the same time. Point-of-sale advertising therefore enjoys closer proximity to the product being advertised than is true of any other form of advertising. The importance of point-of-sale advertising as a purchase-triggering device is underlined by commercial market research findings that significant proportions of purchases in shops are unplanned (Inman & Winer, 1998).

The concerns about point-of-sale promotions in relation to young people's consumption of products that may cause harm to them – such as tobacco and alcohol in excess – centre on the role the might play in triggering the onset of such purchases and maintaining them over time. It is argued that advertising – including that positioned in retail outlets – cause young people to start consuming these products and provides a constant reminder of their availability so discouraging cessation of consumption. The advertisers argue that the role of advertising is not to induce illegal consumption of their products in this way, but to enhance purchase of their brands among mature consumers. There is certainly evidence that point-of-sale displays can increase purchases of featured brands (Grover & Srinivasan, 1992; McKinnon, Kelly & Robison, 1981). This effect, however, can vary across product categories (Wilkinson, Mason & Paksoy, 1982a; Wilkinson, Paksoy & Mason, 1982b) and do not always occur as planned (Achabal et al., 1987; Kumar & Leone, 1988).

Point-of-sale codes of practice

If evidence that retailers readily sell alcohol to underage consumers is reliable, it means that they contravene their own sector's guide on selling alcohol. The Association of Convenience Stores, British Retail Consortium and Wine and Spirit Association produced a guide titled *Responsible Retailing of Alcohol: Guidance for the Off-Trade* (2004). This guide is also supported by the British Institute of Innkeepers, National Federation of Retail Newsagents, Northern Ireland Independent Retailers Trade association and Scottish Grocers' Federation. The guide covers areas such as underage purchases, promotions and advertising, and the location of alcohol products in the store environment.

The guide reminds retailers that it is illegal to sell alcohol to persons aged under 18. It is also against the law to sell liqueur chocolates to anyone under the age of 16. It is acknowledged that it may not always be easy to tell whether someone is aged 18. The guidance offered advises retailers to be cautious, consistent, clear, courteous, conscientious and careful. One rule is to challenge someone to prove their age if they look 'under 21', to reinforce the message through the use of signage that clearly indicates that no alcohol will be sold to people below the age of 18, and to ensure that any such challenge is polite and issued only when the vendor is confident that it will not provoke a violent backlash. Retailers are advised to accept only bone fide proof of age such as a photo driving licence, a passport, of proof of age standards scheme (PASS) cards.

The positioning of alcohol in the store may be restricted by the nature of the local licence to sell alcohol. Even where it is not, retailers must consider placement carefully both to avoid attracting unwanted attention from underage drinkers and to reduce opportunities for theft. Thus, it is advised that alcohol should not be placed in the first few metres inside the door. If extra displays outside the main display are used in the store, again there must be attention given to security issues and underage consumption. Notices indicating the legal position in respect of alcohol sales should be placed with all displays and must be clearly visible for all consumers to see.

Turning to the way alcohol is promoted at the point of sale, the guide states that while consumption of alcohol is not permitted in off-licence premises, the retailer does nonetheless have some duty to ensure that alcohol is promoted in a responsible fashion. A manufacturer or supplier may indicate how they wish their brands to be displayed and promoted. The retailer has a responsibility to check that any such requests are compliant with the *British Code on Advertising and Sales Promotion (BCASP)* and The Portman Group's *Code of Practice on the Naming, Packaging and Promotion of Alcoholic Drinks*.

Point-of-sale promotions have a number of purposes. They can be used to showcase a new brand or product; increase consumer awareness of a product; introduce a product; and to provide information to consumers about special offers. Special offers can include price reductions for limited periods, discounts associated with purchases over a certain quantity and so on. Retailers are advised to ensure that any such onsite promotions do not encourage irresponsible drinking. To this end, the guide indicates that it may be helpful to display information about sensible drinking levels for men and women and to show clearly how these levels equate to consumption of specific types of alcoholic drink. Government guidance for UK adults has indicated that most men can drink up to three or four units of alcohol a day without posing significant risk to their health, while most women can manage two to three units. One unit is equal to half a pint of ordinary strength beer, cider or lager (3.5% alcoholic by volume); a 25 ml (standard pub) measure of spirits (40% alcohol by volume); or a small glass of table wine (9% alcohol by volume).

The nature of alcohol point-of-sale displays

One major study of point-of-purchase alcohol promotion in retail outlets in the US collected observational data from 6031 retail outlets of which 3961 were alcohol retailers in 329 communities across the country. Point-of-purchase alcohol marketing features were catalogued in each store. This included measuring the presence of exterior and interior advertising for alcoholic beverages, health warnings about alcohol, alcohol-branded merchandise such as mats with alcohol company logos, the placement of alcohol products within the store and any low-height advertisement that might be in the line of sight of small children (Terry-McElrath, Harwood, Wagenaar, Slater, Chaloupka, Brewer, & Naimi, 2003).

In the same study, a majority of the alcohol retailers (94%) were found to have some form of alcohol advertising either inside or outside the store. Exterior advertisements were present in four in ten cases (39%). Interior advertising was present in over nine in ten cases (92%). Low-height advertising was found in over four in ten cases (44%). Over half the stores (51%) provided at least one alcohol-branded item.

Further research in this vein corroborated earlier evidence on the prevalence and prominence of in-store advertising and promotions of alcohol products in the US In this case a census of alcohol outlets in ten urban communities in California found that each store contained on average around 35 advertisements for alcohol, mostly for beer. Most of these stores were judged to have placed this advertising in prominent locations and around one in four had failed to display interior alcohol warning signs (Howard et al., 2001).

On the question of the effectiveness of point-of-sale promotions of alcohol sales, evidence has emerged again from the US that certain types of retail environment displays can produce mixed effects upon sales levels. While certain brands can benefit from point-of-sale displays and product organisation, others may suffer purchase downturns. In this instance, retail displays of wines were organised by region rather than by varieties. This resulted in wine selections increasing for wines from preferred regions and decreasing for those from disliked regions as compared to benchmark choice levels made when the wines were not organised by region of production (Areni, Duhan & Kiecker, 1999).

Perhaps the most significant evidence for a point-of-sale advertising effect on alcohol consumption emerged from a longitudinal study in which youngsters were surveyed three times in three years from the ages of 12–15 years (Ellickson et al., 2005). In this case, for youngsters who were non-drinkers in the first survey conducted when they were 12-years old, exposure to in-store, point-of-sale alcohol advertising was more closely linked than exposure to any other form of advertising to drinking onset by the third survey when they were aged 14–15 years. Research from Australia found a variety of different kinds of alcohol-related points-of-sale promotions including gifts with purchases, competitions associated with alcohol brands and special offers. In this case, although point-of-sale promotional impacts were not measured, the authors concluded that the prevalence and salience of such promotions underlined their centrality to the marketing strategies of alcohol companies and had the potential to influence young people's drinking (Jones & Lynch, 2007).

Importance of point-of-sale conditions

Separating out the distinctive effects of point-of-sale advertising upon alcohol consumption among young people from other factors known to be linked to drinking behaviour is a major research challenge. More generally, however, there is evidence that point-of-sale conditions can influence the extent to which young people consume alcohol. In the UK, no retailer or licensed premises may sell alcoholic beverages to individuals who are aged under 18. Yet research has indicated that underage purchases of alcohol are not uncommon and may go unchallenged by retailers. Young people themselves know they can get away with making alcohol purchases even though underage and retailers could display greater vigilance over whom they sell and to a greater diligence in challenging youngsters who try to make illegal alcohol purchases. Challenging alcohol purchase attempts by underage consumers at the point-of-sale can deter such behaviour. Unfortunately, there are many occasions when retailers fail to enforce age-related restrictions of the purchase of alcohol (Willner et al., 2000). Evidence from the US has even indicated that minors were more likely to be able to make alcohol purchases in bars with warning signs against selling to underage purchasers than in bars without such signs (Wolfson et al., 1996a).

The importance of point-of-sale controls over sales of alcohol to underage consumers is underpinned by evidence that the more opportunities that are provided to young people to obtain alcohol the more likely it is that alcohol-related social behaviour problems will occur. Greater densities of premises, including bars, restaurants and shops that sell alcohol in particular locations are associated with increased instances of drunk driving and alcohol-related violence (Jewell & Brown, 1995; Stevenson, Lind

& Weatherburn, 1999). Further evidence from the US has indicated that there are clear relationships between the numbers of alcohol-retailing outlets in specific areas and volumes of sales and occurrences alcohol-related problems (Gruenewald, Millar & Treno, 1993, Gruenewald & Remer, 2006).

Despite age restrictions on alcohol purchases, evidence from the US has indicated that more than eight in ten 17-year olds (83%) and two-thirds of 15-year olds (67%) in that country believed it was easy to get alcohol (Johnston et al., 2004). Furthermore, underage drinkers will frequently obtain alcoholic drinks from retail outlets (Jones-Webb et al., 1997). Indeed, a number of American studies confirmed that underage purchases of alcohol from retail outlets and from bars or restaurants were commonplace across the US (see Forster et al., 1995; Lewis et al., 1996; O'Leary, Gorman & Speer, 1994, Preusser & Williams, 1992; Schofield, Weeks & Sanson-Fisher, 1994). Furthermore, some retail outlets, most notably local convenience stores, were easier targets than other for underage alcohol purchases (Forster et al., 1995; Wolfson et al., 1996a, 1996b).

These American findings have been confirmed in other countries, such as Brazil, where adolescents aged 13–17 years were successful in making alcohol purchases in eight out of ten attempts in over 500 retail outlets surveyed across two urban communities. Furthermore, when outlets that had initially refused to sell alcohol to teenage customers were revisited by girls aged 17 years (who looked more adult-like than younger teenagers in this study), successful purchase were again made in over eight out of ten cases, particularly if the sellers were men aged no more than 30 (Romano et al., 2007).

Further American research has indicated that many premises licensed to sell alcohol for consumption onsite or offsite sold alcohol to young mystery shoppers who were over the legal purchase age but looked younger (Britt et al., 2006). In all, 741 alcohol-selling establishments were visited at least once by 32 male and female mystery shoppers. The overall sales rate was 26 per cent, but at those premises where repeat visits were made, this percentage grew dramatically to 74 per cent. There were variations across different communities ranging from zero per cent to 47 per cent. Restaurants sold alcohol to underage looking customers more often than did bars. Among retail outlets, those with beer-only licences were more likely to sell alcohol to underage looking customers than were those outlets with full liquor licences.

This evidence invites questions about the extent to which under-age purchase attempts are related to the presence of different types of point-of-sale promotions and product displays in stores. Does exterior alcohol advertising draw young consumers into a store to seek alcohol purchases? To what extent is in-store advertising important to triggering purchase requests? Do size, quality and position of point-of-sale advertising make a difference to young shoppers' attention to alcohol in the store environment, their awareness of the brands on sale, and purchase attempts or actual purchases? There is a need to investigate the role played by these variables in the context of young persons' consumption of alcohol.

Product packaging and labelling

One aspect of the point-of-purchase environment is the product display and the packaging of the products. In respect of many product ranges, packaging has come to be regarded as a central component of branding and brand marketing (Hill & Tilley, 2002). Packaging has been found to play a key part in brand development among alcohol products (Casswell, 2004). There are different types of alcoholic products that cater to or attract consumers from distinct markets, for example, beer, cider, lager, spirits, wines and so on. Flavoured alcoholic drinks have also emerged based on earlier generations of cocktails mixed by drinkers or their servers in licensed premises where consumers drink on site. These retailed, ready-to-drink products have proved popular with young drinkers, including underage drinkers largely because of their sweet taste. They are also packaged such that they are readily portable, and this may facilitate illicit consumption by underage drinkers (Mackintosh et al., 1997). Concerns have been raised about these so-called designer drinks or 'alcopops', not just because of their intrinsic qualities that seem to hold great appeal to young drinkers, but also because their manufacturers have, according to some critics, used marketing strategies that are designed to attract the attention of the youth market (Jackson et al., 2000).

Does product packaging actually influence young people's reactions to alcoholic drinks products? One investigation with people aged 12–30 years in Australia held blind tasting and non-blind tastings with a number of alcoholic and non-alcoholic drinks products. In the blind tasting sessions, the identity of the product was withheld from participants, while in the non-blind condition they had full sight of product packaging. Participants rated their liking of each drink and indicated whether it was designed for their age group. The products included beer, lager, spirits and alcopops, as well as coke, fizzy orange, chocolate milk and fruit tea.

In general, young participants felt that the alcohol product packaging was designed to appeal more to older people than to their own age group, while older participants generally agreed. The only exception to this pattern of responding occurred for alcopop drinks where no age effects occurred. Thus, the packaging of these drinks was perceived to be no more or less designed for adults than for teenagers. When looking at the palatability of these drinks, that is, how much participants liked their taste, the presence of product packaging resulted in non-alcoholic drinks being perceived as more suited to younger drinkers and were therefore less well-liked by older drinkers. With most alcoholic drinks, the presence of packaging led to these drinks products being seen as more suited to older drinkers and they were also enjoyed more by those drinkers. With alcopop drinks, the presence of their packaging resulted in these products being progressively less well-liked with age (Gates et al., 2007).

Another feature of product packaging in relation to alcoholic drinks is the presence of labels that provide health-related warnings to consumers about the nature of the product. These labels address issues such as the dangers of drinking and driving or drinking while pregnant. In some countries, these labels are required by law and in other countries there are voluntary agreements involving governments and the alcohol manufacturing industry about warning labels. Countries that require warning labels of alcoholic drinks products by law also frequently stipulate the form and contents of those labels. Countries such as Ecuador, Guatemala, Mexico, Taiwan and Thailand, for example, have stipulated the size of the label of product packages, the font style and colour of the text and the warning message's position on the pack.

Some warnings take the form of general health messages, particularly highlighting risks associated with excessive consumption such as, 'Avoid the risks of excessive alcohol consumption' (Brazil), 'The excessive use of alcohol in harmful to your health' (Columbia), 'Consumption of liquor is injurious to health' (India – State of Assam) and 'The abuse of alcohol beverages can damage the health' (Venezuela). Some health-related warnings are more specific and highlight particular risks associated with alcohol such as, 'Warning: Excessive consumption of alcohol may cause live cirrhosis or liver cancer and is especially detrimental to the mental and physical health of minors' (South Korea). Other warnings focus on the dangers of drinking and driving such as, 'To be safe, don't drink and drive' (Taiwan) and 'Consumption of alcohol impairs your ability to drive a car [or operate machinery, and may cause health problems]' (US). Yet other warnings advise women about risks associated with alcohol consumption when pregnant: 'Warning: Excessive consumption of alcohol may cause liver cirrhosis or liver cancer and, especially, women who drink while they are pregnant increase the risk of congenital anomalies' (South Korea) and 'According to the Surgeon general, women should not drink alcoholic beverages during pregnancy because of the risk of birth defects' (US).

Research evidence has indicated that warning labels can raise consumer awareness about the issues they address, but are less successful at influencing alcohol-related behaviour (Agostinelli & Grube, 2002; Greenfield, Graves & Kaskutas, 1999; Kaskutas & Greenfield, 1997). One major review of the evidence up to the year 2000 concluded that there was little evidence of effects of warning labels on alcohol consumption, although this finding should not be too surprising given methodological limitations that blighted much of the research and the fact that alcohol warning labels up to that time had been fairly small and inconspicuous (Babor et al., 2003).

On a more positive note, some American evidence did emerge that alcohol warning labels could trigger wider public awareness of drink-driving risks. Furthermore, over time, public support for these warnings increased and were particularly well-recalled by high-risk drinkers (Greenfield, 1997). It was in the US that the most comprehensive study of alcohol warning labels was carried out. A series of national surveys were conducted between 1990 and 1994 to assess the impact of alcohol warning labels required by Congress from 1989. Data were collected via telephone interviews and comparisons were made with control samples surveyed at the same times in Ontario, Canada. The study was not without limitations. There was some erosion of response rates in both the US and Canadian surveys. There are also doubts that no exposure to US alcohol product labels occurred among drinkers in Ontario during this period (Stockwell, 2006). Despite these problems, its findings are important.

Between 1990 and 1994, the likelihood of members of the US public having seen an alcohol-warning label increased in prevalence from 30–43 per cent. Heavy drinkers were particularly likely to display some familiarity with these warnings by 1994 (74%). The warning most likely to be recalled was one that made reference to risks of birth defects in new born children among pregnant women who drink alcohol (81%), while recall of the drink-driving warning was much less widespread (46%) (Greenfield, Graves & Kaskutas, 1999). Further data from this study showed that there was widespread public support for the use of warning labels and this support increased over time. Moreover, a growth in support for alcohol warning labels occurred not only in the

US but also among respondents surveyed in Canada. The latter finding suggested that there had been some spillover impact from the US (Room et al., 1995).

Further studies among adolescents and pregnant women yielded mixed evidence of warning label effects. Research among both groups found that awareness and recall of alcohol warning messages increased over time, but there was no conclusive evidence that warning messages had encouraged any shifts in alcohol-related behaviour (Hankin et al., 1993; McKinnon, Nohre, Pentz & Stacy, 2000).

Pricing at point of sale

One of the most significant factors to influence alcohol consumption is pricing (Laixuthai & Chaloupka, 1993). Alcohol consumption is inversely related to price. Rising prices can affect the drinking practices of heavy drinkers as well as occasional drinkers. Hence manipulating prices of alcoholic drinks could affect the extent to which young people drink and the number of young drinkers who drink heavily (Farrell, Manning & Finch, 2003). Pricing interacts with other factors. The vigilance of retailers in checking on age identification of young consumers can affect the behaviour of young drinkers. However, the consequences of these checks – particularly when associated with price offers – can be to encourage bulk buying. Young underage purchasers buy in quantity where they think they will be challenged if they make repeat visits to a store (Meichen et al., 2003).

Another aspect of point-of-sale research associated with pricing has been analysis of the location of retail outlets and in particular how closely located they are to schools and colleges. A number of studies have reported that the use of alcohol promotions, including price reductions, is associated with the type of neighbourhood. Stores in lower-income neighbourhoods with strong ethnic minority representation tend to use alcohol promotions more often than those located in more affluent neighbourhoods (Alaniz, 1998; Alaniz & Wilkes, 1995; Mack, 1997). While the most deprived areas may display the highest concentration of alcohol-selling retail outlets and promotions, the heaviest alcohol consumption has been observed to occur in the least deprived neighbourhoods (Pollack et al., 2005).

One American study found that alcohol-selling retail outlets were often situated close to college campuses and that these outlets made large quantities of alcohol available. Furthermore, they use frequent point-of-sale promotions to encourage people to buy more alcohol. The presence of such outlets and alcohol promotions were associated with higher binge drinking rates on college campuses (Kuo et al., 2003).

Point-of-sale effects and alcohol consumption

Points of sale are not simply locations at which alcoholic beverages can be purchased. They are also sites at which alcohol brands can be promoted. Many alcohol-selling retail outlets provide promotional incentives to purchase, such as free gifts with purchase, competitions and buy some get some free offers (Jones & Lynch, 2007). The next question we need to answer is whether such point-of-sale promotions trigger sales.

Point-of-sale advertising for alcohol has been found to play a part in influencing purchase behaviour and there has been some concern more especially about its role in relation to the shaping of teenage drinking (Skog, 2000; Stout, Sloan, Liang & Davies, 2000). Most research into point-of-purchase and alcohol marketing, however, has focused on the extent to which it occurs and the nature of its visibility within retail store environments. Other research has examined the impact of specific point-of-sale features such as product pricing, and a small amount of research has investigated the effects of exposure to alcohol promotions in retail environments on young people's use of alcohol.

Limited evidence has emerged from research in the US that exposure to point-of-sale promotions is related to alcohol consumption among young people. One study examined the potential effects of several different types of alcohol advertising among 12- to 14-year olds by surveying them repeatedly at ages 12, 13 and 14. It emerged here that those who were non-drinkers at age 12 were more likely to exhibit onset of drinking at age 14, if at age 13 they had been found to have reported exposure to in-store beer displays. Among youngsters who already drank at age 12, amount of exposure to magazines containing alcohol advertisements and attendance at concession stands selling alcohol at sports or music events predicted how often they drank at age 14. Those teenagers who had experienced potential print alcohol advertisements exposure or who had alcohol stands at events drank more at 14, if they had already started drinking at age 12 (Ellicksen et al., 2005).

A second survey examined adolescents' reported exposure to alcohol advertising in stores and to alcohol-branded promotional items and their association with self-reported drinking again amongst a sample of 12- to 14-year olds. The key dependent variables were whether respondents ever or never drank and whether or not they currently drank. Two-thirds of respondents reported visits to stores that sold alcohol at least once a week. Such potential exposure to in-store alcohol promotions and displays predicted a greater likelihood of ever having drunk alcohol, but did not predict whether respondents currently drank.

Ownership of an alcohol-brand-related item of merchandise predicted whether respondents had ever drunk alcohol and whether they currently did. Those who own such promotional items were three as likely as those who did not to report ever having drunk alcohol, and were one and a half times as likely to be current drinkers (Hurtz et al., 2007). The authors concluded that their study provided clear evidence that weekly exposure to alcohol in stores and ownership of alcohol-related promotional items were associated with alcohol consumption. The association between these variables was demonstrated, but whether this relationship can be interpreted as causal and whether it tells us much about the impact of specific in-store promotional features is doubtful. Self-reports of visiting stores that sell alcohol provide little evidence about whether these young consumers actually paid any attention to alcohol displays or related in-store advertising.

There are strict regulations in place to control the way alcohol is retailed that apply to bars and restaurants, off-licences and general-purpose stores that sell alcohol among a range of other products. Issues have been raised about the locations of alcohol points of sale and about the ways they display and promote alcohol at sites of purchase. There have been few studies of the impact of point-of-sale devices on alcohol consumption. Such studies can be complex to set up and are confronted with difficult challenges methodologically in separating out the possible impact of point-of-sale factors from a range of promotional and marketing devices and other environmental and social factors that can influence alcohol consumption.

Within points of sale there are many different promotional devices and techniques that can be applied. Some marketing experts have devised taxonomies of general promotional techniques in retail environments. These techniques may be used single or in complex combinations. Measuring the specific impact of individual promotional devices can provide tricky because of the variety of factors that can interplay within a retail environment to shape the behaviour of consumers.

Point-of-sale devices include product displays and packaging, loyalty reward schemes, coupons, rebates, maps and coasters, counter-top and other in-store signage and exterior signage with pricing information or brand logos, and in-store or exterior poster advertising. Brand-related merchandising is also used with brand logos printed on crockery or items of clothing that are also displayed within the store environment (see Diamond & Johnson, 1990). Such devices can encourage consumer promiscuity and undermine brand loyalty, especially where they are used for competing brands within the same point-of-sale environment. They can encourage consumers to switch around and experiment with different brands (Fearne, Donaldson & Norminton, 1999). There is evidence that for beers and wines, the more frequently consumed alcoholic drinks overall, in-store promotions can boost brand share and help new products become established (Fearne, Donaldson & Norminton, 1999).

Summary and conclusions

Point-of-sale promotions represent an important aspect of alcohol marketing. Alcohol marketers will seek to get their products placed in favourable locations in stores where they are likely to be noticed. In-store notices and price promotions are used alongside product displays to draw the customer's attention to the product on sale and to provide on-the-spot incentives to purchase.

While underage drinkers may find it difficult to make alcohol purchases on premises dedicated to the sale of alcoholic beverages, they can gain ready access to these products in general stores from which they are not banned. Major supermarket stores have become major points of purchase of alcoholic beverages for legal drinkers but also provide environments that underage individuals can legally enter and gain exposure to promotional messages for alcohol.

While legal restrictions exist in most countries concerning the age at which someone is permitted to purchase alcohol products, evidence has emerged from many different national markets that underage purchases still occur and that not all retailers are vigilant in policing these purchases. There is further evidence that although point-of-sale marketing is not without impact, it is less clear whether it represents a trigger mechanism that drives the onset of alcohol consumption among young people. Product displays can be manipulated to influence purchase behaviour, but these influences may be restricted to movements in brand shares rather than in driving total volume sales or causing non-drinkers to take up alcohol. There is evidence that generous price offers on alcoholic products, as are often used in large supermarket stores, can capture a big market share for those retailers. Furthermore, price offers might encourage some drinkers to make bigger volume purchases with the concern that greater volume of consumption could follow on.

So far in this book we have examined the nature and impact of advertising and other promotional techniques used in product marketing to promote alcoholic beverages. Other mass-mediated experiences could also represent part of a wider mix of factors to which young people are exposed that could shape their orientations towards alcohol. The consumption of alcohol can be witnessed in television and in films in a wide range of situations and circumstances. The way drinking behaviour and its consequences are displayed in entertainment and drama content in these media could provide different messages about drinking or demonstrations of behavioural scripts associated with alcohol from which young people could learn. In Chapter 7 we turn to this subject in greater detail to explore whether young people can be influenced by portrayals of alcohol consumption in mediated entertainment contexts.

7

Impact of Alcohol Representation in the Entertainment Media

Concern about the role played by the mass media in relation to alcohol consumption, drinking practices and public beliefs about alcohol and drinking has traditionally focused predominantly on alcohol advertising. The early-1980s, however, saw an interesting diversification of studies on 'media and alcohol'; it was recognised that media images of alcohol and drinking go well beyond commercial advertising. Born to some extent out of frustration with the ambiguity of much 'effects' research on alcohol advertising, the case was put (for example, DHSS, 1981; Gerbner, Morgan & Signorielli, 1982) for a broader consideration of the images of alcohol and drinking which pervade the symbolic environment created by media images generally.

In practice, however, the new concern about the wider range of non-advertising images of alcohol and drinking led mainly to a focus on popular television drama serials or soaps (Lowery, 1980; Wallack, Breed & DeFoe, 1985; Hansen, 1988) with little or no analysis of how public discourse on alcohol may be constructed significantly through factual media genres, news most particularly. Thus, with a few exceptions (see our review and discussion in Chapter 8 of research on the coverage of alcohol in news media), there have been surprisingly few attempts at mobilising the extensive communications research literature on the construction of social problems or on the political agenda-setting role of the mass media (McCombs, 2004) towards an understanding of how alcohol policies and problems are covered and defined by the news media.

In some respects the paths pursued in research on the media and alcohol reflect a traditional division within communication research, namely, between what prominent communications scholar John Corner has labelled the 'public knowledge project' and the 'popular culture project' (Corner, 1991).

[The public knowledge project] is concerned primarily with the media as an agency of public knowledge and 'definitional' power, with a focus on news and current affairs output and a direct connection with the politics of information and the viewer as citizen (...). [The popular culture project] is concerned primarily with the implications for social consciousness of the media as a source of entertainment.

(Corner, 1991: 268)

Informed in considerable measure by the disciplines of social psychology and psychology, and taking its point of departure principally in the traditions of behaviourism, social learning theory and the 'effects' tradition in mass communications research, much of the research on the mass media and alcohol over the last three to four decades has thus been relatively narrowly focused on the question of how individual drinking practices and beliefs about alcohol are 'influenced' by advertising and media entertainment images of alcohol and drinking. By contrast, relatively little research has addressed wider social and political questions about how the 'public agenda' on alcohol is formed, or about how the public and political 'climate of opinion' about how alcohol and drinking in society should be regulated and controlled.

The concern with 'media entertainment images' has focused overwhelmingly on television entertainment programming – popular television serials or 'soaps' in particular – although it has also encompassed considerable but less extensive research on other forms and media such as film (Cook & Lewington, 1979; Denzin, 1991; Herd & Room, 1982; Herd, 1986; Room, 1987; Kulick & Rosenberg, 2001), popular music lyrics (Beckley & Chalfant, 1979; Cruz, 1988; Herd, 2005), popular fiction (Pfautz, 1962; Cellucci & Larsen, 1995; Greenman, 2000) and music videos (Austin, Pinkleton & Fujioka, 2000; DuRant et al., 1997; Robinson et al., 1998; Van den Bulck & Beullens, 2005; Beullens & Van den Bulck, 2008).

Alcohol representations in film and television

While alcohol advertising and promotion may provide the most obtrusive and obvious images and messages about alcohol in the public sphere, there are many other images of drinking present in the mass media that also provide messages to non-drinkers and drinkers alike about alcohol consumption. Regular images on alcohol consumption have been identified in films and television programmes.

Research from the US has recorded that most Hollywood films made for the cinema feature alcohol consumption (Everett, Schnuth & Tribble, 1998). Drinking tends to be shown relatively free of negative consequences for drinkers or for others associated with them. Drinkers are also shown as more socially and sexually successful than non-drinkers, though also as more aggressive at times. Alcohol consumption in films is essentially depicted as normal behaviour (Cape, 2003; McIntosh et al., 1998).

A body of work has emerged since the 1970s that has analysed the representation of alcohol in television programmes. This research, emanating to a significant extent from North America and the UK, has indicated that portrayals of alcohol consumption occur with regularity on peak-time television when young people can be expected to be numerically present in the audience (Breed & DeFoe, 1981; Cafiso et al., 1982). Depictions of alcohol consumption tended to be presented in a positive light. Alcoholic intoxication was seen as fun and often displayed in a humorous context. Sometimes, drinking alcohol was also displayed as a coping mechanism that could be used by someone when under pressure or stressed (Hanneman & McEwan, 1976; Atkin & Block, 1981; Breed, DeFoe & Wallack, 1984). Alcohol consumption on television has tended to be shown as an activity that is free of adverse consequences (Grube, 1993; Mathios et al., 1998).

In a major study of alcohol drinking behaviour on American television, alcohol drinkers were found to be predominantly male. Drinking was also associated mostly with lead characters and, perhaps surprisingly, more with good guys than bad guys (Breed, DeFoe & Wallack, 1984; Wallack, Breed & DeFoe, 1985). The same research revealed that a significant minority of drinking scenes (40%) showed potentially problematic alcohol consumption and nearly one in five scenes (18%) depicted chronic drinkers. Alcohol consumption was recorded in a clear majority (60%) of prime-time television programmes and regular viewers could be expected to witness more than 20 alcohol-related acts per evening (Wallack, Breed & Cruz, 1987).

Research in the UK found that around two-thirds of peak-time programmes on the four TV channels broadcast at that time contained references to alcohol (Hansen, 1986). An average of three drinking scenes per hour was recorded in fictional programmes with the average in soap operas being higher at five per hour. There was generally more alcohol consumption depicted in British-made soap operas than in American or Australian productions. One conclusion reached from this study was that television treats alcohol consumption as normative behaviour and tends to place it in a positive light. Problematic drinking or the association of alcohol consumption with accidents, illness or anti-social behaviour was shown rarely. Two subsequent UK studies followed a similar methodology to that of Hansen and confirmed that verbal or visual alcohol references feature in most peak-time television programmes (Pendleton, Smith & Roberts, 1991; Smith, Roberts & Pendleton, 1988).

A later study of soap operas on British television examined the most watched serialised dramas, including four UK-made and two Australian-made dramas. Five episodes of each serial were recorded over a two-month period in 1994–5. All programmes were coded for depictions of alcohol consumption. A clear majority of the 30 soap episodes (86%) contained any visual or verbal references to alcohol. Such references occurred with regularity occurring once in every 3.5 minutes of programming. Across these programmes, a total of 96 drinking scenes were recorded, giving an average rate of 2.9 scenes per hour. These findings indicated that the amount of alcohol consumption in this type of programming on British television had increased compared with earlier studies conducted in the 1980s (Furnham et al., 1997).

Males outnumbered females among those characters who drank by a ratio of 1.7 to 1. Most drinkers were young to middle-aged adults estimated to be in the 25- to 44-years age range. There were a few drinkers in those soaps who were judged to be aged over 65, but there was no obvious underage drinking depicted (Furnham et al., 1997).

Further increases in the rate of alcohol-related references in British soap operas were recorded by Hansen (2003). This study examined alcohol-related references across news, drama and soaps on peak-time broadcasts (5.30–10.30pm) on one week of terrestrial television output. References to alcoholic drinks and consumption occurred in the great majority (85%) of programmes analysed. Visual scenes of alcohol consumption were far more prevalent in soap operas (10.6 per hour) than in either drama episodes (4.3) or news (1.9). Comparisons of the soap opera data of Hansen (1986) and Furnham et al. (1997) showed that the rate of visual references had increased to 10.6 per hour in 2003 compared with 9.3 per hour in 1994–5 and 5.8 per hour in 1984. Alcohol drinking scenes rose from 3.9 per hour in 1984 to 6.4 in 1994–5 to 7.0 in 2003.

A study by Pitt, Forrest, Hughes and Bellis (2003) explored the potential for exposure to images or messages about alcohol in respect of radio and television. This investigation examined advertising and non-advertising content in both media. Smoking and illicit drug themes were examined alongside that of alcohol. Audience data for television and radio taken from BARB (Broadcasters' Audience Research Board) and RAJAR (Radio Joint Advertising Research) were utilised to identify programmes most watched or listened to by children and teenagers (ages 10–15 and 16–19). The top 15 television programmes for each age group were analysed and covered transmissions on BBC1, BBC2, ITV1 and Channel 4. On radio, content transmitted between 7am and 9am and 3.30pm to 9pm on weekdays and between 9am and 12pm and 3pm to 9pm on weekends was analysed.

Alcohol references were found to be present in programmes broadcast on television before the 9pm watershed that represents the point at which broadcasters may begin to transmit content that may not be suitable for children (aged under-16 years). Such references became more prevalent with each hour approaching 9pm. Positive references to alcohol use were also present before the watershed, with some occurring even before 6pm. In this context a positive reference meant showing alcohol consumption in a favourable light as being good fun or making life better in some way. Negative references to alcohol use were almost equal to positive reference before 6pm but were significantly outnumbered by positive references between 6pm and 9pm.

Recent studies in the UK (Coyne & Ahmed, 2009), in New Zealand (McGee, Ketchel & Reeder, 2007) and in the US (Russell & Russell, 2009) have added further confirmation to the general pattern of findings regarding television entertainment portrayal of alcohol and drinking. Coyne & Ahmed (2009) examined the frequency and portrayal of alcohol use and smoking in soap operas on British terrestrial television. They found that more than 90 per cent of soap opera episodes depicted alcohol-related acts, with an average of 7.65 acts per episode. Assuming that most soap opera episodes are approximately 30 minutes in duration, this figure would indicate a potential further increase in the steady increase identified by Hansen (2003) in the rate of alcohol acts per hour of soap opera programming since the 1980s. Coyne & Ahmed (2009: 345) also found interesting gender-differences in the portrayal of alcohol consumption. Thus female 'characters were drinking alcohol more often than expected and were also more likely to drink at home as a short-term means of coping'. By contrast, 'male characters were more often depicted as social drinkers, with more drinking inside pubs than expected'.

In a study of alcohol imagery in 98 hours of prime-time television programmes and advertising on New Zealand television during June/July 2004, McGee, Ketchel & Reeder. (2007) found an average of one alcohol-related scene every nine minutes. Scenes that depicted uncritical imagery outnumbered scenes showing possible adverse health consequences of drinking by 12 to 1, and a large amount of alcohol imagery was found to be incidental to storylines in programming.

Russell and Russell (2009) reported a comprehensive content analysis of alcohol messages in US prime-time television series. Their study monitored 144 unique episodes, 8 for each of 18 prime-time programmes which included five situation comedies, one cartoon and 12 drama series broadcast over a ten-week period from September to December 2004. Like the British studies discussed above, they found a significant increase in the frequency of alcohol portrayal – alcohol was present in every programme analysed – compared with earlier comparable research by Christensen, Henriksen & Roberts (2000) who found that just over three quarters of prime-time television programmes during the 1998–9 season contained references to alcohol. The Russell and Russell study is particularly noteworthy for its refinement of the distinction between positive and negative portrayals or messages about alcohol. In contrast to many previous studies, they show negative messages about alcohol to be numerically more prominent than positive message. They identify, however, a significant qualitative difference in the way that negative and positive images of alcohol are depicted:

> An overall more negative message about alcohol is related to verbal discussions that affect the plot of the episodes, whereas an overall more positive message is related to visual depictions of the background type. In particular, whenever alcohol is central to the plot of an episode, it tends to be associated with negative elements such as a crime, addiction, or lowered job performance. Overall, messages associating alcohol with positive outcomes, such as having fun or partying hard, are primarily communicated visually in the background.
>
> (Russell & Russell, 2009: 123)

The significance of this finding – that negative messages tend to be foregrounded and central to the narrative, while positive messages are invariably communicated as part of the 'normal' background – lies in the potentially very different interpretation or understanding that these images might give rise to in the viewing audiences. We would argue that this finding adds further ammunition to the argument (for example, Wallack, Breed & Cruz, 1987; Hansen, 1995) that television tends to naturalise alcohol consumption as the unproblematic and positive

norm, while treating problem-drinking, alcoholism and negative outcomes associated with alcohol consumption as 'exceptional'.

Further research conducted with American programming found that
the popular youth-oriented drama series, *The OC*, placed a greater emphasis on non-alcoholic than alcoholic beverages, despite a reputation it
had acquired of focusing on youth and booze themes. When alcohol
portrayals were featured, they tended most often to be situated within
narrative themes of drinking under peer pressure or to escape problems.
Some drinking took place in the context of celebration. There were only
rare depictions of excessively problematic drinking (Van Den Bulck,
Simons, & van Gorp, 2008).

Radio references to alcohol and drinking

Research on the broadcast media has generally overwhelmingly focused
on television rather than radio. Studies of broadcast media portrayals of
alcohol and drinking are no exception to this pattern. Thus, surprisingly
little evidence is available to show either the extent of alcohol referencing across different types of radio programming content or indeed the
nature, function or social implications of such referencing. The relative
absence of research on radio and alcohol undoubtedly can be explained
with reference to the same reasons as for radio research generally, such
as the difficulties of reliably constructing and capturing a representative
sample of the more differentiated and diverse output of radio compared
with television, and the difficulty of reliably coding and analysing
radio output compared with, for example, print media output. But the
relative absence of research on radio and alcohol is perhaps particularly
surprising in light of the increasing concern in recent years about young
drinkers, binge drinking and national cultures of excessive alcohol consumption, particularly when combined with available data showing the
continued popularity – despite the advent of new media and new forms
of media consumption – of radio, not least among younger age groups,
who feature prominently in concerns about binge drinking and excessive alcohol consumption.

A small number of studies in the US have focused radio, although
mainly in the context of alcohol advertising. Thus, a comprehensive
study by the Center on Alcohol Marketing and Youth (CAMY, 2007),
based at Georgetown University in Washington, studied 337,602 alcohol product advertisements placed on stations in 28 of the largest radio
markets in the US in 2006. The study showed that more than a third
of advertising placements for alcohol products were on programming

with an audience of predominantly young people aged 12–20, and that advertisements on programming that youth were more likely to hear than adults accounted for more than half (58%) of youth exposure to alcohol advertising on the radio. The study also showed that 26 of 143 brands placed more than half of their advertisements on programming that youth were more likely to hear than adults.

The British study by Pitt et al. (2003) referred to in the previous section analysed radio programmes most listened to by children and teenagers. They found that between 25 and 50 per cent of half-hour segments analysed each day contained references to alcohol. Within programmes, positive references to alcohol outnumbered negative references, though the latter were still present, confirming what has generally been found with regard to television entertainment programmes, namely, that of a mixed, but predominantly positive, messages environment.

A recent study (Daykin et al., 2009) of weekend programming on six popular radio stations in England during a 9-week period from mid-December 2007 found frequent references to alcohol and drinking, although also some variation by radio station (fewer references on BBC stations than on commercial radio stations) and by type of programme. The study showed that comments encouraging alcohol are most often made in discussions about weekend partying and socialising. The authors go on to conclude that in popular programmes with a high element of audience-interactivity, for example, through phone-ins, emails or similar, 'alcohol is positioned as a natural and necessary marker of the weekend'.

Although other themes and messages exist, the notion that drinking is necessary to have a good time is seldom directly challenged. (Daykin et al., 2009: 110). While acknowledging that references to excessive drinking are not always easily separated from comments about drinking in general, the study shows how a discourse (with a rich vocabulary of drunkenness or excessive drinking) celebrating excessive drinking is prominent in much radio banter. Having a hangover was thus 'often presented as a marker of having had a good night out, with some presenters modelling the idea of having a hangover in the studio'. (p. 108). These researchers also noted that talk 'about excessive drinking often seemed to develop in instances where boundaries, such as the boundary between the broadcasting studio and social spaces occupied by young people, were blurred. Hence, "parties" involving alcohol frequently took place in the studio around the Christmas period'. (p. 109). As the authors point out, the message that this practice conveys is at odds with mainstream social and health messages which discourage drinking at work.

In summary, while the evidence regarding alcohol and drinking-related messages on radio is extremely limited when compared with television, it is clear from what little evidence there is from studies in the US and in the UK that radio may be a potentially important and significant source of perceptions and beliefs about alcohol and its use and abuse in society. Not only do these studies show that alcohol references are prominent in programmes aimed at and attracting a predominantly younger audience, but they also indicate how popular radio chat (including with audience members who phone in and with celebrities of various sorts) often draws on – and in turn perpetuates and reinforces – deep-seated cultural assumptions that stress drunkenness and excessive drinking as fun and amiable/sociable behaviour.

Media exposure and alcohol consumption

As numerous studies conducted since the late-1970s/early-1980s have demonstrated, alcohol and alcohol consumption are widely represented in the media in non-advertising content. The news media cover stories about alcohol misuse and abuse and the social and health problems that can occur as a result of excessive consumption. Alcohol images feature prominently in television programmes and films, and, as demonstrated more recently, in music videos (see Anderson, 2007). These depictions may be capable of cultivating a climate of normality around alcohol consumption and can present illustrative portrayals of the positive and negative aspects of drinking or examples or good and poor conduct surrounding alcohol consumption. There is empirical evidence that supports this last observation. A positive disposition towards drinking has been linked not only to parental and peer-group attitudes, beliefs and behaviour but also to exposure to representations of alcohol consumption in the mass media (Andsager, Austin, & Pinkleton, 2002; Austin & Meili, 1994; Austin, Pinkleton & Fujioka, 2000; Jackson et al., 2000).

There is research that has shown that heavier watching of television and music videos is associated with teenage drinking. The explanation for this relationship might be that both television and music videos contain positive portrayals of alcohol use. The extent to which teenagers used video-recorders to playback videos or play video games, however, was unrelated to their alcohol consumption patterns (Robinson, Chen, & Killen, 1998). This research was longitudinal in nature and surveyed teenagers twice over an interval of 18 months. There were no relationships between any media use and alcohol consumption at the start of the study. Teenagers who already drank during the first survey wave did not differ from those who were non-drinkers in their media behaviours. By the second wave, however, teenagers who had started to drink also watched more television and music videos than did teenagers who had remained non-drinkers.

In a Norwegian study, researchers explored links between 13- to 14-year-olds' alcohol use or intention to drink and their television viewing habits (Thomsen & Rekve, 2006). Norway bans advertising of alcoholic beverages of more than 2.5% alcohol by volume on radio, television, in newspapers and magazines and on billboards. As a result there are limited opportunities for Norwegian youth to experience alcohol advertising. Nonetheless, televised depictions of alcohol can and do occur in programmes. A number of major Norwegian television channels show comedy, drama and factual series imported from the US. Such programmes were presumed by the researchers to contain portrayals of alcohol consumption on the basis of evidence obtained by earlier American content analysis studies (Christensen, Henriksen & Roberts, 2000; Hundley, 1995; Mathios et al., 1998; Wallack et al., 1990).

Among a sample of over 600 respondents, most (63%) had never consumed any alcohol. Evidence emerged that self-reported exposure to American television programmes (measured in terms of endorsed viewing of 14 named US TV series) was related to the belief that drinking is a normal teenage behaviour and to express intention to drink alcohol in the future, but only among adolescents who reported having no friend who drink. Among those who said they had friends who consumed alcohol, reported television viewing was unrelated to beliefs or intentions concerning alcohol. These findings indicate that although television viewing might be associated with teenage intentions to drink alcoholic beverages, this relationship is mediated by peer-group influences.

The influences of media upon alcohol orientations among young people may be subtle and occur at the level of how individuals think about drinking as a phenomenon. Evidence of this type of effect has emerged from a study in which college students were asked to write a story about an individual's consumption of alcohol under stressful circumstances. Instructions to the participants invited some to write the story as if it was about a real-world experience, while others were asked to write it as a TV drama narrative. There were no significant differences in the nature or quality of the storytelling as a function of whether it related a real-world event or a televised event. However, participants who reportedly watched more television in their own lives tended to construct stories in which more alcohol use took place. Other personal experiences with alcohol also appeared to colour the storytellers' tales. Participants who had reportedly passed out from drinking at some point in their own lives were less likely to adopt a negative tone towards alcohol use in their stories (Kean & Albada, 2003).

Further evidence has emerged that the influence of television on teenagers' interest in or consumption of alcoholic beverages may act in quite subtle and often indirect ways. Austin, Pinkleton and Fukioka (2000) surveyed 14- to 17-year olds in California schools about their television viewing habits, perceptions of the realism of television, identification with television portrayals, consumption of alcohol, expectancies about alcohol use, desire for alcohol-related merchandise, and interactions with parents about television. The key dependent variables were reported consumption of alcohol and interest in alcohol-linked merchandise. The latter measure was regarded as particularly important among youngsters who had not yet started to drink alcohol. It revealed an awareness of brands and a preference for items associated with alcohol brand logos.

Boys were more likely to drink than girls and non-white students were slightly more likely to drink than were white students. The main predictors of alcohol consumption, however, were positive expectancies about the use of alcohol and preferences for items associated with alcohol brands. Viewing of late-night talk shows was the only television viewing variables that exhibited a significant link to drinking. Desire for alcohol-themed products was stronger among teenagers who had more positive expectancies about the effects of using alcohol, with viewing of sports programmes and late-night talk shows exhibiting weak relationships to this dependent variable. The desire to emulate media portrayals was not directly linked to use of alcohol, but it did predict to a small, but significant, extent positive expectancies about alcohol use. The latter variable was a key predictor of alcohol use and interest in alcohol-related merchandise among youngsters who have yet to start drinking.

It is not only television that can convey messages about drinking to young people; evidence has also emerged from studies of films and magazines. Films made for cinema have also been found to contain frequent depictions of drinking that usually place alcohol consumption in a positive light. One study reported that out of a sample of 501 contemporary motion pictures, over 90 per cent depicted drinking behaviour. Drinking scenes occupied anything from just under a minute to five minutes of footage time (Sargent et al., 2006). In an accompanying survey of children aged 10–14 years sampled from schools across Vermont and New Hampshire the same researchers examined relationships between claimed watching of 50 different movies and alcohol consumption. Two years after the initial survey they revisited those children who had initially claimed to be non-drinkers. They found that those youngsters with greater movie exposure during that two-year period were also more likely to report that they had started to drink alcohol.

Studies that have adopted more interventionist experimental designs have demonstrated that exposure to film that contain scenes depicting negative consequences of drinking are less likely to encourage young people to want to drink than alternative versions that have these scenes edited out (Bahk, 2001). Even exposure to film clips is sufficient to generate this type of response (Kulick & Rosenberg, 2001). What these findings indicate is that it is not just the depiction of alcohol consumption per se that has an effect upon young viewers but also the depicted consequences of drinking.

Experimental studies on the effects of alcohol imagery on subsequent drinking behaviour have generally been marred by 'limited effects' or contradictory findings as well as the difficulties – inherent to experimental designs – of extrapolating findings from the laboratory environment to people's everyday social context. Early experiments (Rychtarik et al., 1983; Kotch, Coulter & Lipsitz, 1986; Sobell et al., 1986) designed to test the influence of television entertainment programme images of alcohol thus found few or no significant impact on the alcohol-related behaviour of experimental subjects. Sobell et al. (1986: 339) thus conclude,

> The major finding of the present study is that, under the conditions tested in this experiment, neither drinking scenes in television programs nor beer commercials on television precipitated increased drinking by viewers. Male college students who were exposed to a videotaped television program with alcohol scenes and beer commercials consumed approximately the same amount of beer in a subsequent taste test (...) as did subjects who were exposed to videotapes featuring neither alcohol scenes nor beer advertisements.

As Hansen (1988) has noted, despite elaborate experimental designs, meticulous controls and in some cases sophisticated statistical analyses, these studies all failed to demonstrate any of the effects which are usually invoked with reference to modelling theory and with reference to experimental research on television and violence. More interesting than the research results themselves are perhaps the various explanations which the three studies offer in an attempt to account for the seeming lack of influence. Notwithstanding reservations about the size of samples, their possibly self-selective nature, and failure to manipulate the stimulus adequately (Kotch, Coulter & Lipsitz; Rychtarik et al.), the studies offer self-criticism of a more fundamental kind when suggesting that the experimental situation itself may account for the un-expected results.

Sobell et al. point out that their findings must be tempered by a number of caveats, including the fact that 'subjects viewed the program in isolation, rather than in a social context, and in a setting which, although constructed to appear like a home environment may nevertheless have been perceived as a laboratory setting, especially since the study was conducted at the Addiction Research Foundation' (Sobell et al., 1986: 339). They also point out that the stimulus programme used was a programme normally broadcast during prime time (evening), yet the experiment took place during daytime hours. Furthermore, they point out that the experiment allowed only for immediate effects, and did not leave room for the possibility of delayed reactions.

Despite the many caveats pertaining to experimental research, this type of research continues to play a prominent role in efforts to identify the impact of television alcohol images on viewers' perceptions and behaviour. The authors of a recent major experimental study thus feel sufficiently confident about their findings to categorically proclaim in the title of their published research paper that 'Alcohol Portrayal on Television Affects Actual Drinking Behaviour' (Engels et al., 2009).

Rutger Engels and his colleagues (2009), using a naturalistic experimental setting (a bar lab) and a carefully controlled experimental design, tested whether the portrayal of alcohol images in movies and commercials on television promoted actual drinking among experimental subjects, who were young males, aged between 18 and 29 years, in the Dutch university town of Nijmegen. Popular films with and without alcohol portrayal and with/without alcohol advertising were used as stimulus material in the experimental design and alcohol consumption during the experimental session and were carefully monitored.

The results, note the authors, were 'straightforward and substantial: those in the condition with alcohol portrayal in movie and commercials drank on average 1.5 glasses more than those in the condition with no alcohol portrayal, within a period of 1 h' (p. 4). This is unquestionably a carefully designed and tightly controlled study, and the evidence offered by the study is, as the authors put it 'straightforward and substantial', clearly demonstrating a direct causal relationship between exposure to alcohol images and amount of alcohol consumption during the experimental session.

Despite the so-called naturalistic setting of the experiment, the usual criticisms of experimental designs still however remain as relevant and applicable here as many of those mentioned above in relation to experimental studies of the 1980s. Thus, the study is operating with cause-effect measures that can only be described as crude, namely, the relationship between alcohol images/no alcohol images and amount of alcohol consumption during the short period of the experiment. There is thus no detailed analysis of the type (for example, positive/negative) of alcohol images in either the film or advertising content used as stimulus, nor is there any analysis of the types of alcoholic drinks shown and/or consumed during the experiment. But mainly the problem with this kind of evidence remains that, while providing proof of causal effects in the artificially created context of the laboratory experiment, it tells us little or nothing about the interaction of alcohol images and drinking in people's everyday lives and social context.

Cross-sectional, but more particularly longitudinal, surveys by contrast come potentially much closer to showing the relationship between exposure to television and film images of alcohol and viewers' beliefs, perceptions and behaviour with regard to alcohol and drinking. As indicated previously in this section, studies both in the Netherlands (Van den Bulck and Beullens, 2005) and in the US (Sargent et al., 2006) have found a relationship between amount of exposure to alcohol images in television programmes and music videos and subsequent alcohol consumption. In a large study of 5581 German adolescents in 27 schools, Hanewinkel, Tanski and Sargent (2007) found that exposure to movie alcohol images was directly associated with alcohol use (without parental knowledge) and binge drinking. Furthermore, the relationship between exposure and alcohol consumption held up even after controlling for multiple covariates including socio-demographics, personality characteristics and social influences.

In a more recent study, Hanewinkel & Sargent (2009) report on a longitudinal follow-up to the earlier survey (Hanewinkel, Tanski and Sargent, 2007). Their study provides compelling evidence that exposure to movie alcohol depictions predicts problematic alcohol use during adolescence:

This study documents levels of exposure to actors using alcohol in movies that run in the hours, with exposed never-drinker adolescents having a substantially higher risk of trying drinking and binge drinking in the future. The findings suggest that the exposure not only precedes the onset of the behavior but is independent of a number of social influence and personality confounders. Notably,

the finding of a movie effect in Germany occurs in the cultural context of lenience toward teenager alcohol consumption, where teenagers are exposed to multiple other individual and societal prompts
to drink: high per capita consumption of alcohol, little restriction on
alcohol advertising, low alcohol pricing, and legal consumption of
alcohol at age 16.

(pp. 992–3)

In contrast to the findings of some previous studies (Van den Bulck and
Beullens, 2005; Robinson, Chen & Killen, 1998), Hanewinkel & Sargent
(2009) found no relation between hours of television viewing and teenage drinking, which is interestingly similar to the findings of the much
earlier 'cultivation analysis' studies of the early 1980s (for example,
Gerbner, Morgan & Signorielli, 1982).

They go on to question the television exposure finding of two previous studies which had found a relationship between amount of viewing
and teenager drinking, noting that these studies did not assess movie
exposure, nor did they control for parent or peer drinking, personality
(sensation seeking), or parenting style. They make the further interesting and relevant observation that 'having a television in the bedroom' – shown to be an independent predictor of smoking in a study by
Jackson et al. (2007) – rather than signifying increased overall viewing,
may 'be associated with less parental monitoring of media use and more
frequent viewing of adult media venues, which tend to contain more
smoking and drinking.' (Hanewinkel & Sargent, 2009: 994).

The Hanewinkel & Sargent (2009) study is noteworthy for its rigorous
longitudinal design, its large sample and its extensive covariate control
for other social influences, personality and parenting style. But it is
also particularly interesting because it – like studies in the Netherlands
(Engels et al., 2009; Van den Bulck and Beullens, 2005) and in Norway
(Thomsen & Rekve, 2006) – shows that the type of media fare and associated alcohol images are broadly similar, that is, American/US-origi-
nated, across these different cultures (Dutch, German, Norwegian), and
that despite whichever other cultural differences may apply, exposure to
this type of alcohol imagery seems to independently predict adolescent
drinking beliefs and practices.

Conclusion

Numerous studies conducted since the late 1970s have demonstrated
that alcohol and drinking images are prevalent throughout media

content, and particularly in popular media entertainment content such as mass movies and television soap opera and drama series. There is also a growing body of evidence, from both the UK and the US that the frequency of alcohol images in popular television drama serials/series has increased steadily over the last quarter of a century since research first started monitoring in the early 1980s.

These studies have provided a comprehensive picture of the extent, scheduling, and kind of alcohol images in film and television programmes generally, and in popular television series and serials in particular. The findings of these studies show remarkably similar trends in film and television portrayal of alcohol across the different nations and cultures in which studies have been conducted. This is perhaps unsurprising in light of the well-documented Anglo-American and globalised nature of film and television production, characteristic of the last half century or so.

The similarities in findings are, however, also a product to some extent of the similarities of theoretical approaches and methods of analysis employed by these studies. Most studies have taken their point of departure in learning theory and theories of imitative behaviour, and focused on the quantitative measurement (by way of content analysis) of frequency of alcohol scenes, alcohol references/images, types of character, drinking situations, types of drink shown, positive and negative images and consequences associated with the consumption of alcohol. A smaller number of studies have attempted to go beyond the enumeration of key occurrences to a more interpretive analysis of the role of alcohol within the narrative and formal structures of programmes.

The main findings of these studies show, among other things, that alcohol is the most prominent beverage on television, that drinking is on the whole associated with pleasant social interaction, that there is comparatively little portrayal of the negative consequences associated with drinking, and that drinking is frequently portrayed in the context of attractive situations and milieu and as a necessary component of 'having a good time'.

While numerous studies have noted that film and television programmes portray both positive and negative images of alcohol and drinking, a recent study by Russell and Russell (2009) is particularly noteworthy for showing that positive and negative portrayals are qualitatively different. Thus negative messages tend to be foregrounded and central to the narrative, while positive messages are invariably communicated as part of the 'normal' background. We contend that this finding adds further ammunition to the argument (e.g., Wallack, Breed & Cruz, 1987;

Hansen, 1995) that television tends to naturalise alcohol consumption as the unproblematic and positive norm, while treating problem-drinking, alcoholism and negative outcomes associated with alcohol consumption as 'exceptional'.

Studies of the impact of film and television images of alcohol have broadly used either laboratory experimental designs or survey methodology. Much of the experimental research has been marred by the ethical difficulties associated with testing the impact of drinking images on younger audiences, as well as by the inevitably artificial and abstracted nature of the laboratory experimental setting and situation. The evidence of effects of media images has been mixed, although a recent study by Engels et al. (2009) provides compelling evidence that exposure to alcohol images causes increased levels of alcohol consumption in a controlled experimental setting. Given the well-known difficulties, if not impossibility, of extrapolating from laboratory experimental settings to the everyday life context where people normally encounter alcohol images and – perhaps – engage in alcohol consumption, it is perhaps questionable how far experimental research can contribute to a general understanding of the role played by media portrayal with regard to public alcohol-related understanding and practice.

By contrast, both cross-sectional and more particularly longitudinal survey studies of exposure to film/television portrayal of alcohol and involvement in alcohol consumption and excessive drinking have provided significant evidence of a more naturalistic, or true to everyday life, kind. These studies have generally confirmed the similarity across a number of national contexts of the type of film/media content – and associated alcohol images – that viewers are exposed to, and they have provided evidence that exposure to alcohol imagery predicts alcohol consumption and involvement in problematic drinking in adolescence.

Although studies vary considerably in terms of the range of factors controlled for in statistical designs aimed at explaining the co-variance of exposure to alcohol images and subsequent drinking behaviour, these studies have provided compelling evidence that prevalent media portrayal of alcohol and drinking does indeed influence viewers' beliefs and practices with regard to alcohol. Nevertheless, the difficulties, well-known from the past 60–80 years of media and communications research and not least from the vast body of research into the relationship between media images and violence in society, of isolating media influence from all the other factors and influences which play into individuals' alcohol and drinking-related beliefs and practices remain. This difficulty, of separating out media influence from other influences, was recently eloquently characterised by Steven Thomsen (2007: 1):

> [The] ubiquitous nature of mass media in our lives makes it difficult to partial out or detect some of its subtle effects. In many ways, the media is like [a] 'cultural river' whose current moves us down stream. We are often not conscious of the degree, or speed, to which it moves us. As previously suggested, children and teenagers who watch a lot of movies are also likely to watch a lot of television and are equally likely to use other forms of media that also might include incidental portrayals of alcohol use (e.g. magazines, Internet)[.] Because of the cumulative effect of this multitude of consonant messages permeating our lives and simultaneously shaping our culture, it would be difficult to identify how a single message, or messages from a single medium or genre, independently and uniquely cultivate normative beliefs, outcome expectancies, and behavioural intentions – especially in small, subtle increments. This is both an epistemological and methodological issue. As researchers we constantly try to overcome this, but, in the end, we are always forced to acknowledge this key limitation of our work. What is agreed upon by most researchers interested in potential media effects, however, is that the accumulation of all these messages creates a symbolic environment that can become very real – and believable – to us.

8
Impact of Alcohol Representation in the News

Much research on 'media and alcohol' has, as we have shown in the preceding chapters, focused on advertising and on the depiction of alcohol and drinking practices in popular entertainment media. By contrast, surprisingly little research has examined how important messages about alcohol and 'acceptable' drinking practices are communicated through day-to-day news coverage of a wide range of social, political, economic, legislative and health issues. The way that public and political 'climates of opinion' regarding alcohol-related risks, benefits and problems are shaped through news and debate in the public sphere of the mass media is clearly important to understanding how public and political support is garnered and the way paved, for example, for increasing regulation of the promotion, sale and availability of alcohol.

From the press coverage over recent years, an impression has, for example, been created that drinking, and binge drinking in particular, is a major social problem that permeates the country geographically at all levels. The sheer rise to prominence of news stories about binge drinking and associated problems and issues over the last decade is noteworthy. Thus the number of prominent news stories about binge drinking in British national newspapers rose from 118 in 2000/2001 to 616 in 2004/2005 and further still to 710 in 2008/2009 (to 21–September 09).[1] The intense news media attention to alcohol and drinking should of course not be seen as an objective indicator, let alone mirror, of the level of alcohol-consumption or of binge drinking incidents in society, but rather as indicative of public interest and political and legislative activity with regard to alcohol and drinking.

Plant and Plant (2006), in a chapter tellingly titled 'Bar wars: Media frenzy and licensing chaos', thus offer the following characterisation of the intense public debate surrounding the liberalisation of pub-opening hours in England and Wales with the Licensing Act of 2003:

> By the end of 2004 public attention and media interest were becoming increasingly concerned about the social disorder, violence, and other problems associated with heavy drinking and intoxication, especially in town and city centres during weekend evenings. The prospect of liberalised licensing arrangements increasingly came under fire from all quarters and a sustained and quite remarkable onslaught against these changes continued throughout 2005. [...] the press mounted a vigorous and outspoken campaign against Government plans. [...] Media interest built upon and probably amplified a moral panic about binge drinking that had been running for several months.
>
> (Plant & Plant, 2006: 87)

The consumption of alcohol to excess, however, is of course not a new social phenomenon and neither is the occurrence of antisocial behaviour in association with heavy drinking. As is the case with other social problems/issues, media attention and public concern about alcohol-related problems/issues, go through regular cycles of what Downs (1972) referred to as the 'ups' and 'downs' of the 'issue-attention cycle'. What is of interest then is to establish the dynamics that power public, media and political 'issue-attention cycles' with regard to alcohol and drinking in society; in other words, to ask *what, who* or *whose activity* in which public forum 'drives' forward public concern and political and legislative activity with regard to alcohol consumption.

The publicity that binge drinking, for example, receives in mainstream news media is significant in that it raises the salience of excessive alcohol consumption as an issue and may also give rise to the impression that it is more prevalent than it really is. Furthermore, press coverage may raise the prominence of the issue on the political agenda leading government to spend public money dealing with this social 'problem'. Alternatively, government may wish to be seen taking relatively inexpensive public action in the form of tighter restrictions over the sale and promotion of alcoholic drinks products, that may not be welcomed by the alcoholic drinks industry and retailers that sell these products.

In this chapter we explore the achievements of the relatively small body of research on news coverage of alcohol and we argue what is needed is more research designed to show the role of news coverage in the formation of public and political definitions or 'climates of opinion' about excessive alcohol consumption as an economic, health and social

problem for society. Such research can, if taking an appropriately longitudinal perspective, provide important indicators of how public and
political 'climates of opinion' with regard to alcohol and 'acceptable'
drinking practices are formed and changed over time, and particularly
of the role that the news media play in these processes.

News and alcohol

Against the relative wealth of research on the portrayal and influence
of alcohol images in advertising and media entertainment genres, it is
particularly surprising that there has been little research on news and
factual media reporting on alcohol, drinking practices, alcohol policy
and alcohol-related problems. The communications and political science literatures offer significant and powerful theoretical frameworks
for analysing and understanding the role played by the news media in
the public policy process and in the construction of public values and
'climates of opinion' (McCombs, 2004; Best, 1995; Loseke, 2003; Ryan,
1991; Entman, 1993; Reese, Gandy & Grant, 2001; Zaller, 1992).

The key achievement of these frameworks is their departure from
the more conventional focus on individual behavioural and attitudinal
dimensions, characteristic of much research on the influence of alcohol
advertising and their focus instead on how particular problems become
defined as problems for public and political concern, in other words,
how particular issues are elaborated, contested, redefined and eventually removed from the public agenda. Aiming ultimately to chart and
understand the dynamics and public 'careers' of social issues/problems,
these approaches focus on the competition between key claims-makers
(agencies, politicians, organisations, corporations, experts, etc.) in their
attempt at commanding public attention and gaining public legitimacy
for their particular definitions of what constitutes a social problem,
what its causes are and how it should be resolved.

While there have been only limited attempts – and none in the UK –
at pressing these frameworks into service with regard to alcohol, several
studies in the related fields of tobacco/smoking and drugs control have
made considerable strides towards mapping the dynamic interplay
between media reporting, policy, politics, public understanding or
opinion (Chapman, 1989; Menashe & Siegel, 1998; Lima & Siegel, 1999;
Kennedy & Bero, 1999; Durrant et al., 2003; Smith et al., 2005).

To comprehensively identify published research on news coverage of
alcohol and news media roles in relation to alcohol issues, we conducted
searches, using principally combinations of the keyword-stems 'alcohol'

and 'news' in the ISI Web of Science/Web of Knowledge databases (which provide comprehensive indexing of science, humanities and social science publications from 1970 to the present). These searches were complemented with Google searches, with examination of recent reviews/overviews of alcohol research (notably Babor et al., 2003, and Grube, 2004) and with searches on particular institutional archives (e.g., The Prevention Research Center, the Berkeley Media Studies Group and the Alcohol & Public Health Research Unit). The key relevant studies identified through our searches are summarised in Table 8.1, indicating, for each study, the method, media, period, data sets and variables analysed.

The studies singled out for more extensive examination in the following sections have been chosen because they at once represent promising work towards understanding the role of news media in relation to alcohol issues *and* illustrate some of the shortfalls of work in this area. We wish to highlight: (1) the lack of cross-referencing between studies; (2) the need to examine effects of media reporting within appropriate theoretical frames from the media and communications field; (3) the potential power of longitudinal analyses; (4) the mediating role of advocacy or perspective-taking; (5) the significance of message sources; and (6) the significance of the medium in which coverage occurs.

Theoretical and empirical cross-referencing

One issue that has held back theoretical and empirical advancement is the frequent lack of cross-referencing between studies. Researchers working in this field are not always fully aware of each other's work or for other reasons choose not to make reference to the work of others in setting a context for their own research.

In contrast to the considerable amount of research on agenda-setting, framing and advocacy communication in the fields of tobacco/smoking and drugs control, far fewer studies – and none in the UK – have addressed these processes in relation to media news coverage of alcohol issues. Among those that have, there is also considerably less commonality – than among the smoking and drugs studies – of theoretical frameworks used and less cross-referencing.

A recent Finnish study (Törrönen, 2003) of newspaper editorials in the period 1993–2000 thus references previous Finnish work in this area, but makes no reference to key American/Canadian longitudinal research such as Linsky's (1970) classic work on media portrayal of alcoholism, McKenzie and Giesbrecht's (1981) study of Canadian news reporting on alcohol issues, or Lemmens, Vaeth & Greenfield (1999) on alcohol issues

Table 8.1 Key studies of alcohol and news (adapted from Hansen & Gunter, 2007)

Authors/Study	Year of publication	Main method	Media	Period of coverage studied	Key data-sets and analytical variable(s)
S. Casswell	1997	Review and programmatic article	n/a	n/a	Proposed focus: Voices, themes and policies in news coverage
R. JonesWebb, S. Baranowski, D. Fan, J. Finnegan & A. C. Wagenaar	1997	Content analysis	15 Black-oriented and 12 mainstream US newspapers	1993–5	Coverage of alcohol control policy issues
L. Dorfman & L. Wallack	1998	Summary/review of alcohol-relevant findings from a selection of news studies, but mainly a programmatic article on the Advocacy approach and the role for news researchers	Reference to studies of both US broadcast and print media	Studies from selected years between 1990 and 1995	Frequency, positioning and thematic content of references to alcohol; Media advocacy and the role for news researchers
P. Lemmens, P. A. C. Vaeth & T. K. Greenfield	1999	Content analysis	5 national US newspapers	1985–91	Coverage of alcohol and alcoholism; thematic content; positive/negative reporting; sources of information

Author	Year	Method	Source	Period	Focus
I. Yanovitzky & C. Bennett	1999	Content analysis and time-series regression analysis with data on US Congress bills and statistics on Drunk Driving (DD)	2 national US newspapers (*New York Times* and *Washington Post*)	1978 to 1996	News coverage of Drunk Driving (DD); Number of DD-related bills introduced in US Congress; statistics on involvement in DD-behaviour
C. K. Atkin & W. DeJong	2000	Content analysis	Student-run US College newspapers	1994–5	Information on alcohol and other drug use; substance-related problems; control strategies; prevention/treatment efforts; positive/negative portrayal
J. Golden	2000	Content analysis	36 national US network evening news broadcasts (ABC, CBS, NBC).	1977–96	The portrayal of pregnancy and alcohol: thematic content
I. Yanovitzky & J. Stryker	2001	Content analysis and time-series regression analysis with data on US Congress bills and survey data	2 national US newspapers (*New York Times* and *Washington Post*)	1978–96	News coverage ('favourable'/'unfavourable'), policy initiatives/US Congress bills and survey data regarding youth binge drinking
S. L. Myhre, M. N. Saphir, J. A. Flora, K. A. Howard & E. M. Gonzalez	2002	Content analysis	9 California newspapers	Sept 1997–June 1998	Frequency, positioning, framing and authors/sources of alcohol-related articles

(*continued*)

Table 8.1 Continued

Authors/Study	Year of publication	Main method	Media	Period of coverage studied	Key data-sets and analytical variable(s)
I. Yanovitzky	2002	Content analysis and time-series regression analysis with data on US Congress bills and statistics on Drunk Driving (DD)	2 national US newspapers (*New York Times* and *Washington Post*) and the AP wire service	1978–95	News coverage of Drunk Driving (DD); Number of DD-related bills introduced in US Congress; statistics on involvement in DD-behaviour
J. Törönen	2003	Discourse and Narrative analysis	Newspaper editorials on alcohol issues from 6 daily Finnish newspapers	1993–000	'Moral', 'Utopian' and 'Truth' discourses
M. D. Slater, M. Long & V. L. Ford	2006	Content analysis	Representative sample of US local and national television news, local newspapers and national magazines randomly sampled during a 2-year period	2002 and 2003	News stories containing information about alcohol, illegal drugs, violent crimes and injury incidents. Story frames coded: regulatory anti-substance, regulatory pro-substance, enforcement of government or organisational regulations, positive/ negative connotations of substance use, trends in substance use and a miscellaneous category.

coverage in the US press from 1985–1991. While Lemmens et al. (1999) place their research within a general framework of agenda-setting and advocacy communication – although without ultimately pressing these frameworks fully into service – it is perhaps symptomatic of the absence of cross-referencing that Törrönen (2003) makes little or no reference to these specific frameworks, choosing instead to discuss media roles in the less specific discourse of the media as both reflecting and influencing general public climates of opinion. Slater, Long & Ford (2006), while making little or no reference to studies of the 1970s and 1980s or indeed to Törrönen, by contrast draw directly on Lemmens et al. and also reference the important work of Myhre et al. (2002) and of Yanovitzky and Stryker (2001).

Effects of media reporting

Any systematic analysis of media discourses is usually carried out not simply to articulate the way media represent issues but also as a pathway towards understanding or identifying underlying agendas of media owners or producers or potential influences upon media consumers or societies. Bearing this is in mind, it is important therefore for analytical frameworks to be informed, theoretically and in terms of methodological detail, by this objective and to deconstruct media discourses in ways that provide these kinds of insights. The study of news discourses and alcohol issues has begun to explore media discourses for meanings that inform such wider understanding, but there is plenty of scope for further development of research in the future in this context.

Underpinning Törrönen's (2003) research is a clear assumption that news media reporting plays an important role in the processes of public opinion and policy formation, but he stops short of attempting to determine the finer patterns of interaction (reflection and influence) between these key components.

> Editorials may be regarded as responsive 'indicators' of the opinion climate and of the shifts and fluctuations happening in the power relations between societal actors. The newspapers, as collective actors, position themselves in their editorials in the field of politics and try consistently to exert influence. (...) [They] evaluate arguments and decisions happening in the main arenas of society, make an assessment of them and of situations and attempt to influence policy and public opinion.
>
> (Törrönen, 2003: 282)

Törrönen's analysis is particularly useful for its mapping of the changes in media discourse over a period of time characterised by significant changes in Finnish alcohol policy and legislation, and as such it provides evidence on one of the important components – the media – in the dynamics of social values, public opinion, government policy and legislation and media reporting. Törrönen concludes,

> Almost half the editorials discussed alcohol policy in terms of freedom from the restrictive alcohol policy of the state. Encouraging liberalization of alcohol policy peaked in 1996 and 1997. However, as problems of public order became more prominent in the media at the end of the 1990s, claims for the liberalization of alcohol policy died away and between 1998 and 2000 issues of public order dominated those of freedom. In addition, concern about the intoxication-orientated drinking habits of the young and of children became prominent.
>
> (p. 281)

In a slightly earlier study, Yanovitzky and Stryker (2001), working also from the assumption that news media play an important role in constructing the boundaries that define public notions of acceptable behaviour, examined the effects of news coverage on binge drinking over the extended period of 1978–96. Describing their theoretical approach as a 'norm-reinforcement approach', they argue that the news media – together with family, peers and other referents – provide important cues to socially acceptable individual behaviour:

> People can learn about the social acceptability of risky health behaviors just by being exposed to news, commercial advertisements, and entertainment programs (...). Several prominent research traditions (...) have already demonstrated that media portrayals may influence audiences' judgments of social reality, including that of social values and norms (...). It is possible, therefore, that an unfavorable treatment of behaviors by the media will directly reduce their perceived social acceptability among members of society.
>
> (Yanovitzky & Stryker, 2001: 211)

In contrast to the more general formulation offered by Törrönen, they conceptualise 'media effects' within a tightly controlled analytical design enabling the measurement of interactions between the news agenda and public/policy agendas.

Situating their research firmly within agenda-setting and framing theory, Slater, Long & Ford (2006) note that their analysis of news reporting shows distinct 'underreporting' of the role of alcohol in injuries and violent crimes. They surmise that 'If public concern and support for alcohol-control efforts arise, as our survey results suggest is likely, in part as a result of news coverage, then the underreporting of the contribution of alcohol to violent crime as well as unintended injuries may be an obstacle to wider acceptance and use of alcohol-control strategies.' (Slater et al., 2006: 910). In a more recent study, Slater and his colleagues (2009) take the analysis of news media impact on public perception and policy-support further. Through a national survey of just under 1300 randomly selected subjects, they provide evidence that 'attention to news stories about crime and accident influences alcohol-control policy support via concern (and less certainly, risk perceptions)' (p. 272) about the risks associated with alcohol use.

Longitudinal analyses

The role played by the media, and more especially by news media, in shaping public discourses about alcohol consumption cannot be presumed to occur at one point in time. If media coverage of alcohol-related issues has an impact upon public thinking and policy-making, this influence is likely to occur over time. It is important therefore to understand long-term trends in news discourses about alcohol issues and how these are linked to relevant policy and social change over time.

Törrönen's (2003) analysis usefully mapped the changes in media discourse over a period of time characterised by significant changes in Finnish alcohol policy and legislation, and as such it provided evidence on one of the important components – the media – in the dynamics of social values, public opinion, government policy and legislation and media reporting.

Yanovitzky and Stryker (2001), drawing on the traditions of agenda-setting and closely related frameworks, combined three important sets of data from the period 1978–96: secondary analysis of survey data (on young people's 'binge-drinking-related beliefs and involvement in this behaviour' (p. 219)), data on federal legislation against youth binge drinking and primary analysis of press coverage of binge drinking. Yanovitzky and Stryker's study is particularly interesting, because – unlike both Törrönen and Lemmens et al. – their combination, in a rigorous and tightly disciplined research design, of three sets of data enabled them to show that 'media coverage of binge-drinking behavior had a significant positive contribution to the trend in binge-drinking-related congres-sional bills (...)' (p. 222) and '(...) that the impact of news stories on this [binge-drinking] behavior was mediated by policy actions as well as by changes in the social acceptability of this behavior' (p. 230).

Lemmens et al. (1999) examined national newspaper coverage of alcohol issues in the US during the 7-year period 1985–1991. Their study, which consists of a systematic analysis of media coverage, is con-textualised within a general, but relatively brief, discussion about the mass media and the public, touching on questions about agenda-setting and climates of opinion and advocacy communication. Lemmens et al. stress that their 'study was not designed to answer the more fundamen-tal questions about relationship between the mass media and public beliefs, attitudes and opinions about alcohol consumption' (p. 1555). Their analysis is, however, particularly useful for the way in which it demonstrates two key dimensions of news coverage: thematic focus and key sources of alcohol issues information.

Drunk driving was, throughout the period examined, the most promi-nent thematic issue in national coverage. They further found a decrease, in the second half of the period studied, 'of issues related to alcohol abuse and alcoholism and of the ill effects of alcohol on the indi-vidual and society' (p. 1558). Less surprisingly, they found government information sources to be the single most prominent source of media reporting on alcohol, and, by contrast, public health advocates were a relatively infrequent source.

Advocacy and orientation in news discourses

Determining the processes of media effects, whether over the short term or long term, requires an understanding of other mechanisms within media coverage of alcohol issues that may mediate the responses of media con-sumers. One issue in this context is the extent to which a media narrative advocates behavioural change and indicates ways in which such change might be achieved. The orientations taken by the media towards alcohol consumption as a social problem might also shape public reaction, sup-port for policy changes or controls over undesired 'alcohol-related' behav-iours believed to be contingent upon excessive alcohol consumption.

Lemmens et al. (1999) thus examined the general 'slant' (positive, negative, neutral) and overall evaluative stance in newspaper reporting on alcohol issues. While noting that the press evaluations of alcohol use were 'largely neutral or ambivalent and often negative' (p. 1559), they found interesting indications of changing social evaluations of alcohol, and their findings generally confirmed the findings of the much earlier research by Linsky (1970), that 'moralistic' and psychological or 'personality'-focused explanations for alcohol abuse and dependency had, by the latter part of the twentieth century, all but disappeared completely to give way to 'naturalistic/environmental' explanations. While Yanovitzky and Stryker did not succeed in demonstrating a direct impact of media reporting on binge drinking behaviour, their findings showed that news coverage plays an important role in articulating and reinforcing a change in public norms regarding the social acceptability of binge drinking. In this context it is not surprising that the Media Advocacy framework emerges as a useful framework for conceptualising the role of the media:

> Media advocacy, or the strategic use of news and entertainment media to promote social change (Wallack, Dorfman, Jernigan, & Themba, 1993), may be a better strategy to pursue in this respect. The fact that news coverage has been shown to reduce normative ambiguity in this study attests to the promise of this approach. Exposure to information in news and entertainment media is certainly more likely than exposure to any public health communication campaign. Moreover, as behavioral and attitudinal changes tend to be slow and gradual, maintaining public interest and concern requires levels of media attention that cannot be secured even by lavishly funded public health communication campaigns. Last, media attention to health problems is far more likely to attract related policy making and other types of institutional response than discrete campaign messages.
>
> (pp. 231–2)

On the basis of this finding, they convincingly argue that media advocacy (as proposed by Wallack et al., 1993) aimed at influencing news and entertainment media coverage may be considerable more effective than public health communication campaigns in changing social norms with regard to binge drinking.

Importance of message sources

The nature of any agenda set by media, the perceived credibility for the public of media discourses and the ultimate impact of such discourses can be mediated by the sources cited within media reports as sources of critical messages about social issues or policies. Analysis of this component of news reporting of alcohol issues has, so far, been scant.

The study by Lemmens et al. contains many of the right dimensions for understanding media roles in the interplay with public and political agendas, but crucially omits to analyse who the key claims-makers are in the dynamics and development of the public agenda on alcohol. Nor do they make reference to the slightly earlier 'programmatic' article by Dorfman and Wallack (1998), setting out the agenda and task for researchers studying the role of news reporting on alcohol. A more recent study by Myhre et al. (2002), while making considerable headway with a detailed analysis of key content dimensions, similarly omits to examine 'who' articulates/drives the newspaper agenda on alcohol issues. Myhre et al. (2002) do examine 'sources' but by this they mean the 'author/writer' of the individual articles rather than the (authoritative, expert or political) sources who may be quoted or referred to, and who may be the originators of news items.

Significance of medium

With very few exceptions, as indicated in Table 8.1, studies of news coverage of alcohol issues have focused on newspapers, although within this medium some interesting non-mainstream subcategories have been examined (e.g., Myhre et al. (2002), Atkin and DeJong (2000) and Jones-Webb et al. (1997)). The communication medium's significance for the role and social impact of alcohol messages has, however, not received sufficient attention so far.

The significance of medium stems from findings in the general news media literature that the credibility of any news discourse depends not just on the message sources identified, but also upon the medium itself. News suppliers have become 'brands', but the strength of these 'brands' in terms of their reputation for accurate, balanced and credible news often derives from their close association with a specific medium. Thus, television has traditionally been identified in public opinion polls as the most important and most trusted news medium (Gunter, 2005; Lee, 1975; Levy & Robinson, 1986). Newspapers have been rated as more credible than the Internet (Flanagin & Metzger, 2000). However, these distinctions can vary among different media audience communities (Rainie & Packel, 2001).

Lessons from other areas

As indicated earlier, studies of news and tobacco/drugs issues have made further strides – than research on alcohol and news – towards an understanding of the dynamic interplay between news media, pub-lic/political understanding and policy or action. Studies in the tobacco field have thus provided valuable evidence on the relative prominence of tobacco/smoking themes in news coverage, of the different 'frames' used for discussing tobacco themes and legislation, and of the relative prominence of anti- and pro-tobacco control measures in news reporting. While many of these studies make reference to the notion of 'advocacy communication' – the attempt by 'stakeholder' parties in public contro-versy about smoking and tobacco control legislation to influence news media coverage (see Wallack et al., 1993; Chapman & Wakefield, 2001; Chapman, 2004) – it is perhaps only surprising that few have analysed the specific sources of information quoted or referred to in news media coverage of tobacco- and smoking-related issues.

Through the notion of 'advocacy communication', these studies – implicitly if not explicitly – recognise the dynamic and 'constructed' nature of public definitions of tobacco issues, but while they gener-ally put a great deal of emphasis on examining *how* tobacco issues are defined and framed (including in terms of 'valence' dimensions such as positive and negative reporting on tobacco control), they generally do not show who the most successful sources or 'advocates' are in the media and public construction of tobacco issues.

Several agenda-setting studies (Gonzenbach, 1992 and 1996; Fan, 1996) of public understanding and debate about drugs issues have pointed to the complex web of interaction between public opinion, media coverage and political action. Gonzenbach (1992), employing a time-series analysis of media coverage, public opinion and presidential decisions on drugs issues during the period 1984–91, showed media coverage to be an important 'driver' in relation to both public opinion formation and presidential decision-making.

> The results indicate that public opinion mirrors or immediately fol-lows the press, though public opinion also drives the press agenda. Second, the study suggests that the president is following the public agenda, though the president also has strong immediate influence on public opinion. And, finally it suggests the president mirrors and follows the media, in addition to following public opinion.
> (Gonzenbach, 1992: 126)

Studying a similar period, 1985–94, Fan (1996) found evidence that changes in public perception of drugs as a serious problem could be explained by the press increasingly framing the drugs issue as a 'crisis', while other types of framing of the drugs issue contributed only in a limited way to changes in public opinion.

Two key conclusions – with implications for studies of alcohol and news – can be drawn from these studies of news coverage of tobacco and drugs issues: media coverage plays an important role in the building of public and political agendas on such issues as tobacco and drugs control, and the 'terms of discussion' or framing of issues impacts on public understanding of and the formulation of political responses to such issues.

A framework for future analysis

In the remainder of this chapter, we build on the lessons from previous research on news and alcohol-related issues – discussed above – to outline a suitable framework for analysis of the nature and role of news media coverage of alcohol in society. As we have indicated, there is a gap in the literature on media and alcohol consumption that specifically focuses upon the role that news coverage can play in representing the current social climate and relevant social policy-making concerned with problems that arise from excessive or inappropriate alcohol consumption.

As our review of previous research has indicated, the impact of news coverage on public opinion about national and local legislation on alcohol distribution and consumption has been explored sporadically in American studies, but it is also clear that much remains to be understood about it. The news media have been used as platforms for advocacy campaigns designed to promote and enhance the effectiveness of drinking policies. Observations noted that new alcohol-related policies may have been successful in receiving localised media coverage, but whether this coverage had any impact on alcohol consumption practices and other behaviour (e.g., driving) when drinking is less certain (Golden, 2000; Harwood et al., 2005).

In the remainder of this chapter we wish to draw on the lessons from the limited number of studies done so far to propose a number of key dimensions for a framework for analysing news media roles in relation to alcohol. The key dimensions to be considered for a framework of analysis for the study of the role of news media coverage of alcohol consumption and related matters fall under the following three headings: (1) sampling media content, (2) content analysis categories and (3) linking media to public opinion.

(1) Sampling media content

The selection of media content for analysis is a vital component in any study that attempts to present an empirical demonstration of the actual or potential impact of news coverage of alcohol-related issues. One critical question here concerns the audience coverage likely to be achieved by a mass medium or specific outputs of that medium. In other words, we need to know about the kinds of viewers, listeners or readers attracted by a medium and, more specially, the extent to which those media consumers (a) represent social groups that may have been targeted by media messages and (b) are likely to be responsive to those messages in the ways intended. As our review of earlier studies of news coverage of alcohol-related issues has indicated, researchers have so far focused predominantly and with few exceptions on the way these issues have been covered by newspapers. Other important news media, such as television, radio and more recently, the Internet, have rarely been included. Even if the earlier work presents an accurate and comprehensive indication of the nature of print news coverage of alcohol issues, it represents just one part of the range of information sources to which people might turn on their media menu.

In the context of alcohol consumption, for example, an issue such as binge drinking is one that centres on the drinking habits of young people mostly from mid-teens to late 20s. This age group is also the one that is the main focus of attention in respect of alcohol consumption leading to violence or sexual promiscuity. It is not, however, the age group known for its interest in news – or more especially serious forms of news – coverage (Hargreaves & Thomas, 2002). Indeed, there is growing evidence that news consumption in general, and certainly via the principal traditional news sources, is experiencing a downturn (Hargreaves & Thomas, 2002). Nonetheless, information-seeking associated with specific events or issues that are deemed to be socially important to citizens or which deal with matters that create social concern or uncertainty can generate considerable volumes of news consumption.

Some media advocacy research associated with policies designed to produce shifts in alcohol-related behaviour have recognised that multimedia campaigns are needed if the aim is to raise issue awareness across an entire community (Holder & Treno, 1997). If news coverage is part of a wider interventionist campaign, however, it needs to be supplemented by more direct activities on the part of individuals within the community (Treno & Holder, 1997). It could be of value therefore to differentiate between media in terms of a number of criteria relevant to the uptake of information messages. Distinctions between media can be made in terms of the particular groups they reach, the degree of trust placed in media as information sources, and the effectiveness with which people learn from and are persuaded by arguments presented through different media.

We have already noted that young people are not major news consumers. In addition, the news media have different audience profiles. In targeting young people, for example, television may reach significant numbers at certain times, but health campaigners would need to recognise even then that specific programmes are likely to prove more effective than others at attracting young audiences. Newspapers, in contrast, are consumed to a lesser degree by youth audiences. Radio remains a popular medium with young people, but more for its music content than news. The Internet has emerged as a significant medium for young people and has eroded the youth audiences for the longer established news media (Pew Research Center, 2004). Some media may be effective at reaching community or opinion leaders while others may reach the general population.

One further criterion that might influence media content sampling in any study of news coverage of alcohol-related issues is the degree of trust or authority that attaches to particular news suppliers. One of the principal factors according to which the quality of news coverage is assessed by news consumers is its objectivity. This factor is a central ingredient of the 'brand' of a new supplier. The degree of trust placed in a news source may be influenced in part by the medium in which it operates. Television, for example, tends to command greater public trust than newspapers (Gunter, 2005). Some news brands, however, remain strong regardless of the medium in which they operate (YouGov, 2005).

News media can also be distinguished in terms of their respective effectiveness at conveying information to audiences. This point goes beyond differentiating news sources in terms of their perceived importance or credibility for news consumers. In previous research on reporting of alcohol issues, it has been assumed that newspaper reporting can play an important role in public opinion formation (Törrönen, 2003). The significance of newspapers in this context, however, will be determined by how effective print media are compared with broadcast and electronic media at conveying information and persuasive messages to receivers.

Conflicting evidence has emerged about the relative effectiveness of television, radio and newspapers in relation to recall of news by audiences (DeFleur et al., 1992; Furnham & Gunter, 1985; Walma van der Molen & van der Voort, 1997 and 1998). Differences have also been found in the effectiveness of different media in conveying messages designed to elicit resistance to persuasion and attitude change (Pfau et al., 2000).

In monitoring the likely effectiveness of any news-based media advocacy campaign, therefore, it would be relevant to distinguish the nature of the messages conveyed by different media and how appropriate those messages might be in respect of influencing particular groups. Such considerations should take into account the relative efficacy of different media to reach, inform and persuade young people.

A clear differentiation between different media is also important if we are to gain a better understanding of the dynamics which characterise the 'careers' of alcohol issues/problems in public debate. 'Inter-media agenda-setting' is an important concept in this context, that is, we need to ask questions about key national quality newspapers' influence or set the news-agenda for broadcast news or for the national popular/tabloid press, or indeed for regional news media.

(2) Content analysis categories

Many analyses of media content tend to be topic focused. This has certainly been true of analysis of the nature of news coverage. Studies of the changing nature of the news over time have catalogued agenda shifts such that certain topics have been observed to command more space and others less. Thus, in the context of the study of alcohol coverage in the news, researchers have reported on changing levels of representation of alcohol issues and sub-issues over time (Lemmens et al., 1999; Törrönen, 2003).

There have also been some limited attempts at evaluating the nature of coverage in terms of whether it is positive, neutral or negative in its treatment of specific alcohol-related problems (Lemmens et al., 1999; Slater, Long & Ford, 2006). Recent research with the changing nature of news coverage, however, has revealed more subtle ways of profiling news coverage that take into account the probable significance of certain types of narrative and visual presentational styles for the emotional reactions news content can generate among audiences (e.g., Brants & Neijens, 1998; Grabe, Zhou & Barnett, 2001).

Changes in the quality of news that have been examined under the heading of 'tabloidisation', for example, have identified a growth in coverage of what has been referred to by some writers as 'sensational' news coverage (Blumler, 1999; Franklin, 2003) and by others as 'personalised' coverage (van Zoonen & Holz-Bacha, 2000).

Changes in production styles, which are characterised by visual and linguistic changes, have collectively been identified as representing a shift towards the use of techniques that are designed to play on the emotions of news consumers (Brants, 1998). Theoretical models and accompanying empirical methodologies have been developed to investigate this phenomenon (Grabe, Zhou & Barnett, 2001; Uribe, 2004). One reason why the emotionality of news is important is that it can shape not just the audience's emotional state but also the processing of information content (Lang, Bradley & Cuthbert, 1997). Powerful emotional response can impede information processing (Heo & Sundar, 2000; Lang, 2000). Emotional responses can also have a directional impact in determining which content is best remembered (Brosius, 1993; Aust & Zillmann, 1996). Subtle use of emotional cues has been found to determine which information is perceived by the audience as the most compelling or important (Aust & Zillmann, 1996).

When cataloguing the nature of news coverage of alcohol-related issues, insights into the possible impact of media content on audiences could be enhanced from inclusion of 'emotionality' measures in the analytical framework. While some studies have adopted framing models to guide content analysis, frames have been defined primarily in terms of themes of issue coverage (e.g., Champion & Chapman, 2003; Myhre et al., 2002). The inclusion of emotionality elements would further enhance the nature of any analysis of linguistic content of the news and incorporate a theoretically grounded framework for analysis of other non-linguistic news production attributes.

(3) Linking media to public opinion

Linking content to public opinion can be further enhanced through adoption of framing models. The significance of this consideration lies in its centrality to the design of media and community campaigns designed to produce micro-level and macro-level social behaviour change. Iyengar (1991) articulated a model in which distinctions were made between the way news reports argued the case for 'causal responsibility' and 'treatment responsibility' when reporting upon social problems. Causal responsibility identified the nature of a problem and its origins, while treatment responsibility examined sources of power to solve particular problems. In discussing the nature of reporting within television news, Iyengar identified two types of news 'frame' – episodic and thematic. When adopting an episodic news frame, news reports would focus on specific cases or events and represent public issues and social problems in concrete terms. With thematic frames, a more generalised and abstract orientation was adopted in which general outcomes and social conditions would be examined.

In an alcohol-reporting context, a thematic frame might examine general policies about alcohol availability, drinking hours or the nature of alcohol promotions and advertising. In contrast, an episodic frame might focus on stories concerned with specific outbreaks of allegedly alcohol-fuelled violence that might then be used to argue for tighter general restrictions on drinking. According to Iyengar, television tends to prefer episodic frames because they can be readily visualised and this is important for that medium. They can also be more emotionally compelling, which adds to their dramatic value. This is increasingly important in an ever more competitive news environment. We also know that video presentations can be superior to print presentations in the context of presenting persuasive arguments to receivers (Pfau et al., 2000). In the context of using the media to convey messages about alcohol consumption, therefore, it is not simply the nature of the framing of issues that is important, but also the matching of arguments with the medium in which they are likely to be most effective.

What is clear from framing research, however, is that subtle changes to the way an argument is represented can make a radical difference to whether it is accepted or rejected by an audience. Policies that place restrictions upon consumer behaviour are often rejected because they are framed by news stories as developments designed to remove freedom of choice.

Psychological reactance theory has been used to explain why such persuasive approaches tend to be unsuccessful. Individuals react strongly against any steps by an authority to take away their freedom to choose. Restrictions on commodities that consumers have been free to consume may convert them into 'forbidden fruit' rendering them even more attractive. This effect has been observed in relation to age-related restrictions on media content believed to be unsuitable for young media consumers (Bushman & Stack, 1996). Such restrictions can render movies and television programmes even more appealing (Kracmar & Cantor, 1997). Further evidence has emerged that tobacco advertising bans can also make smoking more rather than less attractive to young people. Rather than discouraging smoking, the opposite effect seems to occur, especially among 18- to 24-year olds (Buddelmeyer & Wilkins, 2005).

Conclusion

The news media play an important and significant role in relation to the way that public and political 'climates of opinion' regarding alcohol-related risks, benefits and problems are shaped. Yet, only a small number of mainly American studies have so far addressed key questions about what is being 'said' in the public sphere about alcohol and 'acceptable' drinking practices. Fewer still have investigated the role of news reporting in informing public understanding about alcohol-related risks, in setting public and political agendas on alcohol-issues or in shaping the boundaries within which political, health and economic initiatives regarding alcohol can be articulated and enacted.

We believe there is a need to develop content-coding models that are informed by relevant theories and empirical evidence concerning the way individuals respond to news coverage and to policy developments designed to change their behaviour, especially when these developments take away freedom of choice. So far, studies of news coverage of alcohol issues have adopted more simplistic framing models. We have argued that consideration of empirical evidence on the sensitivities of media audiences to narrative and production treatments in media coverage of social policy issues in the news can lead to the development of more robust and comprehensive coding frames that reveal the presence of coverage features capable of promoting specific types of audience response.

We propose an analytical approach that will not only show the extent and nature of news reporting on alcohol issues, but take into account a range of factors linked to media consumers to guide the sampling of media content and construction of a coding method that will represent frames that are likely to be accepted or rejected by the public. This framing approach will not simply examine sources of policy statements within news reports, but also take into account news source brands and the ways in which arguments for policies are presented, especially as they relate to the freedoms of individuals to choose in relation to the way they behave in different situations. In effect, this approach would be designed to facilitate the mapping of the career of a social issue, to identify the primary definers and claims-makers and therefore who or what drives the public and media discourses on alcohol as a social issue.

9
Alcohol Marketing: Research, Regulation and Compliance

In this book, we have seen that there has been widespread concern about young people's consumption of alcohol for many years, and this concern has been growing. Initially, public attention focused on the prevalence of alcohol consumption among young people. It was noted across many countries that alcohol consumption often started many years earlier than statutory minimum ages for the legal purchase and public consumption of alcoholic beverages. Underage drinking was found to be already prevalent by the time young people reached their early teens, with some drinking registered even among pre-teenage children (Foxcroft et al., 2003; Roche, 2003).

Over many years, the World Health Organisation has taken a lead in prompting national governments to review their laws and regulations concerning the sale and distribution, and the promotion of alcohol and focused attention on the need to protect young people from negative consequences of alcohol consumption, especially when carried out to excess (WHO, 1995, 2004).

In the UK, the British Medical Association has observed that alcohol-related harm can be effectively tackled via alcohol control policies (BMA, 2008). Historically, not all policies of this kind have been successful. In the eighteenth century in the UK a significant rise in alcohol consumption and related social problems followed a reduction in taxation of alcohol (Warner, 2003). In the nineteenth century, the sale of ale, beer and cider was deregulated which resulted in an explosion in premises selling alcoholic drinks. There was also an increase in the rate of drunkenness and other related social problems. The response to this outcome was the assent of new licensing laws to bring the sale of alcohol under tighter control (Plant & Plant, 2006).

In the first half of the twentieth century, during the two world wars and in the intervening period, further restrictions on the sale of alcohol, increased taxation and the loss of large numbers of young men to wartime duty led to a dramatic fall in consumption and in alcohol-related problems (Plant & Plant, 2006).

After the Second World War, alcohol control policies were relaxed in the UK. This was accompanied by steadily increased consumption. This led to growing debates about the status of alcohol consumption in the UK and more especially about the efficacy of government policies and actions (Drummond, 2004; Room, 2004; Hall, 2005; Alcohol Concern, 2004; Anderson, 2007).

Government actions have included educational campaigns and reviews of controls over alcohol purchasing and promotions. Control policies have had mixed effectiveness (Brand et al., 2007). The BMA (2008) recommended a more coordinated strategy involving government and other relevant organisations, though not including the alcohol industry. In fact, the BMA recommended that there should be a movement away from any partnership between industry and government based on voluntary, self-regulation. Its reasoning is that the vested interests of the industry mean that there is a conflict of interest between catering to its business needs and commitment to any system of controls designed to reduce alcohol consumption. A key aspect of effective regulation of drinking must be to control price and availability. Government can introduce laws that affect the affordability of alcohol and to restrict the opportunities for purchase and consumption. One factor that, in the BMA's view, has contributed more than any other to increased consumption of alcohol by young people has been its greater affordability over time. Price increases, triggered through increased government taxation, would be one of the most powerful steps government could take to reduce consumption (Raistrick, Hodgeson & Ritson, 1999; Plant, Single & Stockwell, 1997).

Controlling the availability of alcohol is also believed to have a significant impact on excessive consumption and associated problems. International research evidence from countries as far apart as Australia, Finland and Sweden has indicated that increased hours of alcohol sales was associated with increased deaths on roads and social violence (Sewel, 2002). When opening hours are extended, increased drinking and drink-associated violence follows (Chikritzhs & Stockwell, 2002). Further evidence supportive of this pattern of behaviour has emerged from Nordic countries and from Ireland (Ogilvie, Gruer & Haw, 2005; Plant & Plant, 2006).

It is frequently claimed that alcohol consumption is generally on the rise and that this is reflected in terms of the proportion of the population that drinks alcohol and in the average alcohol consumption rates per capita. A close examination of relevant statistics, however, shows that this statement is not necessarily true (Measham, 2007). When considering drinking trends over time and the direction in which they might be moving, whether alcohol consumption is judged to have risen or fallen can depend upon the time periods over which such trend analysis takes place. For instance, drinking levels have risen between the 1950s and 2000s. Going back another 100 years would show drinking levels at a high level in the nineteenth century and then falling away across the first half of the twentieth century before increasing again (Plant & Plant, 2006).

Although there is evidence, in many developed countries, that youth alcohol consumption has stabilised or even reduced in prevalence, patterns of drinking to excess have been observed among those youngsters who do drink alcohol that seem to be on the increase (Hibbell et al., 2004; WHO, 2004).

Regardless of whether overall prevalence and volumes of drinking are increasing or stabilising, a worrying development in opinions about drinking among young people has been observed. For many teenagers, getting drunk is a primary reason for drinking in the first place and doing so on a regular basis is regarded as acceptable behaviour (Talbot & Crabbe, 2008). There is evidence that young people often go out with the express purpose of getting drunk. The success of a social occasion is defined primarily in terms of how much alcohol was consumed (Engineer et al., 2003). Positive attitudes not simply towards alcohol but towards drunkenness may represent an important backdrop to binge drinking and seeking out extreme intoxication. Evidence from across Europe has indicated that countries that experience the most widespread or serious youth drunkenness problems are those in which the most positive attitudes towards getting drunk are found (Hibbell et al., 2004).

Given the susceptibility of young people to health and social risks associated with excessive alcohol consumption (Bonomo et al., 2004; Wells, Horwood & Fergusson, 2004), there have been repeated calls made by governments, health campaigners and other lobbyists for more efforts to be made to curb this behaviour. One aspect of any intervention designed to discourage alcohol misuse or abuse has been a focus on the way alcoholic rinks are marketed. There is widespread recognition that young people's introduction to alcohol usually occurs at home.

General attitudes towards alcohol and its use are shaped initially by family members and then later by peer-groups context (Adlaf & Kohn, 1989; Fisher & Cook, 1995; Milgram, 2001; Wilks et al., 1989). However, within a broad social mix of influential factors, the way alcoholic drinks are promoted by their manufacturers and distributors is also believed to play a part (Stockdale, 2001).

Explanations for youth drunkenness have also identified both broad social and cultural changes and more specific factors such as alcohol marketing strategies as having significant parts to play. Certainly, it is the case that the drinks industry has diversified in terms of the range of products being taken to market and in the range of drinks venues that have emerged. These developments have created greater market complexity not only in terms of consumer choice but also in the emergence of new niche markets for alcohol consumption. Alcohol beverages such as 'alcopops' have proved to be appealing to young drinkers because they have alcoholic strength and also taste good. Marketing strategies have deployed varied forms of advertising, positioned across different media and often associating alcohol consumption with attractive life-style messages. This phenomenon has been labelled by some writers as the 'recommodification of alcohol' (Barnard & Forsyth, 1998; Measham & Brain, 2005).

In the UK, for example, other social factors have occurred that have created a changed environment for drinking. Licensing hours were extended with 24-hour opening being granted in many parts of the country encouraging an expanded night-time economy that many young people have been attracted to. Alcohol has been priced competitively, especially in retail outlets bringing it comfortably within the financial range of most young people, regardless of their socio-economic background. There have then been actions imposed often by local authorities, taking advantage of new central government legislation, to restrict alcohol consumption and related problematic behaviour. These actions have included more vigilant policing of restrictions on underage drinking, discouraging gatherings of youths in public places where outside or street drinking often occurs, and stronger powers to prosecute alcohol vendors who sell drinks to underage consumers (Measham, 2007).

Those who market alcohol have become skilled in associating alcoholic drinks products with socially attractive attributes and many of those that are used most commonly are believed to hold special appeal to young people (Aitken, 1989). Thus, the suggestion in advertising that an alcohol brand will bring its consumers sexual, social or sporting success or a more affluent lifestyle play on fantasies or aspirations that are especially prominent among young people. Alcohol marketers have also effectively deployed subtle and sophisticated production techniques to enhance the quality and appeal of their commercial promotions. The use of attractive spokespersons, humorous themes, popular music and iconic celebrities are all believed to enhance the attention consumers pay to commercial messages and promote positive attitudes towards the advertising and the brands being advertised (Babor et al., 2003).

In this context, it has become increasingly recognised that the marketing of alcohol needs to be controlled (WHO, 2004). Some nations have gone as far as embodying such controls with their statutes. Regulations and codes of practice for alcohol advertising become legal requirements. In most markets, however, codes of practice are more often voluntary. They are drawn up not by governments or their appointed regulators but by industry trade associations or other networks. Compliance with such codes is also voluntary.

Despite the claims made by health campaigners that alcohol advertising can influence young people's decisions to start drinking and could also influence the way they drink, alcoholic drinks are legal products that can be legally promoted. The medical profession in many countries has spoken out about the nature of alcohol advertising, however, and argued that it frequently uses techniques that seem to be deliberately targeted at young people (Fortin & Rempel, 2005). There is a need therefore for restrictions to be applied to ensure that this advertising does not hold special appeal to children and teenagers.

While acknowledging the seriousness of concerns about young people's misuse of alcohol, some marketing experts have also advised that youth drinking is influenced by a range of factors that may act in concert or independently. It can be difficult to disentangle which societal agents – parents, siblings, friends, peer groups, the mass media, alcohol marketing – have the most significant effects or indeed what the relative contribution of each of these factors might be to the onset of alcohol consumption or any subsequent patterns it may take. Nevertheless, there are indications from the empirical research literature that marketing factors can exert some influences over young people (Hastings et al., 2005; Hastings & Angus, 2009). According to some of the evidence, this influence may stem from a number of distinct marketing variables including exposure to televised advertising, magazine advertising, in-store promotions and product displays (Ellickson et al., 2005). Liking of beer advertisements has been linked to a greater propensity on the part of young people to admit to heavy drinking and drink-related problems

(Wyllie, Zhang & Casswell, 1998). Alcohol consumption among young people has also been found to be heavier in those markets where expenditure on alcohol advertising is highest (Snyder et al., 2006). Alcohol manufacturers have, not surprisingly, disputed whether their marketing practices can be held primarily responsible for drink-related health or social problems among young people. Claims are generally made that alcohol marketing is implemented responsibly within the limits imposed by statutory or voluntary codes of practice (Fortin & Rempel, 2005). It is often further argued that advertising is concerned with promoting brands rather than being purely designed to encourage people – whatever their age – to consume alcohol per se.

Controls over alcohol marketing: International perspective

A number of enquiries have been conducted internationally to assess the extent to which alcohol marketing is effectively controlled. What control in this context means is whether countries have statutory and/ or voluntary codes of practice in place for alcohol marketing, to which aspects of marketing do these codes apply or refer and how are they implemented? Are there regulators in place that monitor compliance with codes of alcohol advertising practice and can they impose penalties on advertisers who breach those codes?

The regulation and control of alcohol advertising in the modern media era has never been easy because advertisers have enjoyed access to a number of disparate advertising media – television, radio, cinema, newspapers, magazines and outdoor billboards and posters (Jernigan & Mosher, 2005). Point-of-sale displays in retail outlets accompanied by local sales promotions represent another marketing platform. The sponsorship of music, sports and other special events represents another form of marketing that is often thought to have special significance with young consumers. Today, the Internet has emerged as an advertising medium of growing significance. It is also a medium that is difficult to regulate.

Reliance on self-regulation versus statutory regulation of alcohol advertising does vary widely between nation states and there remain many countries in which there are few controls implemented of any kind. One survey of 119 countries around the world by the centre for Information on Beverage Alcohol in 1996 found that 44 had enacted statutory regulation, while 20 relied upon industry self-regulation. A further 21 countries had both statutory and self-regulation of alcohol advertising in place. In seven countries, alcohol advertising was banned, while 23 countries had no controls in place at all. The remaining countries had implemented some controls but had no detailed codes of practices (ICAP, 2001).

The World Health Organisation reported a further survey of regulation of alcohol advertising and found that around one in four (range 23–31%) of 117 responding countries had at least partial restrictions in place that varied either by medium or by beverage type (WHO, 2004). Few countries had implemented total bans on alcohol advertising (for example, Algeria, Eritrea, Iceland, parts of India, Iran Jordan, Nigeria and Norway). In another survey, the use of voluntary codes was found to be especially prevalent in Europe. From a sample of 37 countries, clear majorities had prohibitions respectively on spirits advertising (78%) and wine advertising (76%) and a smaller majority restricted beer advertising (62%) (Osterberg & Karlsson, 2003).

The widespread regulation of alcohol advertising in European countries has been underpinned by pan-European action to control it. The 1989 EU directive on broadcasting, *Television without Frontiers* (EEC, 1989), contains rules about the content of alcohol advertising. It is expected that national statutory codes and voluntary codes will reflect the stipulations of the Directive. Doubts have surfaced, however, about whether the Directive's requirements have been successfully and effectively enforced (WHO, 2004). A further discussion paper released by the European Commission focused on concerns about the impact of alcohol advertising on underage drinking and identified targets to reduce youth exposure to such advertising and to ensure that alcohol advertisements did not encourage excessive alcohol consumption (Sanco, 2005). This discussion paper also questioned the effectiveness of voluntary codes of practice. This concern was echoed elsewhere with alcohol industry self-regulation being labelled often as little more than a public relations exercise (EUPHA, 2005).

One review of alcohol marketing regulation examined national regulations of alcohol advertising and marketing in EU member states, applicant countries and Norway (STAP, 2007). It formed part of the ELSA project (Enforcement of national laws and self-regulation on advertising and marketing of alcohol). The total sample of countries surveyed was 24.

The European Commission had presented a series of recommendations about alcohol marketing in 2001 that were specifically designed to protect young people. Alcohol manufacturers were advised not to target young people with their products or promotions and not to include promotional appeals that might prove to be especially attractive to the young. More specifically, alcohol promotions should not use styles associated with youth culture, feature children or people who look young, associate alcohol with consumption or drugs or tobacco, link alcohol to violent or anti-social behaviour, imply that alcohol consumption brings social or sexual success, encourage children or adolescents to drink, advertise during special sporting or music events that might attract significant numbers of children in their audiences, advertise in media outlets targeted at children and adolescents, offer free samples of alcohol or alcohol-related merchandise to children or adolescents.

The STAP (2007) study examined the presence or absence of statutory and non-statutory regulation of alcohol advertising and marketing in each participating country. It distinguished between regulation of volume of advertising and regulation of the content of advertising. The latter comprised a set of variables that reflected recommendations made by the ELSA project and also by the EU Directive 89/552/EEC on alcohol advertising. These recommendations were especially sensitive to the way young people might respond to alcohol advertising.

Thus, a framework of variables was constructed and applied to the alcohol advertising regulatory system in each country producing an audit of regulations across Europe. In examining the volume of alcohol advertising, the analysis considered whether any bans on advertising were in place and how extensive these were. Bans could be defined in relation to six key variables:

- Location: for example, no marketing allowed in specific physical locations such as sports stadiums;
- Time : for example, restrictions on alcohol advertising on television before 9pm;
- Media – channel: for example, no alcohol advertising at the cinema;
- Type of product: for example, no advertising of spirits;
- Target-group: for example, no targeting of people under a specified age;
- Advertiser; for example, restrictions on specific types of advertiser.

The next main set of variables comprised different elements of advertising highlighted by the Council the represented factors believed to facilitate or magnify the impact of alcohol advertising on children. Eleven variables were identified in this context:

(a) Production – beverages produced especially for children.
(b) Styles – use of characters or other variables associated with youth culture.

(c) Children – campaigns featuring children or young people.
(d) Drugs – images or other references associating alcohol consumption with the consumption of other drugs such as tobacco.
(e) Violence – links of alcohol with violent or antisocial behaviour.
(f) Success – association of alcohol with social, sexual or sporting success.
(g) Encouragement – incentives to children and adolescents to drink alcohol such as low prices.
(h) Events – advertising of alcohol during sporting, musical or other special events that attract significant numbers of young people as spectators.
(i) Media – alcohol advertising in media targeted at young people.
(j) Free – distribution of alcoholic drinks to young people and free distribution of alcohol-associated merchandise.
(k) Other – other types of promotion of alcohol drinks to children and adolescents.

Finally, an audit was conducted of the procedures connected to regulation of alcohol advertising in place in different countries. Six different types of procedure were examined:

(1) Pre-launch advice about marketing campaigns before they get underway.
(2) The existence of an organisation that systematically searches for advertising regulation violations.
(3) The availability of a system that allows for complaints to be made about regulation violations.
(4) The existence of a system of appeal against complaints about alleged violations.
(5) The imposition of sanctions against those who violate regulations.
(6) The publication of complaints and results of investigations into them.

In all, 24 countries were included in this research. Between them, they had 79 different regulations about alcohol marketing. Out of these regulations, 49 were statutory (covering 23 countries) and 27 were non-statutory (in 17 countries). There were also three co-regulations (in the UK) comprising agreements between statutory and non-statutory bodies. Six countries had statutory regulation only.

The most comprehensive alcohol advertising codes were found in France, Ireland, Belgium, Estonia and Portugal, followed by Czech Republic,

Germany, Netherlands, Spain and the UK. All these countries had codes for at least nine out of 11 code categories. The least comprehensive codes (six or fewer code categories covered) were found in Bulgaria, Poland, Romania and the Slovak Republic.

There were variations between countries in the presence of regulations or codes concerning different production format or content elements of alcohol advertising. Codes restricting the association of alcoholic brands with some form of success occurred in 23 countries. The use of children or young people or the use of media for alcohol advertising that are targeted at young people were restricted in 22 countries. The use of violent themes in alcohol advertising was restricted in 21 countries. The use of incentives such as cheap prices to encourage young people to drink was banned in 17 countries as was the use of styles linked to youth culture. The distribution of free drinks or alcohol-associated merchandise to young people (14 countries), association of alcohol with other drugs (12 countries) and the provision of beverages especially for young people (9 countries) were all somewhat less widespread. Other types of restriction were present in 12 countries.

Restrictions on themes such as association of alcohol with success (sexual, social, sports-related) and on the use of young people in advertisements were equally likely to occur in statutory regulations (91% in each case) and non-statutory regulations (88% in each case). Restrictions on placement of alcohol advertisements in media targeted at young people were more likely to feature in statutory regulations (91%) than in non-statutory regulations (66%). Codes concerning the use of sponsored events to promote alcoholic brands was more frequently embodied in statutory regulations (55%) than in non-statutory regulations (35%) as was the association of alcohol use with use of other drugs such as tobacco (41% versus 29%). The use of deliberate forms of encouragement to drink alcohol (64% versus 65%) and on the use of free offers (45% versus 41%) were equally likely to occur in statutory or non-statutory regulations. Other attributes were more likely to be found in non-statutory than statutory regulations, including use of characters or themes with youth appeals (82% versus 36%) and use of violence (94% versus 55%).

The STAP analysis examined the distribution and nature of bans on alcohol advertising across Europe. Seventeen countries had bans on the location of alcohol advertising (for example, not in sports stadiums) and the same number of countries had bans on the times when alcohol advertising could be shown (for example, not before 9pm on TV). Fifteen countries had bans that applied selectively to particular types of alcoholic beverage (for example, spirits or wine). Fourteen countries had bans that applied to alcohol advertising in specific media (for example, at the cinema).

These bans occurred more frequently in statutory codes than in non-statutory codes – for location (64% versus 41%), timing (68% versus 29%), medium or channel (55% versus 35%), and type of product (64% versus 29%).

STAP also found that varying numbers of countries operated other procedures linked to regulation of alcohol advertising. In all, 23 countries gave consumers opportunities to complain about alcohol advertising and the same number operated penalties for breaches of codes. Nineteen countries had an organisation that systematically monitored alcohol advertising for code breaches. Fifteen countries had a system in which alcohol advertisers could receive pre-campaign advice about their advertisements and compliance with relevant codes of practice.

The main conclusions reached from this analysis were that most countries operate regulations for alcohol advertising and while there are some similarities across national markets in the nature of these regulations, there are also many differences. What was consistent across countries was the implementation of codes relating to the contents of advertisements. Many countries were less likely to have regulations restricting the volume of alcohol advertising. This was true both of statutory and non-statutory regulations. Of course, it not just the presence of regulations that is important, but also the extent to which they compliance with them occurs. The monitoring of compliance with alcohol advertising codes was more likely to occur in countries with statutory rather than purely voluntarily regulations. This finding indicated that if regulations are really to bite, then governments need to enact legally binding restrictions and ensure through independent monitoring that the industry complies.

Controls over alcohol marketing in the UK

Advertising in the UK is regulated by a combination of statutory and voluntary codes of practice that cover different media and forms of marketing or alcoholic products. The Office of Communications (Ofcom) regulates broadcast advertising (on television and radio) and the Advertising Standards Authority (ASA) is responsible for all forms of non-broadcast advertising. Ofcom was launched at the end of 2003 and replaced the Independent Television Commission and Radio Authority and adopted the advertising codes of each of those bodies.

Both the ASA and Ofcom maintain codes of practice on advertising within which all advertisers are required to operate. Each general advertising code of practice contains codes that are concerned specifically with alcohol advertising. Each organisation also handles advertising complaints from consumers, although from 1 November 2004 Ofcom has sub-contracted broadcast advertising complaints handling to the ASA.

In relation to broadcast advertising, Ofcom adopted the codes of practice previously used by the ITC in respect of television advertising and the Radio Authority in respect of radio advertising. Historically, these advertising codes were regularly reviewed and revised and this practice has continued under Ofcom. Both the Radio and TV Codes for advertising have been adopted by the ASA to which Ofcom sub-contracted advertising regulation and complaints handling in 2004.

The Ofcom advertising codes have been revised in several areas since 2003. Two areas in which there has been a great deal of debate about advertising regulation are alcohol and food. The food advertising debate is ongoing, while the alcohol advertising debate reached a point of resolution – at least for the regulator – when a revised alcohol advertising code was produced after a period of public and industry consultation.

From 1 January 2005, Ofcom introduced its *Final revised alcohol advertising rules* after a period of consultation (15 July 2004–20 December 2004) to consider new proposals for Section 11.8 of the Advertising Standards Code for television advertising. Responses from the alcohol, advertising and television industries were received. New rules were introduced that reinforced the need to divorce links between alcohol consumption and sexual success and to reduce the appeal of alcohol advertising to youth culture. These recommendations were drafted into the revised alcohol advertising code with additional notes of guidance produced by the BCAP.

Section 11.8 of the Ofcom *Code of Advertising Practice* deals with alcoholic drinks. The rules for all advertising are shown in Table 10.3. They require that televised advertisements for alcoholic drinks do not promote alcohol on the basis of social success (with non-drinking implying some kind of weakness), daring and toughness or in association with anti-social themes, links to sexual success, links to overcoming social problems or therapeutic effect, appeal on the grounds of alcoholic strength or consumption before driving or using machinery. Further rules have been drafted that apply specifically to the advertising of alcoholic drinks on radio contained within the Radio Code of the CAP Code and also utilised by Ofcom.

The ASA operates its role in the regulation of broadcast advertising through the Broadcast Committee of Advertising Practice (BCAP). The Broadcast Advertising Copy Clearance (BACC) is another body responsible for ensuring advance compliance on the part of advertisers with broadcast advertising codes of practice, while the ASA performs the same function in respect of non-broadcast advertising copy clearance.

In respect of non-broadcast advertising the ASA implements the Committee of Advertising Practice (CAP) British Code of Advertising, Sales Promotion and Direct Marketing (also known as The CAP Code). CAP is a self-regulatory body that is responsible for drafting, revising and enforcing the Code. The CAP comprises members from the advertising, sales promotion, direct marketing and media sectors. Hence, the relevant industries have voluntarily signed up to this code of practice and abide by ASA judgements in relation to code breaches as identified either by the ASA itself or by consumers or organisations who complain to the ASA by advertisements.

Section 56 of the CAP Code presents a set of guidelines specifically concerned with non-broadcast advertising of alcoholic drinks advertising. Many of the rules laid down about non-broadcast advertising are reflected in the broadcast advertising codes and are concerned with ensuring that advertising for alcoholic products does not make claims that relate consumption to personal enhancement, social or sexual success or encourage excessive consumption or consumption before driving or using dangerous machinery. There are also restrictions imposed on the use of young people in alcohol advertising who might be perceived as underage or who might present as particularly attractive role models to underage drinkers.

In addition, in respect of alcohol marketing, the industry established a voluntary code of practice operated via The Portman Group from 1996. This code covered the naming, packaging and promotion of alcoholic drinks, but does not cover advertising. Complaints about packaging of alcoholic products that go through The Portman Group are assessed by an Independent Complaints Panel, but this Panel has no power to enforce any decisions it takes. Further regulation of alcoholic drinks operates through the Food Safety Act 1990, and Trading Standards Officers have powers to ensure that alcoholic drinks declare their alcoholic strength. Portman reviewed its code in 1997, 2000, 2003 and 2009.

New guidelines were introduced by the Portman Group in 2009 to supplement its Code of Practice on the Naming, Packaging and Promotion of Alcoholic Drinks and the CAP Code. The new guidelines were drafted specifically to cover the use of digital communications to promote alcohol products. Digital communications in this context included blogs, brand websites, instant messaging, mobile messaging, online advertising, podcasts, social networking and video sharing among other online tools. The guidelines reiterated many of the principal codes of the wider marketing code of practices, including avoidance of using online technologies or sites that are widely used by under-18s, caution about featuring actors/models in online content that are under 25 or appear to be under-18, unless in the latter instance, they do not appear to consuming, preparing to consume or having just consumed alcohol. Other recommendations included the inclusion in online sites of age affirmation checks and other indicators of the age of a potential user.

There is growing concern about the use of social networking sites as marketing or promotional tools and the risks such developments pose in terms of exposure of under-18s to such content (Charles, 2009). The Portman Group's new guidelines demonstrated a proactive stance in tackling these concerns face on.

Advertising and promotions for alcohol occur at the points at which it is sold. These include licensed premises such as bars, clubs, off-licences and general retail outlets such as supermarkets and local corner shops. Point-of-sale promotions have a number of purposes. They are used to showcase new brands and products, to increase customer awareness of products, to draw customers' attention to specific products or brands, and to present special offers on established products and brands. Industry bodies such as the British Beer & Pub Association, representing licensed premises, have produced their own marketing guidelines in relation to direct interactions with consumers. In a further spirit of voluntary regulation, some alcohol companies have devised their own marketing codes that cover all forms of marketing and these will be examined later in this chapter.

Corporate marketing codes

Despite criticism that is often levelled at the drinks industry, there have also been signs of increased corporate responsibility on the part of drinks companies and their trade organisations. In the UK, both the Portman Group (2002) and the British Beer and Pub Association (2005) published marketing codes of practice that served as voluntary codes for manufacturers and their advertisers. These codes were combined in the Social Responsibility Standards for the Production and Sale of Alcoholic Drinks in the UK (2005). Alcohol marketers were required by these codes to take care that all forms of marketing avoid the use of content or techniques that might have special appeal to underage drinkers. The industry judged that these voluntary codes were working as they witnessed a drop in complaints about alcohol marketing and more requests from marketers for pre-campaign advice and guidance to ensure that campaigns were code compliant (Poley, 2006). As well as codes of marketing practice introduced by trade bodies representing the manufacturers and distributors of alcohol, some alcohol brewers have introduced their own corporate marketing codes. These codes generally reflect the codes maintained by their trade bodies and by government authorised regulators.

Allied Domecq Spirits and Wine is a major producer of alcoholic beverages and markets its products all over the world. The company has produced its own Spirits and Wine Marketing Code (www.allieddmoecq. com) to promote responsible drinking in recognition that its brands, when sensibly consumed, can form part of a healthy lifestyle, while when consumed irresponsibly could have negative consequences for consumers. The code covers all kinds of brand advertising and marketing communications to consumers across print, broadcast media, labelling, packaging, Internet, consumer promotions, merchandising, point-of-sale materials and sponsorship. The company states that compliance with the code is mandatory for all its executives involved in advertising and marketing activities on behalf of the organisation.

The Allied Domecq marketing code requires that all advertising and marketing communications should be legal, honest, truthful and decent, be prepared with a sense of social responsibility, and should not impugn human dignity or integrity or use culturally offensive symbols. No advertising or marketing of its brands should encourage misuse of alcohol; suggest any association with violent, dangerous or unruly behaviour; cause offense; or encourage underage purchase of alcohol through the use of actors who look younger than 25 years or celebrity role models or images known to be popular with youth or through placement in media likely to be consumed extensively by people aged under-18 years or be placed near schools. All advertising and marketing should display drinking as a mature activity and one that should be engaged with in a responsible fashion. Alcohol consumption should not be depicted before driving or the use of hazardous machinery or in the workplace in general. No advertising or marketing of alcohol should suggest that it has medical or therapeutic qualities. There should be clarity about the alcoholic strength of a brand. There should be no suggestion that alcohol consumption is associated with enhanced mental or physical abilities or social or sexual success. It is clear that the code of practice observed by Allied Domecq resembles in many ways the codes adopted by the major UK advertising regulators and industry trade bodies.

Another major alcoholic drinks corporation, Diageo, engages in a number of 'corporate citizenship activities' through its outlets around the world. It is a founding member of the Portman Group, voluntarily introduced alcohol unit labelling on its product packaging from 1998, and has run responsible drinking campaigns, including with young people. The company has its own marketing code which recognises that although alcohol is a source of pleasure and is an integral part of celebrations in many cultures, it should be consumed responsibly (see Diageo Marketing Code, www.diageo.com/en-row/CorporateCitizenship).

Within its Marketing Code, Diageo undertakes to comply with 'the letter and the spirit of all applicable national laws, local advertising regulations and self-regulatory codes of practice' in respect of all brand marketing activities. Special provisions are made for potential underage drinkers with an assurance given that brand advertising will not be placed in communications where a significant proportion of the audience comprises individuals under the legal drinking age. Furthermore, people shown in the company's advertisements for alcoholic drinks must be and look over 25 years of age. Other steps are taken to minimise the appeal of its advertising to young people under the legal drinking age which cover specific production treatments (use of images, symbols, music, cartoon characters or persons) likely to appeal to the young. The Code also requires its advertising to avoid placing undue emphasis of high alcoholic content as a positive attribute and to desist from making claims about medicinal or therapeutic value of alcoholic brands or to associate drinking with social and sexual success or any anti-social activities.

Diageo requires its marketing staff and any outside agencies that work with the company in respect of its marketing activities to be aware of and to implement the company's Marketing Code. There must be awareness of special cultural nuances and conventions to ensure that its advertising does not cause offence in specific local markets.

InBev is another global brewer with businesses in Asia, Europe and North and South America. Its headquarters are based in Belgium and it is currently one of the biggest alcohol companies in the world with a portfolio of more than 200 brands. InBev published a new Commercial Communications Code that became active in January 2006. The code embraces the company's long-standing corporate responsibility traditions and applies to all aspects of its commercial communications and marketing activities (source: www.inbev.com). Compliance with the Code is mandatory for all of the company's communications and marketing staff and for external advertising, design, public relations, media buying and sales promotions agencies with which the company works.

The overriding principle for all forms of corporate commercial communications involving its brands is that they 'shall be legal, honest, and truthful, and shall not be unethical or otherwise offend or impugn human dignity.' (p. 4) The InBev code endorses the concept of responsible drinking. As such it prohibits the depiction of situations in commercial communications in which excessive or irresponsible drinking are shown. At the opposite end of the drinking continuum the company promises in its code not to present abstinence or moderate drinking in a negative fashion. None of its brand advertising will associate drinking with pregnancy, anti-social behaviour, or drug taking.

Any beer marketing will be aimed only at individuals above the legal drinking age. To reinforce this point, the company undertakes not to employ 'any symbol, image, object, cartoon character, celebrity, music or language that is primarily intended to appeal to children or adolescents' (p. 6). Anyone shown in its advertising must be and appear to be over 25 years of age. Restrictions will be observed in the placement of its advertisements to ensure that at least 70 per cent of the target audience for a medium can be expected to be above the legal drinking age. In addition, no marketing will be undertaken at events where the majority of those in attendance are likely to be below the legal drinking age. No merchandising will contain the company's alcohol brands where it is likely to be used mostly by people below the legal drinking age.

InBev's code further promises to avoid making health and medical claims about its products in its advertising or to make claims about social or sexual success associated with consumption of its brands. All its advertising communications will promote socially responsible drinking and will not create a link between drinking and sporting performance or associate it with potentially hazardous activities.

Code compliance is mandatory for all those involved in marketing communications activities in or on behalf of the company and all marketing communications must achieve clearance in terms of code compliance before reaching advanced stages of production.

Scottish & Newcastle is an international brewer with a beer-led business that operates across Europe and Asia. The company operates a Responsible Marketing Strategy that it rolled out in 2005. The company provides alcohol unit labelling on all its products and has taken a range of initiatives to encourage consumers to drink sensibly. Its Strategy includes a Marketing Code the aim of which is to ensure that the company's marketing communications do no target underage drinkers, encourage illegal, irresponsible or excessive consumption of alcohol or imply that alcohol is a route to social or sexual success. The Responsible Marketing Strategy was guided by codes operated by other organisations including the Portman Group in the UK and the Amsterdam group in Europe. As a brand leader in the market, Scottish & Newcastle accepts that it has a responsibility not just to promote its business but also the socially responsible consumption of alcohol.

The promotion of responsible drinking can occur both through marketing communications and the types of products developed. In some markets, Scottish & Newcastle has introduced low alcohol by volume beers and alcohol-free beers that it claims retain the taste of beer but ensure that alcohol intake is much reduced. In its marketing communications, the company has included warning messages at sponsored events and on product packaging. It launched an anti-drink-drive poster campaign at its Foster's British Grand Prix with messages such as 'If you drink and drive you're a bloody idiot!', 'Know your boundaries – Never Drink and Drive' and 'Designate a 12th man to drive home'.

In its Scottish & Newcastle Social Responsibility Report 2003, the company indicated that it chooses media carefully for its advertising to ensure that no more than 25 per cent of the likely audience is aged under 18 years. It also included an extract from the Portman Group Code on the Naming, Packaging and Promotion of Alcoholic Drinks (3rd edition) as an integral part of its own marketing guidelines.

As the foregoing review has indicated, the alcohol industry abounds with codes of practice for its marketing and advertising activities. The leading breweries in the world, which are also brand leaders in the UK such as Allied Domecq, Diageo, InBev and Scottish & Newcastle all operate their own marketing codes which reflect wider social responsibility corporate values. Many of the corporate codes contain the same or similar clauses and all focus on the same primary features that derive from umbrella trade associations' and advertising regulators' codes of practice for alcohol advertising. Such codes indicate socially responsible intentions. The proof of their effectiveness, however, will be found in the nature of corporate alcohol advertising campaigns.

Are regulations tight enough?

Some critics have argued that advertisers and regulators could go even further than their current codes and practices to safeguard the interests of young people who may be 'at risk' from the potential influences of alcohol advertising. There have been calls for tighter restrictions of advertising of alcohol during peak viewing hours and during broadcast sports events that attract a lot of younger viewers. There has also been concern voiced about the techniques advertisers use to enhance the attractiveness of alcohol brands that may have particularly strong appeal to youngsters (Grube, 1993). The defence that alcohol advertising is not aimed at young people and certainly not at underage drinkers has been challenged on the grounds that advertisements for alcoholic products tend to feature among the most liked television commercials and that they clearly contain ingredients that children and teenagers enjoy (Aitken, 1989).

There is widespread concern about alcohol consumption among young people and the age at which it starts. This concern has been driven by evidence that excessive consumption, especially in binge drinking sessions, can cause harm to those who indulge and to others around them. Outbreaks of anti-social behaviour among young people are frequently fuelled by alcohol. Alcohol also loosens inhibitions in other ways leading to sexual activity that in turn produces underage and unwanted pregnancies. While there is broad recognition that alcohol consumption is influenced by a range of factors associated with the immediate social environment in which a child or teenager lives, there is evidence that youngsters are attentive to alcohol advertising. Awareness of alcohol advertising opens the possibility that it can play a part in instigating drinking among young people or in reinforcing the habit once they have started to drink.

Key social concerns associated with advertising centre on the part it might play in encouraging youth consumption of alcohol at an earlier age than otherwise would have occurred, encouraging youngsters to drink more than they otherwise would do, implying that alcohol consumption bestows the consumer with special social status, and associating alcohol with behaviour that is antisocial or potentially harmful in nature. Advertising is most likely to have an impact when it taps into specific aspects of youth culture. This could endow alcohol with special status that renders it particularly attractive to youngsters searching for their social identity and sensitive to the opinions of their peers.

Regulators in different countries have recognised that whether or not hard evidence exists to back up such claims, there are concerns that alcohol advertising could influence youngsters by playing on images or themes that are important to their social identity and social status. It is important therefore that codes of practice acknowledge these potential influences and proscribe the use of certain types of advertising appeal in relation to alcohol brands.

Research in the UK has indicated that experimentation with alcohol generally begins in early to mid-teens. Some youngsters start to drink alcohol earlier than this. When such youngsters are invited to talk about alcohol advertisements, they do so in similar terms to adults over the legal drinking age. They are able to identify the kinds of brand appeals being used by advertisers and the social values upon which such messages draw (Aitken, 1989).

Many national regulators who impose statutory codes for alcohol advertisers include stipulations that advertisements for alcoholic drinks must not hold actual or potentially strong appeal for people aged under 18 years. Alcohol consumption must be presented as a mature adult pleasure with which, presumably, young teens would not identify. Tastes and fashions, however, especially in youth culture can evolve dramatically from year to year. This means that advertisers must be constantly vigilant to ensure that they do not include elements that could, at some point, be deemed to be youth culture relevant. The specifics of obeying this rule are elaborated upon by national regulations to some degree. Illustrations of this rule include requirements that advertisements for alcoholic beverages should avoid using personalities likely to have credibility for young people, avoid animation likely to be popular with children, avoid use of animals, music styles popular with youngsters and treatments that feature sport. Even the use of humour – a long-standing core ingredient of much alcohol advertising – must be thought about with great care. These are attributes that have been shown by empirical research to attract the attention of children and teenagers (see Aitken, 1989; Hastings, MacKintosh & Aitken, 1992; Nash, Pine & Lutz, 2000; Waiters et al., 2001).

Despite code restrictions on the message appeals of alcohol advertising that might be attractive to underage drinkers, research evidence has continued to emerge that youngsters display high levels of brand recognition (Gentile et al., 2001; Collins et al., 2005). Although even critics of alcohol advertising acknowledge that the onset of interest in alcohol among young people is underpinned by many different social and psychological variables, a sufficient body of research has emerged that marketing factors also play a part in this process (Hastings et al., 2005).

Breaches of codes of practice that are designed to protect the interests of young people at the age of experimentation with alcohol could therefore represent serious matters. Such breaches generally take the form of placement of advertising in locations where actual or potential underage drinkers are likely to receive regular doses of these commercial messages, such as placement in publications with youth readerships, on billboards close to schools, adjacent to television or radio programmes known to attract large numbers of teenage viewers and listeners, and in association with events (for example, music, sports, etc) that are popular with young people.

Despite the presence of regulators and codes of practice governing the positioning and content of alcohol advertising in different media, some critics have argued that there is empirical evidence to show that advertising of alcohol is reaching children below the legal drinking age and having an impact upon them. Production techniques are incorporated into alcohol advertising that can act specifically to enhance its appeal to underage drinkers or potential drinkers. Given that alcohol advertisements have greater appeal to underage drinkers than non-drinkers, some commentators have argued that it may be reinforcing the illegal behaviour of young alcohol consumers (Hastings, MacKintosh & Aitken, 1992).

Research from the US has indicated the alcohol advertising regularly occurs in magazines that are very popular with young people, including ones not yet old enough legally to purchase alcoholic beverages (CAMY, 2006b). This evidence has been reinforced by findings that some alcoholic brands invest significant amounts of their advertising expenditure on placements in magazines widely read by teenagers (CAMY, 2005b; Garfield, Chung, & Rathouz, 2003). Of course, such data sometimes deserve closer attention. Although alcohol advertising may appear in magazines popular with young people in their early to mid-teens, these magazines might predominantly be targeted at young adults, with the same point being true of alcohol advertisements (Nelson, 2005).

Further concern about the effectiveness of voluntary codes of practice for alcohol advertising has arisen in Australia where many breaches were documented. Alcohol products were regularly found to be associated with social, sexual and sporting success. These and other themes were used that were known to hold appeal for young people (Roberts, 2002). The industry also increasingly used the Internet to promote its brands and there also many web sites – though not technically classified as advertising – had promotional purposes and did not keep to the word or spirit of the advertising codes (Carroll & Donovan, 2002).

Although empirical evidence has emerged that indicates that youngsters by their early teens are aware of alcohol advertising, there is less compelling evidence on whether the specific features controlled by advertising codes of practice represent important aspects of young consumers' ideas about alcohol. Even if all signs of sexual success and social status been removed from alcohol advertising, has this lessened its impact? Do alcohol advertisements today have less appeal to young people than those featured in campaigns that would be rejected by current codes of practice?

Youth audience research and codes of practice

Alcohol marketing codes of practice have identified specific content and format attributes of advertisements that are believed to enhance the impact of the advertising message. These features have, in many instances, been identified by empirical research as having mediating effects on the overall influences of advertisements on consumers. Some of these features may be especially potent with young consumers. Such studies have rarely set out to test the efficacy of codes of practice. Yet it is pertinent to enquire about the significance to young consumers of different advertising attributes in relation to the way they engage with alcohol promotions.

Young people have been surveyed for their opinions about how alcohol consumption can be controlled. When asked about the kinds of interventions that would work, restrictions on alcohol advertising did not emerge. Instead, actions on drinking hours, numbers of venues where people can drink, police presence at trouble spots, use of plastic bottle and glasses, and better public transport were identified as the most critical factors (Engineer et al., 2003).

Ofcom and the ASA commissioned important and insightful research with young people to assess their general attitudes towards alcohol and more specifically towards alcohol advertising. This research has fed into consultations concerned with reviews of alcohol advertising codes of practice. This research has been largely qualitative in nature with data obtained from focus group and paired depth interviews with teenagers. Two such studies were commissioned by the regulators in 2004 and 2005 (Cragg, 2004; The Dream Mill, 2005).

Cragg (2004) reported findings from a series of focus groups and depth interviews with young people aged 11–17 years recruited across England, Scotland and Wales. This research was conducted on behalf of Ofcom, the Advertising Standards Authority and the British Board of Film Classification who between them have responsibility for regulation of advertising in broadcasting (Ofcom), at the cinema (BBFC) and in non-broadcast media (ASA). This research used advertising materials as prompts in the interview sessions.

Among the interesting findings to emerge from this investigation was evidence that while young people exhibit some awareness of alcohol advertising and may even like some of it, many of them regard much of it as *not* being targeted at them. Advertising of alcoholic products may be liked because of the actors who appear in it, its humour and, in the case of broadcast or film advertising, its featured music. The one category of alcohol where advertising was seen as being aimed at young people was for 'alcopops'. One of the key elements of appeal in the latter advertising was the use of themes that depicted 'a spirit of kicking against restraints' (Cragg, 2004: 59). Another factor was that alcopops break the mould in that they represent a type of alcoholic drink that young people enjoy, whereas with traditional alcoholic drinks first-time and inexperienced drinkers tend not to enjoy their taste.

What also emerged from this research was that there were age-related differences in opinions about alcohol. These were largely driven by the fact that older teenagers, approaching the legal drinking age, displayed more personal interest in alcohol and its consumption and its side effects represented part of a sub-cultural norm or 'rite of passage'. Pre-teenagers seldom regarded alcohol as having much relevance for them. By mid-teens (15–16 years), many of the respondents in this study reported some consumption of alcohol, though this was generally restricted to special occasions and was associated with going out to parties and having a good time. Alcopops provided a tasty introduction to alcohol consumption for first-time drinkers for whom most beers, wine and spirits had an unpleasant taste.

The intrinsic appeals of alcohol for teenagers were linked to rebelliousness (wanting to engage in something that was legally forbidden); a sign of maturity (grown-ups drink and therefore alcohol consumption indicates that the drinker is more mature than their years); and social conformity (peer pressure to join in).

A high level of awareness of alcohol advertising emerged among young people interviewed in this investigation, especially awareness of brands they already consumed themselves. There were age differences, however, with the youngest respondents (under 12 years) indicating that they paid relatively little attention to alcohol advertisements because they were not relevant to them.

At the time of this study, a number of alcohol advertising campaigns were being carried by the major mass media in which challenges to authority, having a good time and sexual success were prominent themes. All these themes had strong appeals to young people, though only to those for whom these themes had personal and social relevance.

In the second study (The Dream Mill, 2005) which was conducted specifically for Ofcom as part of its review of alcohol advertising codes of practice, focus group interviews were carried out with young people aged 12–17 years, with comparisons being made between three age-bands: 12–13s, 13–15s and 16–17s. Self-reported alcohol consumption emerged among all three age bands, but with drinking tending to predominate in different social settings. Among the youngest respondents (12–13 years) alcohol consumption took place largely with parents and family members on special occasions. At the next age band (13–15 years), drinking was more prevalent and a more relaxed attitude towards it surfaced. Drinking alcohol was regarded as being a part of growing up. The first signs of drinking to the point of getting drunk emerged at this stage of development, though the respondents interviewed here did not describe themselves as binge drinkers. Getting drunk for the first time, once again, was seen by some respondents as a social rite of passage. Among the oldest group, aged 16–17 years, more mature attitudes towards drinking were found. Getting drunk was regarded as acceptable if it occurred at parties as part of having a good time, whereas getting drunk for the sake of it and particularly out in the street, was frowned upon. Getting into pubs under age also held strong appeal for this age band.

Turning to alcohol advertising, respondents in this investigation exhibited some brand awareness and felt broadly positive about the nature of the advertising. One critical point that was raised concerned the failure of television to balance the positive depiction of alcohol consumption with messages about its potentially harmful effects on health. This point applied to programme depictions of alcohol as much as to advertising for alcoholic products. In the three most popular television soaps (*Coronation Street, EastEnders* and *Emmerdale*), for example, much of the action takes place in the local pub. Most of the lead characters are depicted drinking alcohol, and often at lunchtime as well as in the evening.

Alcohol advertising was generally well-liked with specific brands such as Bacardi Breezer being singled out was highly enjoyable to watch because they make drinking alcohol look like fun. However, some of the young people interviewed were able to identify an inherent danger in the intrinsic appeals of such advertising in that the messages gave nothing away about the possible risks associated with excessive drinking.

Ofcom (2007) published follow-up research, sponsored jointly with the ASA, to assess further the appeal of alcohol advertising to young people. Focus group research with young people aged 14–21 years was combined with survey research with 11- to 21-year olds across the UK. This research asked young people about their alcohol consumption and the appeal and memorability of alcohol advertising. Survey respondents and group participants were shown illustrative advertisements to prompt certain responses. Findings revealed fewer unprompted mentions of alcohol advertisements of alcohol advertisements in 2007 than in 2005. The proportions of young people who mentioned any advertisements for beer (76% to 69%), alcopops (50% to 42%), vodka (20% to 16%) and spirits/liqueurs (17% to 7%) all fell in 2007 compared with 2005. Only cider advertisements (up from 6% to 19%) received more widespread recall. This decline in recall also coincided with declines over the same period in amount of expenditure on advertising for beer (down 64%), alcopops (down 71%) and spirits/liqueurs (down 57%). Recall of vodka advertisements declined despite a 28-per cent increase in expenditure on advertising. Finally, the increased mentions of cider advertisements coincided with a 159-per cent increase in expenditure.

What these findings indicate is that the tightening of alcohol advertising codes at the beginning of 2005 was followed by a reduction in overall expenditure on alcohol advertising expenditure on television, but this drop in expenditure was associated with some specific categories of alcohol. In general, if alcohol expenditure declined, so too did young consumer recall of advertising for specific categories (the exception being vodka). If alcohol advertising expenditure increased, as it did dramatically for cider, then recall also improved.

Further analysis by Ofcom (2007) explored the appeals of alcohol advertising and revealed that the appeals mentioned in 2005 were still identified in 2007. Young people continued to like alcohol advertisements just as much, but were less likely in 2007 (7%) than in 2005 (13%) to think that such advertising was aimed at them. At the same time, more young people in 2007 (34%) than in 2005 (25%) exhibited net agreement with the view that alcohol advertisements make the drink being promoted look more appealing. Ofcom asked young people in the focus groups and the survey further questions about the appeals of alcohol advertising. These findings are examined further in the next section, alongside results from the current research, in the context of advertising code issues.

Prevalence of alcohol advertising code violations

Despite the presence of codes of practice operated by industry regulators and the further voluntary codes adopted by alcohol industry trade bodies and alcohol manufacturers, some critics of alcohol marketing, especially the medical profession, believe these codes do not go far enough. One reason for this concern is that alcohol advertising regulation is largely reactive which means that an offence must be committed before an action is taken. In consequence, the damage has already been done even if further enquiry reaches a judgment that an advertisement should be discontinued or changed.

Code violations are still detected in alcohol advertising even though there may be independently and voluntarily self-regulated codes of practice in place. Some of these, relating to the placement of alcohol advertising and their specific message appeals were noted earlier in this chapter. The prevalence of code breaches has varied from country to country. However, they have been observed even in countries with well-established statutory and/or voluntary codes.

One study in Australia found that the majority of magazines popular with young people contained alcohol advertising and over half of these promotions appeared to breach relevant codes of advertising practice (Donovan et al., 2007). In the UK, the Advertising Standards Authority (ASA, 2007) assessed 463 alcohol advertisements in broadcast and non-broadcast media in December (up to Christmas Day) and found just 12 breaches (3% of advertisements). In another UK-based study that compared alcohol advertising from television and print media across 12-month periods before and after the 2005 television alcohol advertising code of practice changes and detected fewer violations in the post-code change period (10%) than in the pre-code change period (17%). The numbers of violations indicate the number of times a code was breached, rather than the number of advertisements that were found in breach, since certain advertisements contained more than one violation (Gunter, Hansen & Touri, 2007).

It emerged that the most commonly violated rule regarded the explicit or subtle link of the advertised brand with the success of a social occasion such as a wedding, (11.8.1(a2)); and the explicit or subtle link of the advertised brand with behaviour that could be potentially dangerous after consuming alcohol. Such behaviour included swimming, diving and use of dangerous machinery. It needs to be clarified that it generally remained unclear whether alcohol had been consumed before a certain type of behaviour/activity took place; however, this could still constitute violation of rule 11.8.1(h), as any such ambiguity should be resolved.

Other violated rules included the connection of the advertised brand with daring and aggressive behaviour (11.8.1(b)–11.8.2(b)); connection of the advertised brand with sexual activity, seduction and enhancement of an individual's attraction (11.8.1(c)–11.8.2 (e)); and participation of people who appeared to be younger than 25-years old (11.8.2(a2)). It also emerged that the majority of violations were found in the Bacardi and Budweiser campaigns followed by Smirnoff and WKD.

Other changes in the nature of appeals utilised in televised alcohol advertisements were noted before and after code of practice revisions. Although the most prominent types of appeal – to taste or flavour and to quality and tradition – did not exhibit any shift in prominence, there was an increase after code of practice changes in the extent to which enjoyment, pleasure and relaxation appeals were used in alcohol advertising. There was a reduction from 2005 in the use of male voice-overs, but an increase was observed in visible depiction of male consumption of alcohol on screen.

The use of sexual appeals reduced after code changes to around one-fifth of their pre-code change level. At the same time, there was an increased use of friendship or belongingness appeals in association with alcohol brands. There was also an increase in the extent to which alcohol advertisements on television used cartoon animation and other special effects from 2005 compared with the earlier pre-code change period. These observed changes do not constitute code breaches in the strictest sense but they do, in some cases, and most notably perhaps in the use of animation special effects, represent attributes that do not always follow the 'spirit' of the codes. It is known that cartoon animation can attract the attention of children and that is one reason why codes of practice highlight the need to take care in the use of these production techniques.

It is recognised that alcohol advertisers must be given some degree of creative licence in the production of their product promotions and must be able to utilise appeals that can effectively establish distinctive brand images for what are, after all, legal products. Nonetheless, some forms of product appeal remain in common practice that may catch the attention of potential underage drinkers. The survey evidence provided in this research indicated that even in the presence of controls for variables such as parental and peer group influences upon alcohol consumption, some measures of alcohol consumption among young legal-age drinkers displayed relationships with reported alcohol advertising exposure. The extent to which young drinkers said they had got drunk in their lifetime, in the past 12 months or in the last month was related to reported exposure to alcohol advertising at the cinema. The extent to which young drinkers claimed to have drunk five alcoholic drinks or more in a row in the past month was predicted by reported exposure to alcohol advertising on television. Finally, claimed consumption of alcopops and of cider was predicted in each case by the amount of exposure to televised advertising for those products. There is some evidence here therefore that exposure to alcohol advertising is selectively related to specific patterns of alcohol consumption among young drinkers.

The research reported by Ofcom (2007) provides further evidence relevant to the interpretation of these links between advertising exposure and alcohol consumption. Cider experienced significant growth in expenditure on televised advertising between 2005 and 2006. Cider advertising also achieved more impacts among 16- to 24-year olds and was more widely recalled by young people surveyed by Ofcom. These changes might offer further insight into why cider advertising exposure has been found to be related positively to consumption of cider by the young people in England (Gunter, Hansen & Touri, 2008).

With alcopops, however, these same variables moved in the opposite direction to that for cider. Advertising expenditure in 2006 was lower than in 2005 on television and in other media, impacts of televised advertising fell by 63 per cent, and recall of alcopops advertisements by 11- to 21-year olds also fell (Ofcom, 2007). These findings might therefore lead to an expectation that exposure to televised advertising for alcopops ought not to predict reported consumption. A closer look at the data from Ofcom provides further insights into this apparent anomaly. Although Ofcom (2007) reported a decline in young peoples' reported consumption of alcopops between 2005 and 2007, which is consistent with the advertising expenditure, impacts and recall data, the fall in consumption did not apply to all brands of alcopops or to all categories of consumer. Consumption of the WKD brand showed a slight increase between 2005 and 2007 for young male alcohol consumers. In the current research, the link between exposure to television alcopop advertising and alcopop consumptions was statistically significant only among males and not among females.

Hastings and Angus (2009) acknowledged that codes of practice exist for alcohol advertising and marketing but believed that neither the codes themselves nor the ways they are implemented go far enough. They cited evidence from the Advertising Standards Authority to show that breaches of the codes occur and under current rules can only be dealt with after the fact. In three years up to the end of March 2009, there were 11 breaches of the broadcast code and 17 breaches of the non-broadcast code. The companies responsible for these advertisements were no longer allowed to broadcast them in their original form. Hastings and Angus also note, however, that no fines were levied, implying that the penalties were no severe enough. Only in the case of television, does pre-vetting of advertisement occur.

For Hastings and Angus this was a weakness in the system and allows breaches and inappropriate advertisements to get out into the public domain. Although the regulators can require advertisements deemed to be in breach to be pulled, by then the damage has been done. The movement towards use of more subtle forms of promotions, below the line rather than above it, was also seen as a worrying trend for Hastings and Angus. Such promotional vehicles can be more difficult to control and breaches may be more difficult to spot, given the reliance of the system on complaints from consumers to trigger punitive action from regulators.

Summary and conclusions

At the beginning of this chapter it was noted that establishing the direction of trends in alcohol consumption among young people is not an exact science. Much depends upon the time period over which these trends are observed. Reduced or stabilising patterns of youth drinking noted in some countries since 2000 are heartening. Whether they represent lasting behaviour patterns is something that only time will tell. Furthermore, binge drinking remains a social problem in a number of developed countries. Assuming that these raw statistics provide useful indicators of actual drinking patterns, even if not perfect ones, they underline an ongoing social problem. The question that arises then is how this problem can be tackled.

More and better regulation of alcohol availability and promotion of alcohol have been identified as two important steps that could and perhaps should be taken. Tighter local codes and laws and their more vigorous implementation can have positive effects on drinking in public places (Squires, 2008). These actions, however, do not necessarily guarantee reduced alcohol consumption per se among young people. They may instead cause the problem to migrate from one location to another. If it becomes more difficult to drink outside, young people may seek to take their drinking into private spaces. This shifts the location of the problem but does not make it go away completely.

In the UK, the BMA (2008) recommended sweeping revision of the regulation of alcohol marketing. The recommendations here largely reflected those voiced by Hastings and Angus (2009). There should be increased taxation on alcoholic beverages, tighter controls over the density of premises selling alcohol in any particular area, a reduction in licensing hours, and more stringent controls of alcohol advertising. The latter should include a ban on all broadcast and cinema advertising likely to be viewed by young people and on sponsorship of events aimed mainly at young people. No alcoholic soft drinks should be marketed to young people.

As things stand, it seems likely that concerns will continue to be articulated about the marketing of alcohol. Across Europe, most European Community member states have statutory and non-statutory regulations in place that are designed to limit the impact of alcohol marketing on young people. These codes display some variations between countries in their contents and in the degree of formal legal underpinning they have received from their governments (ELSA, 2007). Regardless of the level of statutory legal reinforcement of codes, documented cases of code breaches continue to emerge from different countries.

One key area of concern that relates to the wider marketing mix that needs to be addressed, because of its potency to influence consumer behaviour, is pricing (Hastings & Angus, 2009). There is evidence that young people may be especially sensitive to pricing factors (Chaloupka, 2004). Average income has grown faster than the price of alcohol in the UK between 1980 and 2007 rendering alcohol more affordable. The alcohol price index has also increased at a slower rate than the retail price index which means that relatively speaking, alcohol products have become cheaper compared with other product categories (Hastings & Angus, 2009).

Pricing is used as a marketing tool with price offers being made in both the off-premise advertisement on-premise trade. Supermarkets often run price offers on alcohol products to encourage more volume purchase of those products and other product ranges in their stores. Bars offer promotions such as two for one, free drinks for ladies, and so on. Price promotions in bars and retail outlets are sometimes coordinated to form an integrated marketing campaign.

Ultimately, the development and implementation of codes of practice for alcohol advertisers – even if enforced, which is not always the case – may not be sufficient to tackle the problem of youth drinking. Instead, controls over alcohol advertising and over other forms of alcohol marketing probably need to be combined with other forms of community and social action including community-level programmes that tackle head-on the accessibility and use of alcohol among young people (Fortin & Rempel, 2005). Such programmes might involve parents, teachers, local health services and the enactment of local regulations concerning alcohol sales and marketing and effective policing of their implementation. In effect, a number of potential stakeholders have parts to play in creating and implementing a solution to problem alcohol consumption. Alcohol manufacturers and sellers have an obligation to promote drinking responsibly. Attaching primary blame to alcohol advertising is unlikely to get close to tackling a deeper-seated societal problem that can only be reduced through combined action by manufacturers, retailers, bars and clubs, parents, schools, law enforcement agencies, health services and government. Anti-social and harmful drinking will not be reduced simply through restrictions to the way alcohol is advertised, but through the cultivation of responsible social attitudes towards alcohol consumption that promote self-control.

Note

8 Impact of Alcohol Representation in the News

1. A search was carried out on British National Newspapers in the database Nexis, using the search terms alcohol* and binge* (where the asterisk indicates that the search also identifies words starting with these two stems). To ensure that only articles specifically and predominantly about alcohol and binge drinking were selected, the search strategy specified that both of these words must appear in the headline or at the start of the news article. The searches were done for two-year periods starting from 1 January 2000, and yielded the following results: 2000/2001: 118; 2002/2003: 206; 2004/2005: 616; 2006/2007: 596; 2008/2009 (to 21 September 09): 717.

References

Achabal, D. D., McIntyre, S. H., Bell, C. H. & Tucker, N. (1987), 'The effect of nutrition P-O-P signs on consumer attitudes and behaviour'. *Journal of Retailing*, 63(1), 9–24.

Adams, J., Hennessy-Priest, K., Ingimarsdottir, S., Sheeshka, J., Ostbye, T. & White, M. (2009), 'Changes in food advertisements during "prime-time" television from 1991 to 2006 in the UK and Canada'. *British Journal of Nutrition*, 102(4), 584–93.

Adlaf, E. M. & Kohn, P. M. (1989), 'Alcohol Advertising, Consumption and Abuse: A Covariance Structural Modelling Look at Strickland's Data'. *British Journal of Addiction*, 84(7), 749–57.

Agostinelli, G. & Grube, J. W. (2002), 'Alcohol counter-advertising and the media: A review of recent research'. *Alcohol Research and Health*, 26, 15–21.

Aitken, P. (1989), 'Television alcohol commercials and under-age drinking'. *International Journal of Advertising*, 8, 133–50.

Aitken, P. P., Leathar, D. S. & Scott, A. C. (1988a), 'Ten- to sixteen-year-olds' perceptions of advertisements for alcoholic drinks'. *Alcohol and Alcoholism*, 23(6), 491–500.

Aitken, P. P., Eadie, D. R., Leathar, D. S., McNeill, R. E. & Scott, A. C. (1988b), 'Television advertisements for alcoholic drinks do reinforce under-age drinking'. *British Journal of Addiction*, 83, 1399–419.

Alaniz, M. L. (1998), 'Alcohol availability and targeted advertising in racial ethnic minority communities'. *Alcohol Health & Research World*, 22(4), 256–89.

Alaniz, M. L. & Wilkes, C. (1995), 'Reinterpreting Latino culture in the commodity form: The case of alcohol advertising in the Mexican community'. *Hispanic Journal of Behavioral Sciences*, 17(4), 430–51.

Alcohol Concern (2002), *Alcohol and Teenage Pregnancy*. London, UK: Alcohol Concern.

Alcohol Concern (2003, January), *Teenage Drinkers – A Follow-Up Study of Alcohol Use among 15–17-Year Olds in England*. London, UK: Alcohol Concern.

Alcohol Concern (2004), *Young People's Drinking*, Factsheet 1, Summary. London, UK: Alcohol Concern.

Alcohol in Moderation (2003), *Are our children drinking more?* www.aim-digest.com/gateway/pages/underage/articles/children.htm. Accessed 1 May 2005.

Alcohol and Public Health Research Unit (2002), [Internet website]. Available at http://www.aphru.ac.nz/index.htm_[23 August 2006].

Anderson, P. (2007), *The Impact of Alcohol Advertising: ELSA Project Report on the Evidence to Strengthen Regulation to Protect Young People*. Utrecht: National Foundation for Alcohol Prevention.

Anderson, P., de Bruijn, A., Angus, K., Gordon, R. & Hastings, G. (2009), 'Impact of alcohol advertising and media exposure on adolescent alcohol use: A systematic review of longitudinal studies'. *Alcohol & Alcoholism*, 44, 229–43.

Andsager, J. L., Austin, E. W. & Pinkleton, B. E. (2002), 'Gender as a variable in the interpretation of alcohol-related messages'. *Communication Research*, 29, 246–69.

Areni, C. S., Duhan, D. F. & Kiecker, P. (1999), 'Point-of-purchase displays, product organisation and brand purchase likelihoods'. *Journal of the Academy of Marketing Science*, 27(4), 428–41.

Ashley, R. C., Granger, W. J. & Schmalensee, R. (1980), 'Advertising and aggregate consumption: An analysis of causality'. *Econometrica*, 1149–67.

ASA (2005), 'Young people and alcohol advertising. An investigation of alcohol advertising prior to the advertising code changes'. London: Advertising Standards Authority.

ASA (2007), *ASA Compliance Survey 2007*. London, UK: Advertising Standards Authority. Available at: www.asa.org.uk. Accessed 31 October 2008.

Atkin, C. (1993), 'On regulating broadcast alcohol advertising'. *Journal of Broadcasting & Electronic Media*, 37, 107–13.

Atkin, C. & Block, M. (1981), *Content and Effects of Alcohol Advertising*. Report submitted to the Bureau of Alcohol, Tobacco and Firearms, Springfield, VA.

Atkin, C. & Block, N. (1984a), *Content and Effects of Alcohol Advertising*. US National Technical Information Service, Springfield, Virginia.

Atkin, C. & Block, N. (1984b), 'The effects of alcohol advertising'. In T. C. Kinnear (ed.), *Advances in Consumer Research*, vol. 11., pp. 689–93. Provo, UT: Association for Consumer Research.

Atkin, C. K. & DeJong, W. (2000), 'News coverage of alcohol and other drugs in US college newspapers'. *Journal of Drug Education*, 30(4), 453–65.

Atkin, C., Hocking, J. & Block, M. (1984), 'Teenage drinking: Does advertising make a difference?' *Journal of Communication*, 34(2), 157–67.

Atkin, C., Neuendorf, K. & McDermott, S. (1983), 'The role of alcohol advertising in excessive and hazardous drinking'. *Alcohol & Alcoholism*, 23(6), 491–500.

Aust, C. S. & Zillmann, D. (1996), 'Effects of victim exemplification in television news on viewer perception of social issues'. *Journalism Quarterly*, 73, 787–804.

Austin, E. W. & Meili, H. K. (1994), 'Effects of interpretations of televised Alcohol portrayals on children's Alcohol beliefs. *Journal of Broadcasting & Electronic Media*, 38(4), 417–35.

Austin, E. W. & Nach-Ferguson, B. (1995), 'Sources and influences of young school-age children's knowledge about alcohol'. *Health Communication*, 7, 1–20.

Austin, E. W. & Johnson, K. K. (1997), 'Effects of general and alcohol-specific media literacy training on children's decision making about alcohol'. *Journal of Health Communication*, 2, 17–42.

Austin, E. W., Pinkleton, B. E. & Fujioka, Y. (2000), 'The role of interpretation processes and parental discussion in the media's effects on adolescents' use of alcohol'. *Pediatrics*, 105(2), 343–9.

Austin, E. W. & Hust, S. J. T. (2005), 'Targeting adolescents? The content and frequency of alcoholic and nonalcoholic beverage advertisements in magazine and video formats – November 1999–April 2000'. *Journal of Health Communication*, 10(8), 769–85.

Austin, E. W., Chen, M. J. & Grube, J. W. (2006), 'How does alcohol advertising influence underage drinking? The role of desirability, identification and scepticism'. *Journal of Adolescent Health*, 38(4), 376–84.

Austin, E. W. & Knaus, C. (2000), 'Predicting the potential for risky behaviour among those "too young" to drink as the result of appealing advertising'. *Journal of Health Communication*, 5, 13–27.

Babor, T., Caetano, R., Casswell, S., Edwards, G., Giesbrecht, N., Graham, K., Grube, J., Gruenewald, P., Hill, L., Holder, H., Homel, R., Osterberg, E., Rehm, J., Room, R. & Rossow, I. (2003), *Alcohol: No Ordinary Commodity – Research and Public Policy*. Oxford, UK: World Health Organization.

Bahk, C. M. (2001), 'Perceived realism and role attractiveness in movie portrayals of alcohol drinking'. *American Journal of Health Behaviour*, 25, 433–46.

Bandura, A. (1994), 'Social cognitive theory of mass communication'. In J. Bryant and D. Zillmann (eds), *Media Effects Advances in Theory and Research*, Hillsdale, NJ: Lawrence Erlbaum Associates, pp. 61–90.

Bandura, A. (1977), *Social Learning Theory*. New York, NY: General Learning Press.

Barnard, M. & Forsyth, A. J. M. (1998), 'Alcopops and under-age drinking: Changing trends in drink preference'. *Health Education*, 6, 208–12.

Barnes, J. G. (1984), *Per Capita Consumption of Alcohol: An Examination of the Relative Importance of Advertising and Other Factors*. Memorial University of Newfoundland.

Barnes, J. G. & Bourgeois, J. C. (1977), *Factors Which Influence Per capita Consumption of Beverage Alcohol*. Memorial University of Newfoundland and Carleton University for the Non-Medical Use of Drugs Directorate, Health and Welfare, Canada, Ottawa.

Barton, R. & Godfrey, S. (1988), 'Un-health promotion: results of a survey of alcohol promotion on television'. *British Medical Journal*, 4(6), 20–1.

Beckley, R. E. & Chalfant, H. P. (1979), 'Contrasting images of alcohol and drug-use in country and rock music. *Journal of Alcohol and Drug Education*, 25(1), 44–51.

Berkeley Media Studies Group. (2003), Available: http://www.bmsg.org/index. html [23 August 2006].

Best, J. (ed.) (1995), *Images of Issues: Typifying Contemporary Social Problems* (2nd edn). New York: Aldine de Gruyter.

Beullens, K. & Van den Bulck, J. (2008), 'News, music videos and action movie exposure and adolescents' intentions to take risks in traffic'. *Accident Analysis and Prevention*, 40(1), 349–56.

Blumler, J. G. (1999), 'Political communication systems all change'. *European Journal of Communication*, 14(2), 241–9.

BMA (1999), *Alcohol and Young People*. London: BMA.

BMA (2003), *Adolescent Health*, London, UK: British Medical Association.

BMA (2005, March), 'Binge drinking', London, UK: British Medical Association. http://www.bma.org.uk/ap.nsf/content/Hubhotpbingedrinking. Accessed: 4 December 2006.

BMA (2008, February), *Alcohol Misuse: Tackling the UK Epidemic*. London, UK: British Medical Association Broad of Science.

BMA (2009, September), *Under the Influence: The Damaging Effect of Alcohol Marketing on Young People*. London, UK: BMA.

Bonomo, Y. A., Bowes, G., Coffey, C., Carlin, J. B. & Patton, G. C. (2004), 'Teenage drinking and the onset of alcohol dependence: A cohort study over seven years'. *Addiction*, 99, 1520–8.

Borell, S., Gregory, M. & Kaiwai, H. (2005, March), *'If Snoop Dogg was Selling it, I'd Probably Buy It'. Alcohol Marketing and Youth Voices*. SHORE and Te Ropu

Whariki Research centre, Massey University, presentation at ALAC *Working Together* conference, Auckland.

Bourgeois, J. C. & Barnes, J. G. (1979), 'Does advertising increase alcohol consumption?' *Journal of Advertising Research*, 19(4), 19–29.

Boys, A., Marsden, J., Stillwell, G., Hutchings, K., Griffiths, P. and Farrell, M. (2003), *Teenage Drinkers: A Follow-Up Study of Alcohol Use among 1–17-year olds in England*. London: Alcohol Concern.

Bradshaw, P. (2003), *Underage Drinking and the Illegal Purchase of Alcohol*. Edinburgh: The Stationery Office.

Brain, K. & Parker, H. (1997), *Drinking with Design: Alcopops Designer Drinks and Youth Culture*. London, UK: The Portman Group.

Brand, D. A., Saisana, M., Rynn, L. A., Pennoni, F. & Lowenfels, A. B. (2007), 'Comparative analysis of alcohol control policies in 30 countries'. *PLoS Medicine*, 4(4), 752–9.

Brants, K. (1998), 'Who's afraid of infotainment?' *European Journal of Communication*, 13(3), 315–35.

Brants, K. & Neijens, P. (1998), The infotainment of politics'. *Political Communication*, 15, 149–64.

Breed, W. & DeFoe, J. R. (1979), 'Themes in magazine alcohol advertisements: A critique'. *Journal of Drug Issues*, 9, 511–22.

Breed, W. & DeFoe, J. R. (1981), 'The portrayal of the drinking process on prime-time television'. *Journal of Communication*, 31(1), 58–67.

Breed, W. & DeFoe, J. R. (1984) Drinking and smoking on television, 1950–1982. *Journal of Public Health Policy*, 5, 257–270.

Breed, W., DeFoe, D. R. & Wallack, L. M. (1984), 'Drinking in the mass media: A nine-year project'. *Journal of Drug Issues*, 14, 655–64.

British Beer and Pub Association (2005), *Point of Sale Promotions: Standards for the Management of Responsible Drinks Promotions including Happy Hours*. London, UK: BBPA.

Britt. H., Toomey, T. L., Dunsmuir, W. & Wagenaar, A. C. (2006), 'Propensity for and correlates of alcohol sales to underage youth'. *Journal of Alcohol & Drug Education*, 50(2), 25–42.

Brosius, H-B. (1993), 'The effects of emotional pictures in television news'. *Communication Research*, 20(1), 105–24.

Brown, R. A. (1978), 'Educating young people about alcohol use in New Zealand: Whose side are we on?' *British Journal on Alcohol and Alcoholism*, 13, 199–204.

Buddelmeyer, H. & Wilkins, R. (2005), 'The Effects of Smoking Ban Regulations on Individual Smoking Rates', Melbourne Institute Working Paper No. 13-05, University of Melbourne, Victoria, Australia.

Bushman, B. J. & Stack, A. D. (1996), 'Forbidden fruit versus tainted fruit: Effects of warning labels on attraction to television violence'. *Journal of Experimental Psychology: Applied*, 2(3), 207–26.

Cafiso, J., Goodstadt, M. S., Garlington, W. K. & Sheppard, M. A. (1982), 'Television portrayal of alcohol and other beverages'. *Journal of Studies on Alcohol*, 43(11), 1232–43.

Calfee, J. & Scheraga, C. (1994), 'The influence of advertising on alcohol consumption: A literature review and an econometric analysis of four European nations'. *International Journal of Advertising*, 13(4), 287–310.

Campbell, C. (1987), *The Romantic Ethic and the Spirit of Modern Consumerism*. Oxford, UK, Basil Blackwell.

CAMY (2002), *Overexposed: Youth a Target of Alcohol Advertising*. Washington, DC: Center on Alcohol Marketing and Youth.

CAMY (2003), *Youth Exposure to Radio Advertising for Alcohol: United States, Summer 2003* Washington, DC: Center on Alcohol Marketing and Youth. www. camy.org.

CAMY (2004, October 12) *Alcohol Advertising on Television, 2001 to 2003: More of the Same*. Washington, DC: Center on Alcohol Marketing and Youth. www. camy.org. Accessed 10 October 2005.

CAMY (2005a), *Striking a Balance: Protecting Youth From Overexposure to Alcohol Advertisements and Allowing Alcohol Companies to Reach the Adult Market*. Washington, DC: Center on Alcohol Marketing and Youth. http://www.camy. org/research/striking/striking.pdf. Accessed on 15 January 2006.

CAMY (2005b), *Youth Overexposed: Alcohol Advertising in Magazines, 2001 to 2003*. Washington, DC: Center on Alcohol Marketing and Youth. http://www.camy. org/research/mag0405/mag0405.pdf. Accessed on 15 January 2006.

CAMY (2006a), *Still Growing After All These Years: Youth exposure to Alcohol Advertising on Television, 2001–2005*. Washington, DC: Center on Alcohol Marketing and Youth. www.camy.org.

CAMY (2006b), *Youth Exposure to Alcohol Advertising in Magazines, 2001 to 2004*. Washington, DC: Center on Alcohol Marketing and Youth. www.camy.org.

CAMY (2007), *Youth Exposure to Alcohol Advertising on Radio 2006* (CAMY Monitoring Report). Washington, DC: Center on Alcohol Marketing and Youth, Georgetown University.

Cape, G. S. (2003), 'Addiction, stigma and movies'. *Acta Psychiatrica Scandianvia*, 10, 63–9.

Carroll, T. E. & Donovan, R. J. (2002), 'Alcohol marketing on the Internet: New challenges for harm reduction'. *Drug and Alcohol Review*, 21, 83–91.

Casswell, S. (1995), 'Does alcohol advertising have an impact on public health?'. *Drug and Alcohol Review*, 14(4), 395–404.

Casswell, S. (1997), 'Public discourse on alcohol'. *Health Promotion International*, 12(3), 251–7.

Casswell, S. (2004), 'Alcohol Brands in Young People's Everyday Lives: New Developments in Marketing', *Alcohol and Alcoholism*, 6, 471–6.

Casswell, S., Pledger, M. & Pratap, S. (2002), 'Trajectories of drinking from 18 to 26 years: identification and prediction. *Addiction*, 97, 1426–37.

Casswell, S. & Zhang, J. F. (1998), 'Impact of liking for advertising and brand allegiances on drinking and alcohol-related aggression: A longitudinal study'. *Addiction*, 93(8), 1209–17.

Cellucci, T. & Larsen, R. (1995), 'Alcohol education via American literature'. *Journal of Alcohol and Drug Education*, 40(3), 65–73.

Center for Media Education (1998) Alcohol advertising targeted at youth on the internet: An update. http://www.tap.epn.org.

Center for Substance Abuse Prevention (1993), *Prevention Primer: An encyclopedia of alcohol, tobacco and other drug prevention terms*. Rockville, MD: Department of Health and Human Services.

Chaloupka, F. (2004), 'The effects of price on alcohol use, abuse and their consequences'. In R. Bonnie & M. O'Connell (eds), *Reducing Under-Age Drinking: A Collective Responsibility*. Washington, DC: National Academies Press.

Champion, D. & Chapman, S. (2005), 'Framing pub smoking bans: An analysis of Australian print news media coverage, March 1996–March 2003'. *Journal of Epidemiology and Community Health*, 59(8), 679–84.

Chapman, S. (1989), 'The news on smoking – newspaper coverage of smoking and health in Australia, 1987–88'. *American Journal of Public Health*, 79(10), 1419–21.

Chapman, S. (2004), 'Advocacy for public health: A primer'. *Journal of Epidemiology and Community Health*, 58(5), 361–5.

Chapman, S. & Wakefield, M. (2001), 'Tobacco control advocacy in Australia: Reflections on 30 years of progress'. *Health Education & Behavior*, 28(3), 274–89.

Charles, G., (2009), 'A large measure of sense'. *Marketing*, 4 November, p. 17.

Chaudhuri, A. (1998), 'Product class effects on perceived risk: The role of emotion'. *International Journal of Research in Marketing*, 15(2), 157–68.

Chaudhuri, A. & Buck, R. (1995), 'An exploration of triune brain effects in advertising'. In F. Kardes and M. Sujan (eds). *Advances in Consumer Research*, Provo, UT: Association for Consumer Research, vol. 22, pp. 133–8.

Chen, M. J. & Grube, J. W. (2004), 'TV beer and soft drink advertising: What young people like and what effects?' *Alcohol Clinical Experimental Research*, 26(6), 900–6.

Chen, M. J., Grube, J. W., Bersamin, M., Waiters, E. & Keefe, D. B. (2005), 'Alcohol advertising: What makes it attractive to youth?' *Journal of Health Communication*, 10, 533–65.

Chikritzhs, T. & Stockwell, T. (2002), 'The impact of later trading hours for Australian public houses (hotels) on levels of violence'. *Journal of Studies on Alcohol*, 63, 591–9.

Chisholm, D., Rehm, J., Ommeren, M. & Monteiro, M. (2004), 'Reducing the global burden of hazardous alcohol use: a comparative cost-effectiveness analysis'. *Journal of Studies on Alcohol*, 65, 782–93.

Christensen, P. G., Henriksen, L. & Roberts, D. F. (2000), *Substance Use in Popular Prime Time Television*. Los Angeles, CA: Office of National Drug Control Policy: Mediascope.

Coleman, L., & Cater, S. (2005), *Underage 'risky' drinking: Motivations and outcomes*. York, UK: Joseph Rowntree Foundation.

Collins, R. L., Ellickson, P. L., McCaffrey, D. F. & Hambarsoomians, K. (2005), 'Saturated in beer: Awareness of beer advertising in late childhood and adolescence'. *Journal of Adolescent Health*, 37(1), 29–36.

Collins, R. L., Ellickson, P. L., McCaffrey, D. & K. Hambarsoomians (2007), 'Early adolescent exposure to alcohol advertising and its relationship to underage drinking'. *Journal of Adolescent Health*, 40, 527–34.

Comanor, W. S. & Wilson, T. A. (1974), *Advertising and market power*, Cambridge, Mass.: Harvard University Press.

Connolly, G. M., Casswell, S., Stewart, J. & Silva, P. A. (1992), 'Drinking context and other influences on the drinking of 15-year-old New Zealanders'. *Addiction*, 87(7), 1029–36.

Connolly, G. M., Casswell, S., Zhang, J-F. & Silva, P. A. (1994), 'Alcohol in the mass media and drinking by adolescents: A longitudinal study'. *Addiction*, 89, 1255–63.

Cook, J. & Lewington, M. (eds) (1979), *Images of Alcoholism*. London: The British Film Institute.

Corner, J. (1991), 'Meaning, genre and context: The problematics of "public knowledge" in the new audience studies'. In J. Curran & M. Gurevitch (eds), *Mass Media and Society* (pp. 267–84). London: Edward Arnold.

Coulson, N, E., Moran, J. R. & Nelson, J. P. (2001), 'The long-run demand for alcoholic beverages and the advertising debate: A cointegration analysis'. In M. R. Baye & J. P. Nelson (eds), *Advertising and Differentiated Products*, vol. 10. pp. 31–54. Amsterdam: JAI Press.

Covell, K. (1992), 'The appeal of image advertisements: Age, gender and product differences'. *Journal of Early Adolescence*, 12(91), 46–60.

Coyne, S. M. & Ahmed, T. (2009), 'Fancy a pint? Alcohol use and smoking in soap operas'. *Addiction Research & Theory*, 17(4), 345–59.

Cragg, A. (2004), *Alcohol Advertising and Young People*. Research report for the Independent Television Commission and Ofcom, British Board of Film Classification, and Advertising Standards Authority, prepared by Cragg, Ross, Dawson, London.

Cruz, J. D. (1988), 'Booze and blues: Alcohol and black popular music, 1920–1930'. *Contemporary Drug Problems*, 15(2), 149–86.

Daykin, N., Irwin, R., Kimberlee, R., Orme, J., Plant, M., McCarron, L. & Rahbari, M. (2009), 'Alcohol, young people and the media: Astudy of radio output in six radio stations in England'. *Journal of Public Health*, 31(1), 105–12.

DeFleur, M. L., Davenport, L., Cronin, M. & DeFleur, M. (1992), 'Audience recall of news stories presented by newspaper, computer, television and radio', *Journalism Quarterly*, 69, 1010–22.

Denscombe, M. & Drucquer, N. (2000), 'Diversity within ethnic groups: Alcohol and tobacco consumption by young people in the East Midlands'. *Health Education Journal*, 59, 340–50.

Denzin, N. K. (1991), *Hollywood Shot by Shot: Alcoholism in American Cinema*. New York: Aldine de Gruyter.

Department of Health (1995), *Sensible Drinking: The report of an inter-departmental working group*. London: Department of Health.

Department of Health (2005), *Alcohol Needs Assessment Research Project (ANARP): The 2004 National Alcohol Needs Assessment for England*. London, UK: Department of Health.

Department of Health/Home Office (2007), *Safe, Sensible, Social: The next steps in the National Alcohol Strategy*. London, UK: Department of Health, Home Office, Department for Education and Skills, Department for Culture, Media and Sport.

DHSS (1981), *Prevention and Health: Drinking Sensibly*. London: HMSO.

Diamond, W. D. & Johnson, R. R. (1990), 'The framing of sales promotions: An approach to classification'. *Advances in Consumer Research*, 17(1), 494–500.

Donohew, L. (1990), 'Public health campaigns: Individual message strategies and a model'. In E. B. Ray & L. Donohew (eds), *Communication and Health: Systems and Applications*, pp. 136–52. Hillsdale, NJ: Lawrence Erlbaum Associates.

Donovan, K., Donovan, R., Howat, P. & Weller, N. (2007), 'Magazine alcohol advertising compliance with the Australian alcoholic beverages advertising code'. *Drugs and Alcohol Review*, 26(1), 73–81.

Dorfman, L. & Wallack, L. (1998), 'Alcohol in the news: The role for researchers'. *Contemporary Drug Problems*, 25(1), 65–84.

Downs, A. (1972), 'Up and down with ecology – The issue attention cycle'. *The Public Interest*, 28, 38–50.

Dring, C. & Hope, A. (2001), *The Impact of Alcohol Advertising on Teenagers in Ireland*. Health Promotion Unit, Department of Health and Children, Eire, November 2001.

Drummond, D. C. (2004), 'An alcohol strategy for England: The good, the bad and the ugly'. *Alcohol and Alcoholism*, 39, 3767–79.

Duffy, M. (1980), *Advertising, Taxation and the Demand for Beer, Spirits and Wine in the United Kingdom, 1963–1978*. Occasional Paper No. 8009, Department of Management Sciences, University of Manchester, Institute of Science and Technology.

Duffy, M. (1982), 'The effect of advertising on the total consumption of alcoholic drinks in the United Kingdom: Some econometric estimates'. *Journal of Advertising*, 1, 105–17.

Duffy, M. (1985), *Advertising and the Inter-Product Distribution of Demand: A Rotterdam Model Approach Applied to the UK Alcoholic Drinks Market*. Occasional Paper No.8504, Department of Management Sciences, University of Manchester Institute of Science and Technology.

Duffy, M. H. (1987), 'Advertising and the inter-product distribution of demand: A Rotterdam model approach'. *European economic Review*, 31, 1051–70.

Duffy, M. H. (1991), 'Advertising in demand systems for alcoholic drinks and tobacco: A comparative study'. *Journal of Policy Modelling*, 17, 557–77.

Duffy, M. (1995), 'Advertising in demand systems for alcoholic drinks and tobacco: A comparative study'. *Journal of Policy Modeling*, 17, 557–77.

Duffy, M. (2001), 'Advertising in consumer allocation models: choice of functional form'. *Applied Economics*, 33, 437–56.

Duke, S. B. & Gross, A. C. (1993), *America's Longest War: Rethinking Our Tragic Crusade against Drugs*, New York: Tarcher.

DuRant, R. H., Rome, E. S., Rich, M., Allread, E., Emans, J. & Woods, E. R. (1997), 'Tobacco and alcohol use behaviours portrayed in music videos: A content analysis'. *American Journal of Public Health*, 87, 1131–5.

Durrant, R., Wakefield, M., McLeod, K., Clegg-Smith, K. & Chapman, S. (2003), 'Tobacco in the news: An analysis of newspaper coverage of tobacco issues in Australia, 2001'. *Tobacco Control*, 12, 75–81.

Educalcool (2005), *The Effects of Moderate Regular Alcohol Consumption*. Montreal, Canada, Edcualcool. Available at: www.educalcool.qc.ca. Accessed 20 January 2007.

Educalcool (2006), *Alcohol and the Human Body*. Montreal, Canada, Educalcool. Available at: www.educalcool.qc.ca

Edwards, G., Anderson, P., Babor, T. F., Casswell, S., Ferrence, R., Giesbrecht, N., Godfrey, C., Holder, H. & Lemmens, P. H. M. M. (eds) (1994), *Alcohol Policy and the Public Good*. Oxford: Oxford University Press.

EEC (1989), *Television without Frontiers* (TWF), 89/552/EEC 3, October 1989. Brussels: European Union.

Ellickson, P. L., Collins, R. L., Hambarsoomians, K. & McCaffrey, D. F. (2005), 'Does alcohol advertising promote adolescents drinking? Results from a longitudinal assessment'. *Addiction*, 100(2), 235.

ELSA (2007), *Regulation of Alcohol Marketing in Europe*. Utrecht, The Netherlands; National Foundation for Alcohol Prevention in the Netherlands.

Engels, R. C. M. E., Hermans, R., Baaren, R. B. v., Hollenstein, T. & Bot, S. M. (2009)', Alcohol portrayal on television affects actual drinking behaviour'. *Alcohol and Alcoholism*, 23 February (1–6).

Engineer. R., Phillips, A., Thompson, J. & Nichols, J. (2003), *Drunk and Disorderly: A Qualitative Study of Binge Drinking among 18–24-Year-Olds*. Home Office Research Study 262. Home Office Research, Development and Statistics Directorate February 2003. Available at: www.homeoffice.gov.uk/rds/pdf/hors262.pdf. Accessed 27 July 2005.

Entman, R. M. (1993), 'Framing: Toward clarification of a fractured paradigm'. *Journal of Communication*, 43(4), 51–8.

EUPHA (2005), *An Introduction to Co-Regulation and Self-Regulation in the EU: Briefing to Members*. Utrecht: The Netherlands: European Public Health Association.

Everett, S. A., Schnuth, R. L. & Tribble, J. L. (1998), 'Tobacco and alcohol use in top-grossing American films'. *Journal of Community Health*, 23(4), 317–24.

Fan, D. P. (1996), 'News media framing sets public opinion that drugs is the country most important problem. *Substance Use & Misuse*, 31(10), 1413–21.

Farley, J. U. & Lehmann, D. R. (1994), 'Cross-national "laws" and differences in market response'. *Management Science*, 40(1), 111–22.

Farrell, S., Manning, W. G. & Finch, M. D. (2003), 'Alcohol dependence and the price of alcoholic beverages'. *Journal of Health Economics*, 2291), 117–47.

Fearne, A., Donaldson, A. & Norminton, P. (1999), 'The impact of alternative promotion strategies on the spirits category: Evidence from the UK'. *Journal of Product and Brand Management*, 8(5), 430–42.

Fielder, L., Donovan, R. J., & Ouschan, R. (2009), 'Exposure of children and adolescents to alcohol advertising on Australian metropolitan free-to-air television'. *Addiction*, 104(7), 1157–65.

Fillmore, K. (1988), *Alcohol Use across the Life Course: A Critical Review of Seventy Years of International Longitudinal Research*. Toronto, Canada: Addiction Research Foundation.

Fillmore, K., Hartka, E., Jonstone, B., Leino, E., Motoyoshi, M. & Temple, M. (1991), 'A meta-analysis of life course variables in drinking: The Collaborative Alcohol-Related Longitudinal Project'. *British Journal of Addiction*, 86, 1221–68.

Finn, T. A. & Strickland, D. E. (1982), 'A content analysis of beverage alcohol advertising: II. Television advertising'. *Journal of Studies on Alcohol*, 43(9), 964–89.

Fisher, J. C. (1993), *Advertising, Alcohol Consumption and Abuse: A Worldwide Survey*. Westport, CT: Greenwood Press.

Fisher, J. C. (1999), 'Media influences'. In R. T. Ammerman, P. J. Ott & R. E. Tarter (eds), *Prevention and Societal Impact of Drug and Alcohol Abuse*. Mahwah, NJ: Lawrence Erlbaum Associates.

Fisher, J. C. & Cook, P. A. (1995), *Advertising, Alcohol Consumption and Mortality: An Empirical Investigation*. Westport, CT: Greenwood Press.

Fisher, L. B., Williams, M. I., Austin, B., Camargo, C. A. & Colditz, G. A. (2007), 'Predictors of initiation of alcohol use among US adolescents: Findings from a prospective cohort study'. *Archives of Pediatric Adolescent Medicine*, 161, 959–66.

Flanagin, A. J. & Metzger, M. J. (2001), 'Internet use in the contemporary media environment'. *Human Communication Research*, 27, 153–81.

Fleming, K., Thorson, E. & Atkin, C. K. (2004), Alcohol advertising exposure and perceptions: Links with alcohol expectancies and intentions to drink or drinking in under-aged youth and young adults. *Journal of Health Communication*, 9(3), 3–29.

Ford, R., Hawkes, N. & Elliott, F. (2008), 'Alarm over the child drinkers with liver disease'. *Times*, 23rd May. Available at: http://www.timesonline.co.uk/tol/life_and_style/health/article3985004.ece. Accessed 16 July 2008.

Forster, J. L., McGovern, P. G., Wagenaar, A. C., Wolfson, M., Perry, C. L. & Anstine, P. S. (1994), 'The ability of young people to purchase alcohol without age identification in north eastern Minnesota, USA'. *Addiction*, 89, 699–705.

Forster, J. L., Murray, D. M., Wolfson, M. & Wagenaar, A. C. (1995), 'Commercial availability of alcohol to young people: Results of alcohol purchase attempts'. *Preventive Medicine*, 24, 342–7.

Fortin, R. B. & Rempel, B. (2005), *The Effectiveness of Regulating Alcohol Advertising: Policies and Public Health*. Toronto, Canada: Association to Reduce Alcohol Promotion in Ontario. Available at: www.apoinet.ca/arapo. Accessed 15 January 2006.

Foxcroft, D., Ireland, D., Lister-Sharp, D. J., Lowe, G. & Breen, R. (2003), 'Longer-term primary prevention for alcohol misuse in young people: A systematic review'. *Addiction*, 98, 397–411.

Franke, G. R. & Wilcox, G. B. (1987), 'Alcoholic beverage advertising and consumption in the United States, 1964–1984'. *Journal of Advertising*, 16(3), 22–30.

Franklin, B. (2003), 'McJournalism: The McDonalidization thesis and junk journalism'. Paper presented at the Political Studies Association Annual Conference, The University of Leicester, 15–17 April 2003, Leicester.

Free Speech, Advertising Educational Foundation (AEF) (2005), Available at http://www.aef.com/on_campus/classroom/speaker_pres/data/3003. Accessed on 18/03/2009.

Fuller, E. (2008), *Smoking, Drinking and Drug Use among Young People in England in 2007*. London: Information Centre for Health and Social Care.

Furnham, A. & Gunter, B. (1985), 'Sex, presentation mode and memory for violent and non-violent news'. *Journal of Educational Television*, 11, 99–105.

Furnham, A., Ingle, H., Gunter, B. & McClelland, A. (1997), 'A content analysis of alcohol portrayal and drinking in British television soap operas'. *Health Education Research*, 12(4), 519–29.

Garfield, C. F., Chung, P. J. & Rathouz, P. J. (2003), 'Alcohol advertising in magazines and adolescent readership'. *Journal of the American Medical Association*, 289, 2424–9.

Gates, P., Copeland, J., Stevenson, R. J. & Dillon, P. (2007), 'The influence of product packaging on young people's palatability rating for RTDs and other alcoholic beverages'. *Alcohol and Alcoholism*, 42, 1–5.

Gentile, D., Walsh, D., Bloomgren, J., Atti, J. & Norman, J. (2001, April), 'Frogs sell beer: The effects of beer advertisements on adolescent drinking knowledge, attitudes and behaviour'. Paper presented at the biennial conference of the Society for Research in Child Development, Minneapolis, Minnesota.

Gerbner, G. (1995), 'Alcohol in American culture'. In S. E. Martin (ed.), *The Effects of the Mass Media on Use and Abuse of Alcohol*, Bethesda, MD: National Institutes of Health, pp. 3–29.

Gerbner, G., Morgan, M. & Signorielli, N. (1982), 'Programing health portrayals: What viewers see, say, and do'. In D. Pearl, L. Bouthilet & J. Lazar (eds), *Television and Behavior: Ten Years of Scientific Progress and Implications for the Eighties. Vol 2: Technical Reviews* (pp. 291–307). Rockville, Maryland: U.S. Department of Health and Human Services.

Gill, J. S., Donaghy, M., Guise, J. & Warner, P. (2007), 'Descriptors and accounts of alcohol consumption: methodological issues piloted with female undergraduate drinkers in Scotland'. *Health Education Research*, 22(1), 27–36.

GINA (2005, October), *Making the Links: Domestic Abuse and Substance Misuse*, Conference Report, Scottish Women's Aid/ Gender Issues network on Alcohol, Glasgow. http://www.scottishwoemensaid.co.uk/mainevents/imageupload/index/php?conference. Accessed 15 January 2006.

Gius, M. P. (1995), 'Using panel data to determine the effect of advertising on brand-level distilled spirits sales'. *Journal for Studies on Alcohol*, 56, 73–6.

Godfrey, C. (1988), 'Licensing and the demand for alcohol'. *Applied Economics*, 20, 1541–58.

Golden, J. (2000), '"A tempest in a cocktail glass": Mothers, alcohol, and television, 1977–1996'. *Journal of Health Politics Policy and Law*, 25(3), 473–98.

Gonzenbach, W. J. (1992), 'A time-series analysis of the drug issue, 1985–1990 – the press, the president and public opinion. *International Journal Of Public Opinion Research*, 4(2), 126–47.

Gonzenbach, W. J. (1996), *The Media, the President, and Public Opinion: A Longitudinal Analysis of the Drug Issue, 1984–1991*. Mahwah, NJ: Lawrence Erlbaum Associates.

Grabe, M. E., Zhou, S. & Barnett, B. (2001), 'Explicating sensationalism in television news: Content and the bells and whistles of form'. *Journal of Broadcasting & Electronic Media*, 45(4), 635–55.

Grabowski, H. G. (1976), 'The effects of advertising on the interindustry distribution of demand'. *Explorations in Economic Research*, 3 (Winter), 21–75.

Greenberg, B. S., Fazal, S. & Wober, M. (1986), *Children's Views on Advertising*. London, UK: Independent Broadcasting Authority, Research Report.

Greenfield, T. K. (1997), 'Warning labels: Evidence on harm-reduction from long-term American surveys'. In M. Plant, E. Single and T. Stockwell (eds), *Alcohol: Minimizing the Harm*. London, UK: Free Association Books.

Greenfield, T. K., Graves, K. L. & Kaskutas, L. A. (1999), 'Long-term effects of alcohol warning labels: Findings from a comparison of the United States and Ontario, Canada'. *Psychology and Marketing*, 16, 261–82.

Greenman, D. J. (2000), 'Alcohol, comedy, and ghosts in Dickens's early short fiction'. *Dickens Quarterly*, 17(1), 3–13.

Grewal, D., Monroe, K. B. & Krishnan, R. (1998), 'The effects of price-comparison advertising on buyers' perceptions of acquisition value, transaction value and behavioral intentions'. *Journal of Marketing*, 62 (Apr), 46–59.

Grover, R. & Srinivasan, V. (1992), 'Evaluating the multiple effects of retail promotions on brand loyal and brand switching segments'. *Journal of Marketing Research*, 29, 76–89.

Grube, J. W. (1993), 'Alcohol portrayals and alcohol advertising on television: Content and effects on children and adolescents'. *Alcohol Health Research World*, 17, 54–60.

Grube, J. W. (2004), 'Alcohol in the media: Drinking portrayals, alcohol advertising, and alcohol consumption among youth'. In R. J. Bonnie & M. O'Connell (eds), *Reducing Underage Drinking: A Collective Responsibility* (pp. 597–624). Washington, DC: National Academy Press.

Grube, J. W. Madden, P. A. & Fries (1996), 'The effects of television alcohol advertising on adolescent drinking'. Poster presented at the Annual Meeting of the Research Society on Alcoholism, Washington, DC, June 1996.

Grube, J. W. & Wallack, L. (1994), 'Television beer advertising and drinking knowledge, beliefs, and intentions among schoolchildren'. *American Journal of Public Health*, 84(2), 254–9.

Grube, J. W. & Walters, E. (2005), Alcohol in the media: Content and effects on drinking beliefs and behaviours among youth. *Adolescent Medicine*, 16, 327–43.

Gruenewald, P. J., Ponicki, W. R. & Holder, H. D. (1993), 'The relationship of outlet densities to alcohol consumption: A time series cross-sectional analysis'. *Alcoholism: Clinical and Experimental Research*, 17, 38–47.

Gruenewald, P. J. & Remer, L. (2006), 'Changes in outlet densities affect violence rates'. *Alcoholism: Clinical and Experimental Research*, 30, 1182–93.

Gunter, B. (2005), 'Trust in the news on television'. *Aslib Proceedings*, 57(5), 384–97.

Gunter, B., Hansen, A. & Touri, M. (2007), *The Representation and Reception of Meaning in Alcohol Advertising and Young People's Drinking: A Report for the Alcohol Education and Research Council*. Leicester: University of Leicester, Department of Media and Communication.

Gunter, B., Hansen, A. & Touri, M. (2009), 'Alcohol advertising and young people's drinking', *Young Consumers*, 10(1), 4–16.

Hackbarth, D. P., Silvestri, B. & Cosper, W. (1995), 'Tobacco and alcohol billboards in 50 Chicago neighbourhoods: Market segmentation to sell dangerous products to the poor'. *Journal of Public Health Policy*, 16(2), 213–30.

Hall, W. (2005), 'British drinking: A suitable case for treatment'. *British Medical Journal*, 331, 527–8.

Hammersley, R. & Ditton, J. (2005), 'Binge or bout? Quantity and rate of drinking by young people in the evening in licensed premises'. *Drugs: Education, Prevention and Policy*, 12(6), 493–500.

Hanewinkel, R. & Sargent, J. D. (2009), 'Longitudinal study of exposure to entertainment media and alcohol use among German adolescents'. *Pediatrics, 123*(3), 989–995.

Hanewinkel, R., Tanski, S. E. & Sargent, J. D. (2007), 'Exposure to alcohol use in motion pictures and teen drinking in Germany'. *International Journal of Epidemiology*, 36, 1068–77.

Hankin, J., Firestone, I., Sloan, J., Ager, J., Goodman, A., Sokmol, R. & Martier, S. (1993), 'The impact of the alcohol warning label on drinking during pregnancy'. *Journal of Public Policy and Marketing*, 12(1), 10–18.

Hanneman, G. & McEwen, W. (1976), 'The use and abuse of drugs: An analysis of mass media content'. In R. E. Ostman (ed.), *Communication Research and Drug Education* (pp. 65–88). Beverly Hills, CA: Sage.

Hansen, A. (1986), 'The portrayal of alcohol on television'. *Health Education Journal*, 45(3), 127–31.

Hansen, A. (1988), 'The contents and effects of television images of alcohol: Towards a framework of analysis'. *Contemporary Drug Problems*, 15(2), 249–79.

Hansen, A. (1995), 'Viewers' interpretation of television images of alcohol'. In S. E. Martin (ed.), *The Effects of the Mass Media on the Use and Abuse of Alcohol* (pp. 151–6). Bethesda, MD: National Institutes of Health.

Hansen, A. (2003), 'The portrayal of alcohol and drinking in television news and drama programmes'. London: Alcohol Concern. Available at http://www.alcoholconcern.org.uk/servlets/doc/682. Accessed 23 August 2006.

Hansen, A. & Gunter, B. (2007), 'Constructing public and political discourse on alcohol issues: Towards a framework for analysis'. *Alcohol and Alcoholism*, 42(2), 150–7.

Hargreaves, I. & Thomas, J. (2002), *New News, Old News*. London: Independent Television Commission.

Harrison, L. & C. Godfrey (1989), 'Alcohol advertising controls in the 1990s'. *International Journal of Advertising*, 8, 167–80.

Harwood, E. M., Witson, J. C., Fan, D. P. & Wagenaar, A. C. (2005), 'Media advocacy and underage drinking policies: A study of Louisiana news media from 1994 through 2003'. *Health Promotion Practice*, 6(3), 246–57.

Hass, A. (2005), *Reducing Alcohol Advertisements Kids See Won't Cost Industry Adult Market*. Washington, DC: Center on Alcohol Marketing and Youth. www.camy. org. Accessed 15 January 2006.

Hastings, G., B., Anderson, S., Cooke, E. & Gordon, R. (2005), 'Alcohol marketing and young people's drinking: A review of the research'. *Journal of Public Health Policy*, 26, 296–311.

Hastings, G. & Angus, K. (2009, September), *Under the Influence: The Damaging Effect of Alcohol Marketing on Young People*. London, UK: British Medical Association.

Hastings, G. B., MacKintosh, A. M. & Aitken, P. P. (1992), 'Is alcohol advertising reaching the people it shouldn't reach?' *Health Education Journal*, 51(1), 38–42.

Hayward, K. & Hobbs, D. (2007), 'Beyond the binge in "Booze Britain": Market-led liminalization and the spectacle of binge drinking'. *British Journal of Sociology*, 58, 437–56.

Health Care Technology (2002), 'Alcohol Consumption increasing in US'. www. health-care-technology-llc.com/frbalcohol.htm. Accessed 17 May 2005.

Heath, D. B. (2000), *Drinking Occasions: Comparative Perspectives on Alcohol and Culture*. Philadelphia, PA: Brunner/Mazel.

Henriksen, L., Schleicher, N. C., Feighery, E. C. & Fortmann, S. (2008), 'Receptivity to alcohol marketing predicts initiation of alcohol use'. *Journal of Adolescent Health*, 42, 28–35.

Heo, N. & Sundar, S. S. (1998), 'Source Perception and Electrodermal Activity'. Paper presented at the conference of the Association for Education in Journalism and Mass Communication, Theory and Methodology Division, August 5–8 1998, Baltimore.

Herd, D. (1986), 'Ideology, melodrama, and the changing role of alcohol problems in American films'. *Contemporary Drug Problems*, 13(2), 213–47.

Herd, D. (2005), 'Changes in the prevalence of alcohol use in rap song lyrics, 1979–97'. *Addiction*, 100(9), 1258–69.

Herd, D. & Room, R. (1982), 'Alcohol images in American Film 1909–1980'. *Drinking & Drug Practices Surveyor*, 18, 24–35.

Hibbell, B., Andersson, B., Ahlstrom, S., Balakireva, O., Bjarnasson, T., Kokkevi, A. & Morgan, M. (eds) (2000), *The 1999 ESPAD Report – The European School Survey Project on Alcohol and Other Drugs: Alcohol and Other Drug Use Among Students in 30 European Countries*. Stockholm: The Swedish Council for Information on Alcohol and Other Drugs (CAN), Co-operation Group to Combat Drug Abuse and Illicit Trafficking in Drugs (The Pompidou Group).

Hibbell, B., Andersson, B., Ahlstrom, S., Balakireva, O., Bjarnasson, T., Kokkevi, A. & Morgan, M. (eds) (2004), *The 2003 ESPAD Report – The European School Survey Project on Alcohol and Other Drugs: Alcohol and Other Drug Use Among Students in 30 European Countries*. Stockholm: The Swedish Council for Information on Alcohol and Other Drugs (CAN), Co-operation Group to Combat Drug Abuse and Illicit Trafficking in Drugs (The Pompidou Group).

Hill, H. & Tilley, J. (2002), 'Packaging of children's breakfast cereal: Manufacturers versus children'. *British Food Journal*, 104, 766–77.

Hill, L. (1999), 'What it means to be a Lion Red man: Alcohol advertising and Kiwi masculinity'. *Women's Studies Journal*, 15(1), 65–83.

Hill, L. & Casswell, S. (2000), 'Alcohol advertising and sponsorship: Commercial freedom or control in the public interest?' In N. Heather et al. (eds), *International Handbook on Alcohol Dependence and Related Problems*. Chichester, UK: John Wiley.

Hoadley, J. F., Fuchs, B. C. & Holder, H. D. (1984), 'The effect of alcohol beverage restrictions on consumption: A 25-year longitudinal analysis'. *American Journal of Drug and Alcohol Abuse*, 10, 375–401.

Holbrook, M. B. (1986), 'Emotion in the consumption experience: Toward a new model of the human consumer'. In R. A. Peterson (ed.), *The Role of Affect in Consumer Behavior: Emerging Theories and Applications*, Lexington, MA: Heath, pp. 17–52.

Holbrook, M. B. & Batra, R. (1987), 'Assessing the role of emotions as mediators of consumer responses to advertising'. *Journal of Consumer Research*, 14 (December), 404–20.

Holder, H. D. & Treno, A. J. (1997), 'Media advocacy in community prevention: News as a means to advance policy change'. *Addiction*, 92(Suppl. 2), S189–99.

Hollingworth, W. & Ebel, B. E. (2006), 'Prevention of deaths From harmful drinking in the United States: The potential effects of tax increases and advertising bans on young drinkers'. *Journal of Studies on Alcohol*, 67, 300–8.

Horgan, M. M. (1986, May), *The Relationship of Alcoholic Beverage Advertising and Drinking Behaviour: A Digest of the Literature*. Report for the Brewers Association of Canada.

Houghton, E., & Roche, A. M. (eds) (2001), *Learning About Drinking*. Philadelphia, PA: Brunner-Routledge.

Hovius, B. & Solomon, R. (2001), *Alcohol Advertising: A Legal Primer (2nd edn)* Toronto, Ontario: Association to Reduce Alcohol Promotion in Ontario.

Howard, K. A., Flora, J. A., Schleicher, N. & Gonzalez, E. M. (2001), 'Alcohol point-of-purchase marketing in ten California communities'. Paper presented to the 129th Annual Meeting of APHA (American Public Health Association). Atlanta, Georgia, 21–5 October 2001. See www.apha.confex.com/apha/129am/techprogram/paper_24197. Accessed 9 June 2004.

Hundley, H. L. (1995), 'The naturalization of beer in *Cheers*'. *Journal of Broadcasting & Electronic Media*, 39(3), 350–9.

Hughes, K., MacKintosh, A. M., Hastings, G., Wheller, C., Watson, J. & Inglis, J. (1997), 'Young people, alcohol and designer drinks: Quantitative and qualitative study'. *British Medial Journal*, 314, 414–18.

Hurtz, S., Henriksen, L., Wang, Y., Feighery, E. & Fortmann, S. (2007), 'The relationship between exposure to alcohol advertising in stores, owning alcohol promotional items and adolescent alcohol use'. *Alcohol & Alcoholism*, 42(2), 143–9.

ICAP (2001), 'Self-regulation of beverage alcohol advertising'. *ICAP Reports 9*. Washington, DC: International Center for Alcohol Policies.

ICHS/NCSR/NFER (2007), *Smoking, Drinking, and Drug Use among Young People in England in 2006*. London, UK: Information Centre for Health and Social Care, National Centre for Social Research, National Foundation for Educational Research.

Inman, J. J. & Winer, R. S. (1998), 'When the rubber meets the road: A model for in-store consumer decision making'. *Marketing Science Institute Working Paper*, No. 98–122, October 1998.

Iredale, W. (2007), 'Teenage girls drink boys under the table'. *Sunday Times*, July 22, p. 8.

Iyengar, S. (1991), *Is Anyone Responsible? How Television Frames Political Issues*. Chicago: University of Chicago Press.

Jackman, S. & Hill, L. (2003), *Global Perspectives on Alcohol Marketing: Issues for Young People*. 4th International Conference on Drugs & Young People, Wellington, New Zealand, 26–8 May 2003.

Jackson, C., Brown, J. D. & L'Engle, K. L. (2007), 'R-rated movies, bedroom televisions, and initiation of smoking by white and black adolescents'. *Archives Of Pediatrics & Adolescent Medicine*, 161(3), 260–8.

Jackson, M. C., Hastings, G., Wheeler, C., Eadie, D. & MacKintosh, A. M. (2000), 'Marketing alcohol to young people: Implications for industry regulation and research policy'. *Addiction*, 95 (Supplement 4), 5597–608.

Jefferis, B. J., Power, C. & Manor, O. (2005), 'Adolescent drinking level and adult binge drinking in a national birth cohort'. *Addiction*, 100(4), 543.

Jernigan, D. & O'Hara, J. (2004), 'Alcohol advertising and promotion'. In R. J. Bonnie & M. E. O'Connell (eds), *Reducing Underage Drinking: A Collective Responsibility*, Washington, DC: The National Academic Press.

Jernigan, D. H. & Mosher, J. F. (2005), 'Editors' introduction: Alcohol marketing and youth public-health perspectives'. *Journal of Public Health Policy*, 26(3), 287–91.

Jernigan, D. H. & Ostrom, J. (2006), 'Youth exposure to alcohol advertising on radio – Unite States, June-August 2004'. *Morbidity and Mortality Weekly Report*, 55, 937–40.

Jewell, R. T. & Brown, R. W. (1995), 'Alcohol availability and alcohol related motor vehicle accidents'. *Applied Economics*, 27, 759–65.

Johnston, L. D., O'Malley, P. M., Bachman, J. G. & Schulenberg, J. E. (2004), *Monitoring the Future National Survey Results on Drug Use, 1975–2003. Volume 1: Secondary School Students*. NIH Publication No. 04-5507. Bethesda, MD: National Institute on Drug Abuse.

Jones, S. C. & Lynch, M. (2007), 'A pilot study investigating the nature of point-of-sale alcohol promotions in bottle shops in a large Australian regional city'. *Australian and New Zealand Journal of Public Health*, 31(4), 318–21.

Jones-Webb, R., Baranowski, S., Fan, D., Finnegan, J. & Wagenaar, A. C. (1997), 'Content analysis of coverage of alcohol control policy issues in black-oriented and mainstream newspapers in the US'. *Journal of Public Health Policy*, 18(1), 49–66.

Jones-Webb, R., Toomey, T., Miner, K., Wagenaar, A. C., Wolfson, M. & Poon, R. (1997), 'Why and in what context adolescents obtain alcohol from adults: A pilot study'. *Substance use & Misuse*, 32, 219–28.

Jung, J. (1995), 'Parent-child closeness affects the similarity of drinking levels between parents and their college-age children'. *Addictive Behaviors*, 20(1), 61–7.

Kaskutas, L. A. & Greenfield, T. K. (1997), 'The role of health consciousness in predicting attention to health warning messages'. *American Journal of Health Promotion*, 11, 186–93.

Kean, L. G. & Albada, K. F. (2003), 'The relationship between college students' schema regarding alcohol use, their television viewing patterns and their previous experience with alcohol'. *Health Communication*, 15(3), 277–98.

Kelly, K.J. & Edwards, R. W. (1998), 'Image advertisements for alcohol products: Is their appeal associated with adolescents' intention to consume alcohol?' *Adolescence*, 33(129), 47–59.

Kelly, K. J., Slater, M. D. & Karan, D. (2002), 'Image advertisements' influence on adolescents' perceptions of the desirability of beer and cigarettes'. *Journal of Public Policy & Marketing*, 21(2), 295–304.

Kennedy, G. E. & Bero, L. A. (1999), 'Print media coverage of research on passive smoking'. *Tobacco Control*, 8(3), 254–60.

Kohn, P. M. & Smart, R. G. (1984), 'The impact of television advertising on alcohol: An experiment'. *Journal of Studies on Alcohol*, 45(4), 295–301.

Kohn, P. M. & Smart, R. G. (1987), 'Wine, women, suspiciousness and advertising'. *Journal of Studies on Alcohol*, 48(2), 161–6.

Kohn, P. M., Smart, R. G. & Ogborne, A. C. (1984), 'Effects of two kinds of alcohol advertising on subsequent consumption'. *Journal of Advertising*, 13(1), 34–9.

Kotch, J. B., Coulter, M. L. & Lipsitz, A. (1986), 'Does televised drinking influence children's attitudes towards alcohol'. *Addictive Behaviors*, 11(1), 67–70.

Krank, M. D. & Kreklewestz, K. L. (2003), Exposure to alcohol advertising increases implicit alcohol cognitions in adolescents (abstract). Fort Lauderdale, FL: Research Society on Alcoholism.

Krank, M. D., Wall, A., Lai, M. D., Wekerle, C. & Johnson, T. (2003), Implicit and explicit cognitions predict alcohol use, abuse and intentions in young adolescents (abstract). Fort Lauderdale, FL: Research Society on Alcoholism.

Kracmar, M. & Cantor, J. (1997), 'The role of television advisories and ratings in parent-child discussion of television viewing choices'. *Journal of Broadcasting & Electronic Media*, 41, 393–411.

Kulick, A. D. & Rosenberg, H. (2001), 'Influence of positive and negative film portrayals of drinking on adolescents' alcohol outcome expectancies'. *Journal of Applied Social Psychology*, 31, 1492–9.

Kumar, V. & Leone, R. P. (1988), 'Measuring the effect of retail store promotions on brand and store substitution'. *Journal of Marketing Research*, 25, 178–85.

Kuther, T. L. & Higgins-D'Alessandro, A. (2003), 'Attitudinal and normative predictors of alcohol use by older adolescents and young adults'. *Journal of Drug Education*, 33(1), 71–90.

Kuo, M. C., Wechsler, H., Greenberg, P. & Lee, H. (2003), 'The marketing of alcohol to college students – The role of low prices and special promotions'. *American Journal of Preventive Medicine*, 25(3), 204–11.

Lader, D. (2009), *Drinking: Adults' Behaviour and Knowledge in 2008. Opinions (Omnibus) Survey Report No.39*. Newport: Office for National Statistics.

Laixuthai, A. & Chaloupka, F. J. (1993), 'Youth alcohol use and public policy'. *Contemporary Policy Issues*, 11(4), 70–81.

Lancaster, K. M. and Lancaster, A. R. (2003), 'The economics of tobacco advertising: spending, demand and the effects of bans'. *International Journal of Advertising*, 22, 41–65.

Lang, A. (2000), 'The limited capacity model of mediated message processing: A framework for communication research'. *Journal of Communication*, 50(1), 46–70.

Lang, P. J., Bradley, M. M. & Cuthbert, B. N. (1997), 'Motivated attention: Affect, activation and action'. In P. J. Lang, R. F. Simmons & M. T. Balaban (eds), *Attention and Orienting Sensory and Motivational Processes*. Hillsdale, NJ: Lawrence Erlbaum Associates.

Lariviere, E., Larue, B. & Chalfant, J. (2000), 'Modeling the demand for alcoholic beverages and advertising specifications'. *Agricultural Economics*, 22, 147–62.

Laroche, M., Kim, C. & Zhou, L. (1996), 'Brand familiarity and confidence as determinants of purchase intention: An empirical test in a multiple brand context', *Journal of Business Research*, 37(2), 115–20.

Lavack, A. M. & Toth, G. (2006), 'Tobacco point-of-purchase promotion: Examining tobacco industry documents'. *Tobacco Control*, 15, 377–84.

Lee, B. & Tremblay, V. J. (1992), 'Advertising and the US market demand for beer'. *Applied Economics*, 24, 69–76.

Lee, R. (1975), 'Credibility of newspaper and TV news'. *Journalism Quarterly*, 55(2), 282–7.

Leiber, L. (1998), 'Commercial and character slogan recall by children aged 9 to 11 years: Budweiser frogs versus Bugs Bunny'. Centre on Alcohol Advertising www.traumfdn.org/trauma/alcohol/advertisements/budstudy.html. Accessed 20 January 2006.

Leifman, H., Osterberg, E. & Ramstedt, M. (2002), *Alcohol in Postwar Europe, ECAS II: A Discussion of Indicators on Alcohol Consumption and Alcohol-Related Harm.* Sweden: National Institute of Public Health.

Leigh, B., & Lee, C. (2008), What motivates extreme drinking? M. Martinic & F. Measham (2008), *Swimming with Crocodiles: The Culture of Extreme Drinking.* London, UK: Routledge, pp. 53–78.

Lemmens, P. H., Vaeth, P. A. C. & Greenfield, T. K. (1999), 'Coverage of beverage alcohol issues in the print media in the United States, 1985–1991'. *American Journal of Public Health*, 89(10), 1555–60.

Levy, M. & Robinson, J. (1986), *The Main Source.* Beverly Hills: Sage.

Lewis, R. K., Paine-Andrews, A., Fawcett, S. B., Francisco, V. T., Richter, K. P., Copple, B. & Copple, J. E. (1996), 'Evaluating the effects of a community coalition's efforts to reduce illegal sales of alcohol and tobacco products to minors', *Journal of Community Health*, 21, 429–36.

Lieberman, L. R. & Orlandi, M. A. (1987), 'Alcohol advertising and adolescent drinking'. *Alcohol Health and Research World*, 12(1), 30–43.

Lima, J. C. & Siegel, M. (1999), 'The tobacco settlement: An analysis of newspaper coverage of a national policy debate, 1997–98'. *Tobacco Control*, 8(3), 247–53.

Linsky, A. S. (1970), 'Theories of behaviour and the image of the alcoholic in popular magazines 1900–1966'. *Public Opinion Quarterly*, 34, 573–81.

Lipsitz, A., Brake, G., Vincent, E. J. & Winters, M. (1993), 'Another round for the brewers: Television advertisements and children's alcohol expectancies'. *Journal of Applied Social Psychology*, 23(6), 439–50.

Lister Sharp, D. (1994), Underage drinking in the United Kingdom since 1970: public policy, the law and adolescents and longitudinal analyses'. *Alcohol & Alcoholism*, 29, 525–31.

Loseke, D. R. (2003), *Thinking about Social Problems: An Introduction to Constructionist Perspectives.* (2nd edn). New York: Aldine de Gruyter.

Lowery, S. A. (1980), 'Soap and booze in the afternoon: An analysis of the portrayal of alcohol use in daytime serials'. *Journal of Studies on Alcohol*, 41(9), 829–38.

Lyons, A. C., Dalton, S. I. & Hoy, A. (2006), '"Hardcore drinking" Portrayals of alcohol consumption in young women's and men's magazines'. *Journal of Health Psychology*, 11(2), 223–32.

MacAskill, S., Cooke, E., Eadie, D., & Hastings, G. (2001), *Perceptions of Factors that Promote and Protect against the Misuse of Alcohol amongst Young People and Young Adults*. Glasgow, UK: Centre for Social Marketing, University of Strathclyde.

MacKintosh, A. M., Hastings, G., Hughes, K., Wheller, C., Watson, J. & Inglis, J. (1997), 'Adolescent drinking – the role of designer drinks'. *Health Education*, 6, 213–24.

Mack, R. (1997), 'Bringing down the walls of state pre-emption: California cities fight for local control of alcohol outlets'. *African-American Law and Policy Report*, 3(1), 295–324.

MacRae, F. (2007), 'Alcohol abuse claims twice as many female lives as 15 years ago'. *Daily Mail*, 22 October, p. 21.

Madden, P. & Grube, J. (1991), 'Alcohol and tobacco advertising on sports and prime-time television'. Paper presented at the American Public Health Association meetings, Atlanta, GA, November 13.

Madden, P. A. & Grube, J. W. (1994), 'The frequency and nature of alcohol and tobacco advertising in televised sports, 1990 through 1992'. *American Journal of Public Health*, 84(2), 297–99.

Makowsky, C. R. & Whitehead, P. C. (1991), 'Advertising and alcohol sales: A legal impact study'. *Journal of Studies on Alcohol*, 52, 555–67.

Martinic, M. & Measham, F. (2008a), *Swimming with Crocodiles: The Culture of Extreme Drinking*. London, UK: Routledge.

Martinic, M. & Measham, F. (2008b), 'Extreme drinking'. In M. Martinic and F. Measham (eds), *Swimming with Crocodiles: The Culture of Extreme Drinking*. London, UK: Routledge, pp. 1–12.

Mathios, A., Avery, R., Shanahan J. & Bisogini, C. (1998), 'Alcohol portrayals on prime-time television: Manifest and latent messages'. *Journal of Studies on Alcohol*, 59(3), 305–10.

Maxwell, C., Kinver, A. & Phelps, A. (2007), *Scottish Schools' Adolescent Lifestyle and Substance Use Survey (SALSUS) National Report: Smoking, Drinking and Drug Use among 13- and 15-Year Olds in Scotland in 2006*. London, BMRB Social Research.

McCarty, D. & Ewing, J. A. (1983), 'Alcohol consumption while viewing alcoholic beverage advertising'. *International Journal of Addiction*, 18, 1011–18.

McClure, A., Dal Cin, S., Gibson, J. & Sargent, J. D. (2006), 'Ownership of alcohol-branded merchandise and initiation of teen drinking'. *American Journal of Preventive Medicine*, 30, 277–83.

McCombs, M. (2004), *Setting the Agenda: The Mass Media and Public Opinion*. Cambridge: Polity.

McCreanor, T., Barnes, H. M., Kaiwai, H., Borell, S. & Gregory, A. (2008), 'Creating intoxigenic environments: Marketing alcohol to young people in Aotearoa New Zealand'. *Social Science and Medicine*, 67, 938–46.

McCreanor, T., Moewaka Barnes, H., Gregory, M., Kaiwai, H. & Borell, S. (2005), 'Consuming identities: Alcohol marketing and the commodification of youth experience'. *Addiction Research and Theory*, 13, 579–90.

McGee, R., Ketchel, J. & Reeder, A. I. (2007), 'Alcohol imagery on New Zealand television'. *Substance Abuse Treatment Prevention and Policy*, 2(6), 1–6.

McGuiness, T. (1980), 'An econometric analysis of total demand for alcoholic beverages in the UK, 1956–1975'. *Journal of Industrial Economics*, 29, 85–109.

McGuinness, T. (1983), 'The demand for beer, spirits and wine in the UK, 1956–79'. In M. Grant, M. A. Plant and A. Williams (eds), *Economics and Alcohol*, London: Croom Helm.

McIntosh, W. D., Smith, S. M., Bazzini, D. G. & Mills, P. S. (1998), 'Alcohol in the movies: Characteristics of drinkers and non-drinkers in films from 1940 to 1989'. *Journal of Applied Social Psychology*, 29, 1191–9.

McKeganey, N., Forsyth, A., Barnard, M. & Hay, G. (1996), 'Designer drinks and drunkenness amongst a sample of Scottish school children'. *British Medical Journal*, 313, 401.

McKenzie, D. & Giesbrecht, N. (1981), 'Changing perceptions of the consequences of alcohol consumption in Ontario, 1950–1981'. *Contemporary Drug Problems*, 10, 215–42.

McKinnon, D., Nohre, L., Pentz, M. & Stacy, A. (2000), 'The alcohol warning and adolescents: 5-year effects'. *American Journal of Public Health*, 90(10), 1589–94.

McKinnon, G. F., Kelly, P. & Robison, E. D. (1981), 'Sales effects of point-of-purchase in-store signing'. *Journal of Retailing*, 57, 49–63.

McMahon, J., Jones, B. & O'Donnell, P. (1984), 'Comparing positive and negative alcohol expectancies in male and female social drinkers'. *Addiction Research*, 1, 349–65.

Measham, F. (2006), 'The new policy mix: Alcohol, harm, minimisation and determined drunkenness in contemporary society'. *International Journal of Drug Policy*, 17, 258–68.

Measham, F. (2007), 'The turning tides of intoxication: Young people's drinking in Britain in the 2000s'. *Health Education*, 108(3), 207–22.

Measham, F. (2008), 'A history of intoxication: Changing attitudes to drunkenness and excess in the United Kingdom'. In M. Martinic & F. Measham (2008), *Swimming with Crocodiles: The Culture of Extreme Drinking*. London, UK: Routledge, pp. 13–36.

Measham, F., Aldridge, J. & Parker, H. (2001), *Dancing on drugs: Risk, health and hedonism in the British club scene*. London, UK: Free Association Books.

Measham, F. & Brain, K. (2005), '"Binge" drinking, British alcohol policy and the new culture of intoxication'. *Crime, Media, Culture: An International Journal*, 1(3), 263–84.

Meichen, K., Wechsler, H., Greenberg, P. & Lee, H. (2003), 'The marketing of alcohol to college students: The role of low prices and special promotions'. *American Journal of Preventive Medicine*, 25, 1–8.

Menashe, C. L. & Siegel, M. (1998), 'The power of a frame: An analysis of newspaper coverage of tobacco issues – United States, 1985–1996'. *Journal of Health Communication*, 3(4), 307–25.

Midanik, L. T. (1999), 'Drunkenness, feeling the effects and 5+ measures'. *Addiction*, 94, 887–97.

Midanik L. T. & Room R. (1992), 'The epidemiology of alcohol consumption'. *Alcohol Health and Research World*, 16, 183–90.

Milgram, G. G. (2001), 'Alcohol influences: The role of family and peers'. In E. Houghton & A. M. Roche (eds), *Learning About Drinking*. Philadelphia: Brunner-Routledge, pp. 85–108.

Miller, P. & Plant, M. A. (1996), 'Drinking, smoking and illicit drug use among 15 and 16 year olds in the United Kingdom'. *British Medical Journal*, 313, 394–7.

Miller, P. & Plant, M. A. (2001), 'Drinking and smoking among 15- and 16-year-olds in the United Kingdom: A re-examination'. *Journal of Substance Use*, 5, 285–9.

Montes-Santiago, J., Muniz, M. L. A. & Bazlomba, A. (2007), 'Alcohol advertising in written mass media in Spain'. *Anales De Medicina Interna*, 24(3), 109–12.

Montonen, M. (1996), *Alcohol and the Media*. WHO Regional Publication Series, No. 62. Helsinki: World Health Organisation.

Mosher, J. F. & Johnsson, B. (2005), 'Flavoured alcoholic beverages: An international marketing campaign that targets youth'. *Journal of Public Health Policy*, 26, 326–42.

Myhre, S. L., Saphir, M. N., Flora, J. A., Howard, K. A. & Gonzalez, E. M. (2002), 'Alcohol coverage in California newspapers: Frequency, prominence, and framing'. *Journal of Public Health Policy*, 23(2), 172–90.

Nash, A. (2002, August), 'Children's responses to alcohol advertising on television: A summary of recent research'. Report to the Office of Communications, Department of Psychology, University of Hertfordshire, Hatfield, UK.

Nash, A., Pine, K. & Lutz, R. J. (2000), 'TV alcohol advertising and children – a longitudinal study: Analysis of the first data collection'. Paper presented at the British Psychological Society Development Conference, Brighton.

Nash, A. S., Pine, K. J. & Messer, D. J. (2009), 'Television alcohol advertising: Do children really mean what they say'? *British Journal of Developmental Psychology*, 27, 85–104.

National Institute on Drug Abuse (1998), *National Survey Results on Drug Use from the Monitoring the Future Study, 1975–1997, Volume 1: Secondary School Students*. Rockville, MD: Department of Health and Human Services.

National Statistics online (2006, November) 'Alcohol-related deaths'.At http://www.statistics.gov.uk/eci/nugget.asp?id=1091 Accessed 4 December 2006.

Nelson, J. P. (1990a), 'State monopolies and alcoholic beverage consumption'. *Journal of Regulatory Economics*, 2, 83–98.

Nelson, J. P. (1990b), 'Effect of regulation on alcoholic beverage consumption: Regression diagnostics and influential data'. In R. R. Watson (ed.), *Drug and Alcohol Abuse Reviews: Prevention*, Clifton, NJ: Humana Press, pp. 223–43.

Nelson, J. P. (1999), 'Broadcast advertising and US demand for alcoholic beverages'. *Social Economic Journal*, 65, 774–90.

Nelson, J. P. (2004), 'Advertising bans in the United States', EH.Net Encyclopaedia. Available athttp://eh.net/encyclopedia/article/Nelson.AdBans. Accessed on 25/03/2009.

Nelson, J. P. (2005), 'Beer advertising and marketing update: Structure, conduct and social costs'. *Review of Industrial Organization*, 26, 269–306.

Nelson, J. P. & Moran, J. R. (1995), 'Advertising and US alcoholic beverage demand: System-wide estimates'. *Applied Economics*, 27, 1225–36.

Nelson, J. P. & Young, D. J. (2001), 'Do advertising bans work? An international comparison'. *International Journal of Advertising*, 20, 273–96.

Neuendorf, K. (1985), 'Alcohol advertising and media portrayals'. *Journal of the Institute for Socioeconomic Studies*, 10, 67–78.

Neuendorf, K. (1986), 'The marketing of alcohol as beverage: Youth and general population reactions'. Department of Communication, Cleveland State University, Ohio.

Neuendorf, K. (1987), 'Alcohol advertising: Evidence from social science'. *Media Information Australia*, 43, 15–20.

Newcombe, R., Measham, F. & Parker, H. (1995), 'A survey of drinking and deviant behaviour among 14/15 year olds in North West England'. *Addiction Research*, 2, 319–41.

News-Medical.Net (2004), 'Polls show more teen girls see "alcopop" advertisements than women aged 31–44'. www.news-medical.net. Accessed 16 May 2005.

NHS Health and Social Care Information Centre (2006), *Drug Use, Smoking and Drinking among Young People in England in 2005: Headline Figures*. London, UK: Author.

NHS Information Centre (2007), 'Statistics on Alcohol: England, 2007 Report'. From NHS Information Centre for Health and Social Care. Available at http://www.ic.nhs.uk/statistics-and-data-collections/health-and-lifestyles/alcohol/statistics-on-alcohol:-england-2007-[ns]. (Accessed 10 August 2007).

NHS Information Centre (2008), 'Statistics on Alcohol: England, 2008 Report'. From NHS Information Centre for Health and Social Care. Available at http://www.ic.nhs.uk/statistics-and-data-collections/health-and-lifestyles/alcohol/statistics-on-alcohol:-england-2008-[ns]. (Accessed 10 December 2008).

NHS National Services Scotland (2007), *Alcohol Statistics Scotland*. Edinburgh, Scotland: Author.

O'Brien, S., Sinclair, H., Soni, S., O'Dowd, T. & Thomas, D. (2001), 'Trends in alcohol consumption in undergraduate third level students; 1992–1999'. *Irish Journal of Medical Science*, 170(4), 224–7.

Ofcom (2007, November), *Young People and Alcohol Advertising: An investigation of alcohol advertising following changes to the Advertising Code*. London: Office of Communications and Advertising Standards Authority. Visit: www.ofcom.org.uk

Office for National Statistics (1999), *First release: Living in Britain 1998, General Household Survey*. London: Office for National Statistics.

Office for National Statistics (2002), *Living in Britain 2002, General Household Survey*. London: Office for National Statistics.

Office for National Statistics/Department of Health (2004), *Living in Britain 2002* London, UK: Office for National Statistics.

Office for National Statistics (2006), *General Household Survey 2005*. London: The Stationery Office.

Office for National Statistics (2008), *General Household Survey 2006: Smoking and Drinking among Adults*. Cardiff: ONS.

Ogborne, A. C. & Smart, R. G. (1980), 'Will restrictions on alcohol advertising reduce alcohol consumption?' *British Journal of Addiction*, 75, 293–6.

Ogilvie, D., Gruer, L. & Haw, S. (2005), 'Young people's access to tobacco, alcohol and other drugs'. *British Medical Journal*, 331, 393–6.

Olney, T. J., Holbrook, M. B. & Batra, R. (1991), 'Consumer responses to advertising: The effects of advertisement content, emotions, and attitude toward the advertisement on viewing time'. *Journal of Consumer Research*, 17 (March), 440–53.

O'Leary, D., Gorman, D. M. & Speer, P. W. (1994), 'The sale of alcoholic beverages to minors'. *Public Health Reports*, 109, 816–18.

Ornstein, S. L. & Hanssens, D. M. (1985), 'Alcohol control laws and the consumption of distilled spirits and beer'. *Journal of Consumer Research*, 12, 200–13.

Osterberg, E. & Karlsson, T. (2003), *Alcohol Policies in EU Member States and Norway: A Collection of Country Reports*. Brussels: European Commission.

Park, J. & Stoel, L. (2005), 'Effect of brand familiarity, experience and information on online apparel purchase'. *International Journal of Retail & Distribution Management*, 33(2), 148–60.

Parliamentary Office of Science and Technology (2005), *Binge Drinking and Public Health*. London: Parliamentary Office of Science and Technology.

Pasch, K. E., Komro, K. A., Perry, C. L. Hearst, M. O. & Farbakhsh, K. (2007), 'Outdoor alcohol advertising near schools: What does it advertise and how is it related to intentions and use of alcohol among young adolescents?' *Journal of Studies in Alcohol and Drugs*, 68, 587–96.

Pechmann, C., Levine, L., Loughlin, S. & Leslie, F. (2005), 'Impulsive and self-conscious: Adolescents' vulnerability to advertising and promotion', *Journal of Public Policy and Marketing*, 24(2), 202–21.

Pegler, M. M. (1995), *Visual Merchandising and Display* (3rd edn.) New York: Fairchild Publications.

Peles, Y. (1971a), 'Economics of scale in advertising beer and cigarettes'. *Journal of Business*, 44, 32–7.

Peles, Y. (1971b), 'Rates of amortization of advertising expenditures', *Journal of Political Economy*, 79, 1032–58.

Pendleton, L. L., Smith, C. & Roberts, J. L. (1991), 'Drinking on television: A content analysis of recent alcohol portrayal'. *British Journal of Addiction*, 86, 769–74.

Pew Research Center (2004), *Online News Audiences Larger, More Diverse: News Audiences Increasingly Politicized*. The Pew Research Center, Washington, DC. Avaliable online at: http://www.people-press.org. (Accessed 5 January 2006).

Pfau, M., Holbert, R. L., Zubric, S. J., Pasha, N. H. & Lin, W-K. (2000), 'Role and influence of communication modality in the process of resistance to persuasion'. *Media Psychology*, 2, 1–33.

Pfautz, H. (1962), 'The image of alcohol in popular fiction: 1900–1904 and 1946–1950'. *Quarterly Journal for Studies on Alcoholism*, 23, 131–46.

Phillipson, L. & Jones, S. C., 'Awareness of alcohol advertising among children who watch televised sports'. Proceedings of the Australian and New Zealand Marketing Academy (ANZMAC) Conference, 2007, 2803–10.

Pinsky, I. & Silva, M. T. A. (1999), 'A frequency and content analysis of alcohol advertising on Brazilian television'. *Journal of Studies on Alcohol*, 60(3), 394–9.

Pitt, G., Forrest, D., Hughes, K. & Bellis, M. A. (2003), *Young People's Exposure to Alcohol: The Role of Radio and Television*. Liverpool John Moores University and Knowsley Primary Care Trust.

Plant, M. L. (1997), *Women and Alcohol: Contemporary and Historical Perspectives*. London, UK: Free Association Books.

Plant, M. A. & Plant, M. L. (2006), *Binge Britain: Alcohol and the National Response*. Oxford, UK: Oxford University Press.

Plant, M., Single & Stockwell, T. (1997), *Alcohol: Minimising the Harm. What Works?* London: Free Association Books.

Plant, M. A. & Miller, P. M. (2000), Drug use has declined among teenagers in United Kingdom. *British Medical Journal*, 320, 1536–7.

Plant, M. & Miller, P. (2001), 'Young people and alcohol: An international insight'. *Alcohol & Alcoholism*, 36(6), 513–15.

Plant, M., & Plant, M. (2006) *Binge Britain: Alcohol and the National Response*. Oxford, UK: Oxford University Press.

Pollack, L. E., Cubbin, C., Ahn, D. & Winkleby, M. (2005), Neighbourhood deprivation and alcohol consumption: Does the availability of alcohol play a role?' *International Journal of Epidemiology*, 34, 772–80.

Pollay, R. W. (2007), 'More than meets the eye: On the importance of retail cigarette merchandising'. *Tobacco Control*, 16, 270–4.

Poley, D. (2006), 'Response of The Portman Group to World Health Organisation stakeholder consultation on health problems related to alcohol consumption'. Available Online at: www.portmangroup.org.uk/assets/documents/WHO%20consultation%20Sept%202006

POPAI (2001), *P-O-P Measures Up: Learnings from the Supermarket Class of Trade*. Alexandria, VA: Point-of-Purchase Advertising International. Available at: www.popai.com.

Portman Group (2002), *Code of Practice: On Naming, Packaging and Promotion of Alcoholic Drinks*, 3rdedn. London, UK: The Portman Group.

Portman Group (2009, October), *Responsible Marketing of Alcoholic Drinks in Digital Media*. London, UK: Portman Group.

Preston, C. (2000), 'Are children seeing through ITC advertising regulations?' *International Journal of Advertising*, 19(1), 117–36.

Preusser, D. F. & Williams, A. F. (1992), 'Sales of alcohol to underage purchasers in three New York counties and Washington DC'. *Journal of Public Health Policy*, 13, 306–17.

Prevention Research Center. (2006), [Internet website]. Available: http://www.prev.org/ [23 August 2006].

Prime Minister's Strategy Unit (2003), 'Interim Analytical Report for the National Alcohol Harm Reduction Strategy'. London, UK: Prime Minister's Strategy Unit.

Rainie, L. & Packel, D. (2001, February 18), *More Online, Doing More*. Pew Internet & American Life Project. www.pewinternet.org. [Accessed 24 October 2006].

Raistrick, D., Hodgeson, R. & Ritson, B. (1999), *Tackling Alcohol Together: The Evidence Base for UK Alcohol Policy*. London, UK: Free Association Books.

Ranzetta, L., Fitzpatrick, J. & Seljmani, F. (2003, August), *Megapoles: Young People and Alcohol: Final Report*. London, UK: Greater London Authority.

Reese, S. D., Gandy, O. H. & Grant, A. E. (eds) (2001), *Framing Public Life: Perspectives on Media and Our Understanding of the Social World*. Mahwah, NJ: Lawrence Erlbaum Associates.

Responsible Retailing of Alcohol: Guidance for the Off-Trade (2004, June). Produced by the Association of Convenience Stores, British Retail Consortium and Wine and Spirit Association. www.efrd.org. Accessed 1 August 2006.

Richardson, A. & Budd, T. (2003), *Alcohol, Crime and Disorder: A Study of Young Adults. Home Office Research Study 263*. London: Home Office Communication Development Unit.

Roberts, G. (2002, May), 'Analysis of alcohol promotion and advertising'. Melbourne: Centre for Drug Studies, Australia.

Robinson, T. N., Chen, H. L. & Killen, J. D. (1998), 'Television and music video exposure and risk of adolescent alcohol use'. *Pediatrics*, 102(5), E541–E546.

Robinson, S. & Lader, D. (2009), *Smoking and Drinking among Adults 2007. General Household Survey 2007*. Newport: Office for National Statistics.

Roche, A. (2003), 'Alcohol advertising and promotion'. *Of Substance: The National Magazine on Alcohol, Tobacco and Other Drugs*, 1(1), 3–4.

Romano, M., Duailibi, S., Pinsky, I. & Laranheira, R. (2007), 'Alcohol purchase survey by adolescents in two cities of State of Sao Paulp, Southeastern Brazil'. *Rev Saude Publica*, 41(4), 1–6.

Room, R. (1987), 'Alcoholism and Alcoholics Anonymous in U.S. films, 1945–1962: The party ends for the "Wet Generations"'. In P. Paakkanen & P. Sulkunen (eds), *Cultural Studies on Drinking and Drinking Problems* (pp. 147–50). Helsinki: Alko.

Room, R. (1989), 'Alcoholism and alcoholics anonymous in U. S. films, 1945–1962: The party ends for the "wet generations"'. *Journal of Studies on Alcohol*, 50, 368–83.

Room, R. (2004), 'Disabling the public interest: Alcohol strategies and policies for England'. *Addiction*, 99, 1083–9.

Room, R., Graves, K., Giesbrecht, N. & Greenfield, T. (1995), 'Trends in public opinion about alcohol policy initiatives in Ontario and the US 1989–1991'. *Drug & Alcohol Review*, 14, 35–47.

Rorabaugh, W. (2003), 'Drinking in the "Thin Man" films, 1934–47'. *The Social History of Alcohol and Drugs*, 18, 51–68.

Russell, D. W. & Russell, C. A. (2008), 'Embedded alcohol messages in television series: The interactive effect of warnings and audience connectedness on viewers' alcohol beliefs'. *Journal of Studies on Alcohol and Drugs*, 69(3), 459–67.

Russell, C. A. & Russell, D. W. (2009), 'Alcohol messages in prime-time television series. *Journal Of Consumer Affairs*,' 43(1), 108–28.

Ryan, C. (1991), *Prime Time Activism: Media Strategies for Grassroots Organizing*. Boston, MA: South End Press.

Rutherford, P. (1994), *The New Icons? The Art of Television Advertising*. Toronto, London: Toronto University Press.

Rychtarik, R. G., Fairbank, J. A., Allen, C. M., Foy, D. W. & Drabman, R. S. (1983), 'Alcohol use in television programming: Effects on children's behaviour'. *Addictive Behaviors*, 8, 19–22.

Saffer, H. (1991), 'Alcohol advertising bans and alcohol abuse: An international perspective'. *Journal of Health Economics*, 10, 65–79.

Saffer, H. (1997a), 'Alcohol advertising and youth'. *Journal of Studies on Alcohol*, Supplement no.14, 173–81.

Saffer, H. (1997b), 'Alcohol advertising and motor vehicle fatalities'. *Review of Economics and Statistics*, 79, 431–42.

Saffer, H. & Chaloupka, F. (2000), 'The effect of tobacco advertising bans on tobacco consumption'. *Journal of Health Economics*, 19, 1117–37.

Saffer, H. & Dave, D. (2002a), 'Alcohol advertising and youth'. *Journal of Studies on Alcohol*, Supplement no. 14, 173–81.

Saffer, H. & Dave, D. (2002b), 'Alcohol consumption and alcohol advertising bans'. *Applied Economics*, 1325, 1325–34.

Saffer, H. & Dave, D. (2003), *Alcohol Advertising and Alcohol Consumption by Adolescents*. National Bureau of Economic Research, Working paper 9676.

Sanco, D. G. (2005), Discussion paper on the EU Strategy on Alcohol. Available at: www.europa.eu.int

Sargent, J. D., Wills, T. A., Stoolmiller, M., Gibson, J. & Gibbons, F. X. (2006), 'Alcohol use in motion pictures and its relation with early-onset teen drinking'. *Journal of Studies on Alcohol*, 67, 54–65.

Schofield, M. J., Weeks, C. & Sanson-Fisher, R. (1994), 'Alcohol sales to minors: A surrogate study'. *Preventive Medicine*, 23, 827–31.

Schultz, D. E. (2006), 'Challenges to study on alcohol advertising effects on youth drinking'. *Archives of Pediatric Adolescent Medicine*, 160, 857.

Scribner, R., Mason, K., Threall, K., Simonsen, N., Schneider, S. K., Towvim, L. G. & DeJong, W. (2008), 'The contextual role of alcohol outlet density in college drinking'. *Journal of Studies on Alcohol and Drugs*, 69, 112–20.

Seldon, B. J. & Jung, C. (1993), 'Derived demand for advertising messages and substitutability among the media'. *Quarterly Review of Economics and Finance*, 33, 71–86.

Selvanathan, E. A. (1989), 'Advertising and alcohol demand in the UK: Further results'. *International Journal of Advertising*, 8(2), 181–8.

Sewel, K. (2002), *International Alcohol Policies: A Selected Literature Review*. Edinburgh, Scottish Executive.

Siegel, M., King, C., Ostroff, J., Ross, C., Dixon, K. & Jernigan, D. H. (2008), 'Comment-alcohol advertising in magazines and youth readership: Are youths disproportionately exposed?' *Contemporary Economic Policy*, 26(3), 482–92.

Sivarajasingam, V., Matthews, K. & Shepherd, J. P. (2006), 'Price of beer and violence-related injury in England and Wales'. *Injury*, 37, 388–94.

Simon, J. L. (1969), 'The effect of advertising on liquor brand sales'. *Journal of Marketing Research*, VI, 301–13.

Simpson, C. L., Beirness, D., Mayhew, D. & Donelson, A. (1985), *Alcohol Specific Controls: Implications for Road Safety*. Ottawa, ON: Traffic Injury Research Foundation of Canada.

Skog, O. (2000), 'An experimental study of a change from over-the-counter to self-service sales of alcoholic beverages in monopoly outlets'. *Journal of Studies in Alcohol*, 61, 95–100.

Slater, M. D., Rouner, D., Murphy, K., Beauvais, F., Van Leuven, J. K. & Rodriguez, M. D. (1996), 'Male adolescents' reactions to TV beer advertisements: The effects of sports content and programming context'. *Journal of Studies on Alcohol*, 57, 425–33.

Slater, M. D., Rouner, D., Domenech-Rodriguez, M., Beauvais, F., Murphy, K. & Van Leuven, J. K. (1997), 'Adolescent responses to TV beer advertisements and sports content/context: Gender and ethnic differences'. *Journalism and Mass Communications Quarterly*, 74, 108–22.

Slater, M. D., Long, M., & Ford, V. L. (2006), 'Alcohol, illegal drugs, violent crime, and traffic-related and other unintended injuries in US local and national news'. *Journal of Studies On Alcohol*, 67(6), 904–10.

Slater, M. D., Lawrence, F. & Comello, M. L. G. (2009), 'Media influence on Alcohol-control policy support in the US adult population: The intervening role of issue concern and risk judgments'. *Journal of Health Communication*, 14(3), 262–75.

Small, M. A. (1980), 'Alcohol portrayal in the mass media'. *Alcohol Health and Research World*, Fall, 30–4.

Smart, R. G. (1988), 'Does Alcohol Advertising Affect Overall Consumption? A Review of Empirical Studies'. *Journal of Studies on Alcohol*, 49(4), 314–23.

Smart, R. G. & Cutler, R. E. (1976), 'The alcohol advertising ban in British Columbia: Problems and effects on beverage consumption'. *British Journal of Addiction*, 71, 13–21.

Smart, R. G. (2006), 'Limitations of study of alcohol advertising effects on youth drinking'. *Archives of Pediatric Adolescent Medicine*, 160, 857.

Smith, L. A. & Foxcroft, D. R. (2009), *Drinking in the UK: an exploration of trends*. London, UK: Joseph Rowntree.

Smith, C., Roberts, J. L. & Pendleton, L. L. (1988), 'Booze on the box. The portrayal of alcohol on British television: A content analysis'. *Health Education Research*, 3, 267–72.

Smith, K. C., Terry-McElrath, Y., Wakefield, M. & Durrant, R. (2005), 'Media advocacy and newspaper coverage of tobacco issues: A comparative analysis of 1 year's print news in the United States and Australia'. *Nicotine & Tobacco Research*, 7(2), 289–99.

Snyder, L. B., Fleming, M., Slater, M., Sun, H. & Strizhakova, Y. (2006), 'Effects of alcohol advertising exposure on drinking among youth'. *Archives of Pediatrics & Adolescent Medicine*, 160, 18–24.

Sobell, L. C., Sobell, M. B., Riley, D. M., Klajner, F., Leo, G. I., Pavan, D. & Cancilla, A. (1986), 'Effect of television programming and advertising on alcohol – consumption in normal drinkers'. *Journal of Studies On Alcohol*, 47(4), 333–40.

Sobell, L. C., Sobell, M. B., Toneatto, T. & Leo, G. I. (1993), 'Severely dependent alcohol abusers may be vulnerable to alcohol cues in television programs'. *Journal of Studies on Alcohol*, 54(1), 333–40.

Social Responsibility Standards for the Production and Sale of Alcoholic Drinks in the UK (2005). Available at: www.bii.org/uploads/documents/social%20-responsibility%20standards%20final. Accessed 20 January 2006.

Squires, P. (2008), *ASBO Nation: Anti Social Behaviour – Critical Questions and Key Debates*. Bristol, UK: Policy.

Stacy, A., Zogg, J., Unger, J. & Dent, C. (2004), 'Exposure to televised alcohol advertisements and subsequent adolescent alcohol use'. *American Journal of Health Behaviour*, 28(6), 498–509.

STAP (2007), *Regulation of Alcohol Marketing in Europe: ELSA Project Overview on the Existing Regulations on Advertising and Marketing of Alcohol*. Utrecht, The Netherlands: National Foundation for Alcohol Prevention in the Netherlands. Available at www.stap.nl. Accessed 15 January 2008.

Steele, J. (2006, November 29th), 'Last orders for those ladettes'?' *Metro*, p. 13.

Stevenson, R., Lind, B. & Weatherburn, D. (1999), 'The relationship between alcohol sales and assault in New South Wales, Australia'. *Addiction*, 94, 397–410.

Stewart, D. W. & D. H. Furse (1986), *Effective Television Advertising: A Study of 1000 Commercials*, Lexington, MA: Lexington Books.

Stockwell, T. (2006, February), *A Review of Research into the Impacts of Alcohol Warning Labels on Attitudes and Behaviour*. Centre for Addictions Research of BC. Report commissioned by Health Canada. University of Victoria, British Columbia, Canada.

Stout, E. M., Sloan, F. A., Liang, L. & Davies, H. H. (2000), 'Reducing harmful alcohol-related behaviours: Effective regulatory methods'. *Journal of Studies in Alcohol*, 61, 402–12.

Strickland, D. E. (1981, September), 'The advertising regulation issue: Some empirical evidence concerning advertising exposure and teenage consumption patterns'. Paper presented at the conference on Control Issues in Alcohol Abuse Prevention, Charleston, South Carolina

Strickland, D. E. (1982), 'Alcohol advertising: orientation and influence'. *Journal of Advertising*, 1, 307–19.

Strickland, D. E. (1983), 'Advertising exposure, alcohol consumption and misuse of alcohol'. In M. Grant, M. Plant & A. Williams (eds), *Economics and Alcohol: Consumption and Controls*. New York: Gardner Press, pp. 201–22.

Strickland, D. E. (1984), 'Content and effects of alcohol advertising'. Comment on NTIS Pub. No. PB82-123142. *Journal of Studies on Alcohol*, 45, 87–93.

Strickland, D. E. & Finn, T. A. (1984), 'Targeting of magazine alcohol beverage advertisements'. *Journal of Drug Issues*, 14(3), 449–67.

Strickland, D. E., Finn, T. A. & Lambert, M. D. (1982), 'A content analysis of beverage alcohol advertising'. *Journal of Studies on Alcohol*, 42, 655–82.

Stockdale, J. E. (2001), 'The role of the media'. In E. Houghton & A. M. Roche (eds), *Learning About drinking*. Philadelphia, PA: Brunner/Routledge.

Substance Abuse and Mental Health Services Administration (1999), *National Household Survey on Drug Abuse Main Findings 1997*. Rockville, MD: Department of Health and Human Services.

Talbot, S. & Crabbe, T. (2008), *Binge Drinking, Young People's Attitudes and Behaviour: A Report Commissioned by Positive Futures*. London, UK: Positive Futures Team, Crime Concern.

Terry-McElrath, Y. M., Harwood, E. M., Wagenaar, A. C., Slater, S., Chaloupka, F. J., Brewer, R. D. & Naimi, T. S. (2003), 'Point-of-purchase alcohol marketing and promotion by story type – United States, 2000–2001'. *MMWR Weekly*, 52(14), 310–13.

The Dream Mill (2005), *Consultation with Young People on the Proposed Ofcom Broadcasting Code: A research consultation with under18s*. Report published by Office of Communications, September 2005.

Thomsen, S. R. (2007), 'Commentary: Searching for media effects'. *International Journal of Epidemiology*, 36, 1078–9.

Thomsen, S. R. & Rekve, D. (2004), 'The differential effects of exposure to "youth-oriented" magazines on adolescent alcohol use'. *Contemporary Drug Problems*, 31(1), 31–59.

Thomsen, S. R. & Rekve, D. (2006), 'The relationship between viewing US-produced television programs and intentions to drink alcohol among a group of Norwegian adolescents'. *Scandinavian Journal of Psychology*, 47, 33–45.

Törrönen, J. (2003), 'The Finnish press's political position on alcohol between 1993 and 2000'. *Addiction*, 98(3), 281–90.

Tremblay, V. J. & Okuyama, K. (2001), 'Advertising restrictions, competition and alcohol consumption'. *Contemporary Economic Policy*, 19(3), 313–21.

Treml, V. G. (1975), 'Production and consumption of alcoholic beverages in the USSR: A statistical study'. *Journal of Studies on Alcohol*, 36(3), 285–320.

Treno, A. J. & Holder, H. D. (1997), 'Community mobilization, organizing, and media advocacy. A discussion of methodological issues'. *Evaluation Review*, 21(2), 166–90.

Trottman, R., Wyllie, A. & Casswell, S. (1994), *Content Analysis of Television Alcohol Advertisements*. University of Auckland, Auckland: Alcohol and Public Health Research Unit.

Unger, J. B., Anderson Johnson, C. & Rohrbach, L. A. (1995), 'Recognition and liking of tobacco and alcohol advertisements among adolescents: Relationships with susceptibility to substance abuse'. *Preventive Medicine*, 24, 461–6.

Unger, J., Schuster, D., Zogg, J., Dent, C. & Stacey, A. (2003), 'Alcohol advertising exposure and adolescent alcohol use: A comparison of exposure measures'. *Addiction Research and Theory*, 11(3), 177–93.

Uribe, R. (2004), *Emotionality on British TV News: An Examination of its Methodological and Empirical Aspects*. Doctoral thesis, Department of Journalism Studies, University of Sheffield.

Van den Bulck, J. & Beullens, K. (2005), 'Television and music video exposure and adolescent alcohol use while going out'. *Alcohol and Alcoholism*, 40(3), 249–53.

Van den Bulck, H., Simons, N. & van Gorp, B. (2008), 'Let's drink and be merry: The framing of alcohol in the prime-time American youth series *The OC'*. *Journal of Studies on Alcohol and Drugs*, 69, 6, 933–40.

Van Zoonen, L. & Holz-Bacha, C. (2000), 'Personalisation in Dutch and German politics: The case of talk shows'. *Javnost – The Public*, 7(2), 45–56.

Wagenaar, A. C. & Perry, C. L. (1994), 'Community strategies for the reduction of youth drinking: Theory and application'. *Journal of Research on Adolescence*, 4, 319–45.

Waiters, E., Treno, A. J. & Grube, J. W. (2001), 'Alcohol advertising and youth: A focus group analysis of what young people find appealing in alcohol advertising'. *Contemporary Drug Problems*, 28, 695–718.

Wallack, L., Breed, W. & Cruz, J. (1987), 'Alcohol on prime-time television'. *Journal of Studies on Alcohol*, 48, 33–8.

Wallack, L., Breed, W. & DeFoe, J. R. (1985), 'Alcohol and soap operas: Drinking in the light of day'. *Journal of Drug Education*, 15, 365–79.

Wallack, L. M., Cassady, D. & Grube, J. (1990), 'Beer commercials and children: exposure, attention, beliefs and expectations about drinking as an adult'. AAA Foundation for Traffic Safety, Washington, DC.

Wallack, L., Dorfman, L., Jernigan, D. & Themba, M. (1993), *Media Advocacy and Public Health*. Newbury Park, CA: Sage.

Wallack, L. M., Grube, J. W., Madden, P. A. & Breed, W. (1990), 'Portrayals of alcohol on prime-time television'. *Journal of Studies on Alcohol*, 51(5), 428–37.

Walma van der Molen, J. H. & van der Voort, T. H. (1997), 'Children's recall of television and print news: A media comparison study'. *Journal of Educational Psychology*, 89, 82–91.

Walma van der Molen, J. H. & van der Voort, T. H. (1998), 'Children's recall of the news: TV news stories compared with three print versions'. *Educational Technology Research and Development*, 46(1), 39–52.

Walsh, B. M. (1980), *Drinking in Ireland*. The Economic and Social Research Institute, Dublin.

Warner, J. (2003), *Craze: Gin and Debauchery in an Age of Reason*. London, UK: Profile.

Waterson, M. (1989), 'Advertising and alcohol: An analysis of the evidence relating to two major aspects of the debate'. *International Journal of Advertising*, 8, 111–31.

Wechsler, H., Davenport, A., Dowdall, G., Moeykens, B. & Chatillo, S. (1994), 'Health and behavioural consequences of binge drinking in college: A national survey of students at 140 campuses'. *Journal of the American Medical Association*, 272, 1672–7.

Wechsler, H. & Nelson, T. F. (2006), 'Relationship between level of consumption and harms in assessing drink cut-points for alcohol research: Commentary on "Many college freshmen drink at levels far beyond the binge threshold"' by White et al. *Alcoholism: Clinical and Experimental Research*, 30, 922–7.

Wechsler, R. (2001), 'Alcohol propaganda. Analyzing and countering alcohol industry advertising'. *Prevention Tactics*, 5(2), available at http://www.emt.org/userfiles/Tactic52.pdf. Accessed on 19/04/2009.

Wells, J. E., Horwood, L. J. & Fergusson, D. M. (2004), 'Drinking patterns in mid-adolescence and psychosocial outcomes in late adolescence and early adulthood'. *Addiction*, 99, 1529–41.

WHO (1995), *Global Status report: Alcohol policy*. Geneva: World Health Organization. Available at: www.who.int.

WHO (2001), *Global Status Report on Alcohol*. Geneva, World Health Organization.

WHO (2004), *Global Status report: Alcohol policy*. Geneva: World Health Organization. Available at: www.who.int.

Wicki, M., Gmel, G., Kuntsche, E. et al. (2006), 'Is alcopop consumption in Switzerland associated with riskier drinking patterns and more alcohol-related problems?' *Addiction*, 101, 522–33.

Wilkinson, J. B., Mason, B. & Paksoy, C. H. (1982a), 'Assessing the impact of short-term supermarket strategy variables'. *Journal of Marketing Research*, 19, 72–86.

Wilkinson, J. B., Paksoy, C. H. & Mason, B. (1982b), 'A demand analysis of newspaper advertising and changes in space allocation'. *Journal of Retailing*, 57, 30–48.

Wilks, J., Callan, V. J. & Austin, D. A. (1989), 'Parent, peer and personal determinants of adolescent drinking'. *British Journal of Addiction*, 84(6), 619–30.

Willner, P., Hart, K., Binmore, J., Cavendish, M. & Dunphy, E. (2000), 'Alcohol sales to underage adolescents: An unobtrusive observational field study and evaluation of a police intervention'. *Addiction*, 95, 1373–88.

Winter, M. V., Donovan, R. J. & Fielder, L. J. (2008), 'Exposure of children and adolescents to alcohol advertising on television in Australia'. *Journal of Studies on Alcohol and Drugs*, 69(5), 676–83.

Wolfson, M., Toomey, T. L., Forster, J. L., Wagenaar, A. C., McGovern, P. G. & Perry, C. L. (1996a), 'Characteristics, policies, and practices of alcohol outlets and sales to youth'. *Journal of Studies on Alcohol*, 57, 670–4.

Wolfson, M., Toomey, T. L., Murray, D. M., Forster, J., Short, B. J., & Wagenaar, A. C. (1996b), 'Alcohol outlet policies and practices concerning sales to underage people'. *Addiction*, 4, 589–602.

World Health Organization (2003), 'Industry views on beverage alcohol advertising and marketing, with special reference to young people'. Prepared for the World Health Organization by the International Center for Alcohol Policies on behalf of its sponsors. Available at http://www.icap.org/LinkClick.aspx?fileticket= uBV8L5W870U%3D&tabid=105. Accessed on 10/07/2009.

Wright, N. R. (2006), 'A day at the cricket: The breath alcohol consequences of a type of very English binge drinking'. *Addiction Research and Theory*, 14, 133–7.

Wyllie, A., Casswell, S. & Stewart, J. (1989), 'The response of New Zealand boys to corporate and sponsorship alcohol advertising on television'. *British Journal of Addiction*, 84(6), 639–46.

Wyllie, A., Millard, M. & Zhang, J. F. (1996), *Drinking in New Zealand: A National Survey 1995*. Auckland, NZ: Alcohol & Public Health Research Unit.

Wyllie, A., Zhang, J. F. & Casswell, S. (1998), 'Responses to televised alcohol advertisements associated with drinking behaviour of 10–17 year olds'. *Addiction*, 93, 361–71.

Yanovitzky, I. (2002), 'Effect of news coverage on the prevalence of drunk-driving behavior: Evidence from a longitudinal study'. *Journal of Studies On Alcohol*, 63(3), 342–51.

Yanovitzky, I. & Bennett, C. (1999), 'Media attention, institutional response, and health behavior change – The case of drunk driving, 1978–1996'. *Communication Research*, 26(4), 429–53.

Yanovitzky, I. & Stryker, J. (2001), 'Mass media, social norms, and health promotion efforts – A longitudinal study of media effects on youth binge drinking'. *Communication Research*, 28(2), 208–39.

YouGov (2005), 'Press Gazette Poll: The most trusted news brands'. Available online at: http://www.yougov.co.uk/extranets/ygarchives/content/pdf/OMI050101003_2.pdf. (Accessed 5 May 2005)

Young, B. M. (2003, March), 'A review of the literature on the role of advertising in the consumption of alcohol products by younger people'. Report to the Office of Communications. School of Psychology, University of Exeter.

Young, D. J. (1993), 'Alcohol advertising bans and alcohol abuse' [Comment]. *Journal of Health Economics*, 12(2), 213–28.

Zaller, J. R. (1992), *The Nature and Origins of Mass Opinion*. New York: Cambridge University Press.

Zwarun, L. & Farrar, K. M. (2005), 'Doing what they say, saying what they mean: Self-regulatory compliance and depictions of drinking in alcohol commercials in televised sports'. *Mass Communication & Society*, 8(4), 347–71.

Index